ENDORSEMEN

"Ralph Steele's memoir will be of great value, an inspiration for many who are seeking release from ignorance and suffering."

— *Ajahn* **Sumedho**
Senior-most Western disciple of *Ajahn* Chah
Founder of Chithurst Forest Monastery and
Amaravati Buddhist Monastery in England and other
branch monasteries in the West

"Ralph has written an engaging and inspiring account of his life. His unique background and extensive spiritual experience are related with energy, compassion, and candor. *Tending the Fire* leaves one with hope for ourselves, that the truths of the Buddha are within reach if we are willing to practice, and that those truths have the power to transform not just ourselves, but the world around us."

— **Abbot Pasanno Bhikkhu**
Abhyagari Buddhist Monastery

"Ralph Steele takes us on an extraordinary and compelling journey as he unfolds the chapters of his life in *Tending the Fire*. His story opens doors into many diverse worlds and welcomes us in to meet the characters of his life. Ralph's commitment to healing and deep confidence in the Buddha's Path of Awakening conveys strength, encouragement, and wonder at what can be possible when we cultivate our heart and mind. This is a journey not to be missed."

— **Anandabodhi Bhikkhuni**
Co-Founder of Aloka Vihara,
A Theravada Buddhist Nuns' Community
in the Forest Tradition

"In *Tending the Fire*, Ralph Steele leads us on an amazing journey, weaving together the deep spiritual roots of his childhood on Pawleys Island, South Carolina, the harrowing experiences of Vietnam, and a life-changing pilgrimage to the great Buddhist meditation masters and monasteries of Southeast Asia. Ralph's revealing honesty about the deep-seated racism he encountered in this country, his own struggles with drugs, and his profoundly transforming spiritual practices illuminates so much of our human condition. One can't help but marvel at his extraordinary life."

— **Joseph Goldstein**, author of
Mindfulness: A Practical Guide to Awakening

"Ralph Steele's *Tending the Fire* offers a glimpse into worlds few of us will ever experience—and yet the humanity he shares with us is something we all can resonate with. His is an extraordinary journey of healing and transformation—but as we read, this feels accessible within each one of us. We are truly blessed by this deeply inspiring and transformative book."

— **Alexandra Kennedy**, M.A., LMFT, psychotherapist and
author of *Honoring Grief:*
Creating a Space to Let Yourself Heal; and
Losing A Parent: Passage to a New Way of Living

"Buddha was a Kshatriya; he came from the warrior class. Ralph Steele, too, is a warrior who, like Buddha, had to climb the walls of his enclosures to breathe the fresh air. And he did it with an adept's fortitude. He tended a fire by which many might be warmed. Sit in this fire yoga that purifies, with dharma-doctor Ralph Steele."

— **Stephen and Ondrea Levine**, authors of
Becoming Kuan Yin: The Evolution of Compassion; and
The Healing I Took Birth For

"If you're interested in stepping up to the plate in your own life spiritually, read this book. Ralph Steele offers an inspiring invitation to all of us to get it together. Truthful and spacious, he's your brother. Funny, deep and wise, he's an Elder. Do pay attention with love!"

— Amadea Morningstar,
Ayurvedic Teacher and author of
*The Ayurvedic Guide to Polarity Therapy:
Hands-on Healing A Self-Care Guide;* and
*Ayurvedic Cooking for Westerners:
Familiar Western Food Prepared with Ayurvedic Principles*

"Few contemporary writers are able to describe the subtleties of authentic spiritual practice. Fewer still can skillfully reveal the complex internal journey a young man travels when, suddenly a soldier, he lands in the confusing fog of deadly war.

Ralph Steele is uniquely qualified to do both, and he does them brilliantly. As a rural son of the South, he takes us through every step of his odyssey—as soldier, student, monk, and teacher. His unbridled curiosity explores the question of what it means to be fully human and fully awake, in the best and worst of times in any human life.

Ralph is able to show us, in an unflinchingly graphic story, what is at once intimate and honest, heart-shredding and tender. He invites us to look behind the curtain into a world that Hollywood portrays as a glamorous, seductive lie. Ralph's odyssey of evolving mindfulness is nourished by an impossibly enormous heart, which he shares freely and generously with all who cross his path.

Most importantly, Ralph shows us how to tell the truth— about the wars in the world and about the wars in our own hearts. I cannot begin to explain what Ralph has given us. It is raw, it is magnificent, and it is real. He is a kind and patient guide. And if you walk beside him for a while, you will learn more about yourself than you ever imagined."

— Wayne Muller, M.Div., author of
*Sabbath: Finding Rest, Renewal, and
Delight in Our Busy Lives;* and
A Life of Being, Having and Doing Enough

"This is an extraordinary journey narrated by an extraordinary individual. In these pages, Ralph Steele leads us from the people, life, and wildlife of Pawleys Island, South Carolina, to the people and forests of Buddhist monasteries in Myanmar and Thailand; from the traumas of racism and war to the peace and bliss of mindfulness. This remarkable story is worth telling and well worth reading! *Yahman!*"

— **Jan Willis**, author of
*Dreaming Me: Black, Baptist and Buddhist—
One Woman's Spiritual Journey*

"A beautifully written, humbling, uplifting, and profoundly sweet and electrifying life story illustrating the transformative value of the cultivation of mindfulness in the face of endemic racism, war, PTSD, addiction, peacefulness, and beauty—and a society and wider world in endless flux on every level. I met Ralph almost thirty years ago, but the details of his story are almost all news to me—the kind of news that will touch you and wake you up and warm you to humanity at its loving/knowing best, including perhaps even your own. A book in a class of its own."

— **Jon Kabat-Zinn**, author of
*Full Catastrophe Living:
Using the Wisdom of Your Body and Mind to
Face Stress, Pain, and Illness*

"This is the book for all of us who struggle with honoring our devotional path while living in the everyday world. Allow yourself to settle down as Ralph Steele describes his journey through a childhood on Pawleys Island, growing up in the military, living in Japan, serving in Vietnam, and taking robes as a Buddhist monk, then leaving those robes, while trying to honor his family lineage as a community spiritual leader. Share in the very best kind of spiritual teaching: the kind that comes with peeling away layer after layer of storytelling."

— **Melinda A. Garcia**, Ph.D.
Community, Clinical, Organizational Psychology

"*Tending the Fire* is an extraordinarily engaging memoir. Ralph Steele tells the story of his passionate inner experiences in diverse cultural contexts from the Vietnam War to his total surrender to life as a forest monk in Myanmar. He communicates the ethos of his childhood in Pawleys Island, South Carolina, and his work with the dying as well as his modern psychotherapy practice where he heals the complexity of trauma from war and racism. These dharma stories gave me new insights and respect for his life lived with a passion for practice. I would recommend this book to my colleagues and friends. It will become part of my teaching curriculum."

— **Janet M. Schreiber**, Ph.D.
Director of the Graduate Program in
Trauma, Grief, and Renewal
Southwestern College, Santa Fe, New Mexico

"Within the depths of Ralph Steele's early childhood on an island, his spraying of Agent Orange over villages in Vietnam, his work with death and dying, and his life as a monk in a monastery—there is not a person who, after reading all he has lived through, will not be grateful for his or her own life."

— **Frank L. Eastland**
Ret. Chief Warrant Officer 4 (CWO4)
175th Assault Helicopter Company,
Bear Cat Vietnam 1970-1971

TENDING THE FIRE

TENDING THE FIRE

Through War and The Path of Meditation

Ralph Steele

ISBN: 978-0-9896593-2-1
ISBN: 0989659321
Library of Congress Control Number: 2014935800

Cover and Text Design by: Miko Radcliffe,
   www.drawingacrowd.net
Cover Photos of Ralph Steele as a Monk by:
   Venerable Tan Pannavuddho Bhikku
Recent Back Cover Photo of Ralph Steele by: David Hoptman,
   www.davidhoptman.com

Sacred Life Publishers™
SacredLife.com
Printed in the United States of America

This book is dedicated to

anyone who has the courage to

tend his or her fire

CONTENTS

FOREWORD

Ralph Steele's *Tending the Fire* is a pathfinder. Pursuing the truth of one's life, no matter what, is the way of the strong. Justice may or may not follow. Ralph Steele's steadfast journey masterfully takes on the hard realities of his life while pursuing the depth of spirituality. To fully appreciate the wide stance of Ralph's path, it is helpful to look at the American landscape Ralph so aptly walks us through.

I first met Ralph in a car pool up the California Coast to a Buddhist Meditation Retreat I would be co-leading. During the long drive we had a chance to get to know one another while others slept. Meeting for the first time, I naturally asked Ralph where he was from. He said, "I grew up in a place that you may never have heard of: Pawleys Island. My first language was Gullah."

I shared with Ralph that when I was born my grandparents built a house on the South Carolina coast so that the fresh salt air would protect me from contracting polio. As a child, I walked under the low-hanging moss-covered trees on the pathways of Brookgreen Gardens. Down the road was the Pawleys Island Hammock Store on Pawleys Island. Familiar with where Ralph's life began, I also knew the pulse of the times.

During the decades before the civil rights movement, the language of racism was embedded in the unspoken. The dichotomy of the segregated South under the pseudonym *separate but equal* was upheld by sign and symbol. Laws upheld injustice. On the South Carolina Grand Strand, some of the most beautiful coastline in the United States, black women in their long cotton day dresses walked along the steaming hot sands of the beach with the white children they watched over. These caregivers were forbidden to go beyond the shoreline to swim in the cool waters of the ocean on the same beach as white people.

The false pretense of *separate but equal* meant that a white store owner or gasoline station attendant could keep the restrooms locked for black people, conveniently having misplaced the key some time ago. If there was a paved road it may very well stop before the segregated section of town. In most cases, white men called black men by their first names while black men were to address white men as *Mister.* Also, many knew who the Ku Klux Klan members were—by their shoes. Men only had two pairs of shoes, one for weekdays and one for Sundays. And everyone shopped locally at the same small department stores. Quiet fear insulated the minds of many people.

If word got out that a white woman had given a handsome tip to a black household worker, her yard would fill with protesting neighbors; "Just what did she think she was doing?" Those white folks, who gave to black folks, gave secretly. Polite veneers covered a sea of unexamined misperception until the Civil Rights Act of 1964.

Ralph's courageous journey of truth is more than a memoir, more than a meditation guide; Ralph has carved a way to engage life, historical circumstance, and choice.

May we all benefit from Ralph Steele's heroic journey.

— **Jacqueline Schwartz-Mandell**
Director and Founding Teacher of Samden Ling,
A Sanctuary of Meditative Contemplation
Portland, Oregon

First, one must get to know oneself. Then, having become familiar with oneself, one can live one's life more deeply. Living one's life more deeply is the meaning of Dharma.
                                  – Ogyen Trinley Dorje

1. DECIDING AND GETTING TO MYANMAR (1997-1999)

Once upon a time, I was in a doctoral program in psychology, but I was already feeling that I didn't need to absorb all those academic belief systems in order to get to Ralph. I was also three years into a four-year teacher-training program that Jack Kornfield, a psychologist and meditation teacher, had been leading at Spirit Rock Meditation Center in Woodacre, California, for several decades; and I was bored and he knew it. Vipassana meditation is one of the great Buddhist traditions; however I was the only Vipassana teacher of color in his group, and the total of all European and North American Vipassana teachers of color together was less than one percent. So after the retreat, we talked about it. He knew the love I have for the Buddha's teachings, but we both knew that I needed to take some time off.

I wanted to experience being with people who have truly awakened through the process of meditation. Was it really possible or just pie in the sky? I wanted to get some extended mileage into my practice and understand more deeply how to tend to my own neuroses. I wanted to get way down in there and practice *tending the fire*, which is my phrase for mindfulness. Jack said, "Of course it is possible. I was a monastic for five years, and I am still digesting my experience—which words do very little to describe, as you notice in my books, Ralph."

I also needed something else. It came to me when I took a week to go fishing with my friend John on a river off of the Cook Inlet in Alaska. He had a friend named Richard who took his retirement investment and made Alaska his home. Richard was in his late sixties and about six feet eight inches tall. He had two homes, one in town and one at his hunting lodge in the woods. At his lodge, over the years he had collected various animals and mounted their heads. He said, "Ralph, instead of building a relationship with a psychiatrist and meditation, I decided to get more involved with what I love to do. Hunting and fishing is my stress management."

I said, "What an exciting way to tend your fire."

Richard had enough guns and fishing rods to open up one of those wilderness outfitters shops. John had not seen him since he retired, and John was getting close to retirement himself. John's partner Carolyn was recently diagnosed with cancer and he was considering leaving her. Their relationship was fifteen-plus years. That was an iceberg decision involving another one of many emotionally abused women in our society; this left a sad feeling in me. John wanted to see how Richard was taking care of himself, and it looked like he was doing an excellent job. John and I were going through a transition. Both of us were contemplating leaving our relationships for different reasons. I wonder who am I to say that he was cultivating emotional abuse by leaving his partner.

I said to myself, "Ralph, going away could be called emotional abuse to your partner, Sabine, as well. Just because it is a spiritual quest that you are contemplating, does that make it right?" And in addition, I found out that I had a kid in this realm—16 years after his birth. His mother had given him away, but after knowing of him for one year, I found him in New York and vowed to be a serious foundation for him so that he could live his life.

Richard said, "John told me that you practice meditation."

"Yes," I replied.

"What is walking meditation like?" he asked.

I began to explain the process of being mindful of the breath and movement of one's feet and body (see appendix for further instruction). Richard responded, "That sounds exactly like what I do when I go hunting. I become so relaxed and concentrated, I feel at one with nature." John was listening to Richard's interesting response to our conversation.

We all went to bed; it was a little difficult to sleep because of the stuffed animal heads (elk, bear, big horn sheep, and moose) hanging on the walls. Some of them were the size of a desk. I finally said a prayer and I was able to rest my bones.

I recall standing next to the river at four-thirty in the morning. In the dark, I was thinking about what I could do to get a better understanding of my relationship with life. As the darkness transformed into light, I felt a presence behind me, so I slowly turned my head around and noticed that there were at least fifty eagles perched there, hanging out or waiting for the day. In that moment I realized that my life needed to be more connected with nature, the kind of beauty I knew as a child, on Pawleys Island, South Carolina. It was in my bones: I needed some nature. *Yahman* (meaning everything's going to be all right); this was a mantra I learned from being with my grandmother Sister Mary.

After much deliberation, I decided to discontinue the doctoral program in psychology that I had been pursuing; at this time, colleagues in my Vipassana teacher study group responded to my desire for a more direct experience of Buddhist psychology and suggested that I take robes in Myanmar and Thailand. I had practiced with some Burmese monks at the Joshua Tree retreat center in Southern California and heard many stories about the forest monasteries in Myanmar and Thailand. I came to thinking I would go there and live a monk's life—at least for a year. I had not been in Asia since the Vietnam War. This time around, instead of wearing a uniform and fighting for a cause that wasn't mine, I would be there as a Buddhist monk. I had thought that a year was more what I wanted, but I also took into consideration that I might never return.

At this time Sabine and I discussed that we would part with no strings attached. We were not married at the time, although we had been partners for thirteen years, and she was a veteran of "no strings attached" experiences. Previously she had made a two-year journey to India to finalize her research in anthropology from Heidelberg University. That journey led her to a master Tantric teacher that helped to validate her understanding of self and life. So letting go was not even close to a foreign concept to her. Our first date was at a conference taught by Sufi master Pir Vilayat Inayat Khan. Our spiritual exploration had continued as a couple; and we have also supported each other's individual journey since then.

Sabine is about five feet five inches with red hair that comes down to the middle of her back. She is German and has Slavic cheekbones, emerald green eyes, and a soft smile that lights up the room. Her voice can be strong and demanding and also respectful and loving; she has an incisive intellect and is very articulate, to the point of being elegant with her words. Her personality is always upbeat.

She is very strong both physically and emotionally, which has been an excellent foundation for getting through two occurrences of breast cancer. Sabine's determination is unbelievable. When she was first diagnosed with cancer, she made the decision to not tell her parents—in order to protect them from excessive worry with their daughter living in another country. I supported her and it ended up being a healthier decision for us.

I am strongly attracted to her intellectual capabilities and our common interest in world culture; with her graduate degree in cultural anthropology she has always had an interest in community awareness. She does not like to be in debt; that really turns me on. Sabine is the embodiment of compassion; her presence is soft and electrifying.

What made this journey so special was that we decided not to have any attachment with regard to having a sexual relationship ever again. We talked about our relationship.

I said, "In some monastic traditions, you can have a relationship."

Sabine replied, "But in this tradition we cannot have the same kind of relationship."

I told her, "Relationship is an interesting process."

"Yes," she replied, "And the most powerful medicine in humanity is love."

4

"Yes, I agree. Sabine, the body is the greatest attachment, and I am beginning to feel the loss of this relationship. I am also feeling the joy of starting out on this unknown journey."

"Yes, Ralph, I am having both feelings as well."

I responded, "From my experience of assisting people through the process of dying, this is what it is like. You cultivate an extraordinary relationship with the dying during the process of caring for that person. Then the body dies. The relationship continues except that adjustments are made since the physical body is no longer there."

"Mmm," Sabine replied, "You are right. I will miss your smell, and all these sensual experiences will just be a memory. The body is a huge attachment, and relationships mirror that. This will be, and has already begun to be, an incredible journey for us."

I spoke next, "You are an incredible person."

"Yes, I am and don't you forget it!"

We had a tearful laugh.

The independence with which Sabine lives is impeccable. She shows that in all aspects of her personality. My grandmother, Sister Mary, once said to me after I moved to New Mexico: "Why do you have to live so far away from home? You are so darn independent. Who made you like that?"

"You did," I replied.

She laughed and said, "That's a good thing. Just keep God in your heart and be kind to others." Sabine has that same kind of character. This was what we were facing in our relationship—the ultimate experience of letting go of one love for another additional love: which was my journey to Asia.

Since I was letting go of a life that I knew to go into a monastic life that I didn't know, there were many doubts which arose. As I didn't want my doubting mind to get the better of me, I decided to visit Abhayagiri Buddhist Monastery in Redwood Valley, California, to get a feel of what being a monk would be like. I spent some time with *Ajahn* Pasanno (who was co-abbot with *Ajahn* Amaro who was not around). Of modest height and slender like most

5

forest monks, *Ajahn* Pasanno is originally from Canada. He had to leave Thailand because his popularity had become overwhelming.

We met in his administrative room.

"So you want to become a monk?" he asked.

"Yes," I replied.

"We had an African-American man who considered ordination; however, he went away to think it over and never returned."

I put my hands together in prayer, in a show of respect. "Well, I am planning to ordain and have made up my mind to go to Asia to practice. With everyone darker than me, hopefully, I will only have other issues to deal with."

In a soft voice he replied, "That's not the reason he left. His life had been complicated, and he has had difficulties finding balance."

"*Ajahn*, I'd rather go to Asia and practice. My love for practice is so deep; it has helped me to cope with post war trauma and heroin addiction. This practice continues to give me insight into my behavior; that's why I would like to study with some Buddhist psychology masters."

Ajahn and I just sat there for a moment; his eyes began to glow and a smile jumped off his face.

He walked over to a box sitting on the bookshelf, reached in, pulled out a knitted cap, and gave it to me (to keep my head warm when it was cool). Then he left to attend to his administrative duties.

While I was sitting on the floor having tea with a few of the monks at Abhayagiri, I noticed a picture on the wall of a monk that made me feel good inside. I pointed to that picture and asked the monks who that person was. Simultaneously, that person walked through the door and sat down in front of me. Wow, here was this six-foot-four monk, with a shiny head the size of a volleyball, big fat lips, red cheeks, and a voice that sounded like James Earl Jones (the voice of Darth Vader in the original *Star Wars* movie!). As he spent some time with me, I was so overcome by the power of his presence that I felt as though I was in elementary school.

He proceeded to tell me a few things about life as a monk, while at the same time giving me instructions about my sitting posture. I noticed that he moved his legs from one side to the other side about every five or ten minutes; as I started doing the same thing, I realized that this posture stretched the adductor muscles in the inside of my legs. The tension from the pain of sitting there for two hours soon went away. He said that I would do okay if I took good care of myself; also he warned me that I would have some sexual issues but that these would pass in my late fifties. Finally he said that I was very psychic and hoped that I would develop maturity with it.

He wished me well and told me I would see him again. He got up and walked out the door. I later found out that he was the most senior Western monk—*Ajahn* Sumedho. My doubting mind was at ground zero. This was going to be my next life if I wanted it.

After returning to Santa Fe, Sabine and I had many discussions about my decision.

I said, "Are you ready to let go?"

Her response was, "Spare me. I am not a child."

"Okay, Sweetness, let's do this," I replied. "We need to talk about this again and again."

We needed to make sure that I would not be leaving her in a stressful situation, since the plan was not to return to lay life. We made arrangements that she would come over to visit in a year, around the time of my fiftieth birthday, to make sure this was what I wanted to continue doing. We took our time with this as we both wanted to feel okay with the situation.

This was a big fire, and I wanted to make sure this was the right thing to do. I had walked out on my first wife Sandy after seven years. At the time we had tried marital counseling but it had made things worse because I did not realize that I was suffering from complex trauma. I did not want to repeat the past. While Sabine and I planned in great detail my possible stay in the monastery, I also made sure she would be all right living in Santa Fe.

I left on June 21st, the last summer solstice of the century. Sabine came with me from our home in Santa Fe to the airport in Albuquerque, New Mexico. Sabine, my partner and best friend for nearly thirteen years, was an amazing human being with her own breathtaking story to tell. When she first took me to her home in Germany to meet her parents, they met us at the airport, and her father was carrying a rose, which he gave to me and said: "I've never met a black man before, you are most welcome." He accepted me, as I was. So here we were, saying goodbye, and she cried, knowing we would not see each other again for a long time.

In Los Angeles, I had to wait some hours for my flight to Thailand. It was after midnight, and I sat alone in the airport dining room. I had only been able to sleep two hours the previous night, and tonight it looked like zero rest. The lack of sleep was kicking in; I was going into dream mode.

In the depth of my tiredness, I could feel my emotions, like someone playing a piano that's in tune and out of tune—with the piano being emotions and the keys my various mental states. I thought about Vietnam, and felt the rhythm of grief and sadness, with happiness just coming in and out. This trip to Myanmar and Thailand had a rhythm of joy and happiness, with grief and sadness just coming in and out. The ultimate rhythm comes when you learn how *not* to hit those keys, just observe and listen, like a bird flying across the sky. *Yahman*, that's why I was on this journey to the Mother Country of Buddhism—to learn that tune and how to dance with it.

Styling my brown straw hat and walking out to the gate, I was already feeling like a *bhikkhu*, a Buddhist monk who lives by alms and sees the cycle of birth, life, death, and rebirth. How special it was to have this time to just practice training my mind.

It was a long flight with plenty of time to reflect and entertain my mental states. Lobsang Lhalungpa, my Tibetan teacher for eleven years, gave me a book to read during my flight, titled *The Life of Milarepa*. I read that Milarepa came to be known as one of the most famous meditation practitioners and teachers; he was the rascal of rascals. Since I had studied him in college for my undergraduate degrees in humanistic psychology and religious studies, I said to Lobsang, "I don't need him."

"Yes, you do. Read it again."

"Okay."

Lobsang saw my anger and rage; he was the exact opposite, kind and gentle. He had assigned the Tara mantra practices for 100,000 recitations. After four months, I said "Okay, I am complete."

"Now do a million," he responded.

When any one of his students attempted to bow, he would quickly come closer and stick his hand out, with a soft smile on his face that would melt butter; his response was that a handshake would do. At a conference that His Holiness the Dalai Lama was hosting, His Holiness walked off the stage into the audience and greeted Lobsang. That was just a confirmation for us that we had found a true gem. Lobsang's father had been the Dalai Lama's Oracle. It was a privilege to have him in my life. He was the Senior Elder who took me and less than twenty others under his wing.

I had decided to fly on Korean Airlines because several people had told me they had a bad safety record, *and yet,* the service was excellent! Their kindness made the flight so enjoyable; I offer a deep bow to Korean Airlines. I found myself thinking about how I got into meditation and my spiritual education and all the people who helped along the way, and that took me back to drugs, the war, and racism; and *that* took me back to my childhood, and my first spiritual teacher—Sister Mary. So that's where I want to begin.

2. CHILDHOOD ON PAWLEYS ISLAND
(1950s)

I was born on Pawleys Island off the coast of South Carolina, and Sister Mary was my grandmother on my mother's side. At that time, Pawleys was a paradise of apricots, plums, blackberries, pecans, walnuts, and many other fruit trees growing in the wild. We had water lilies and assorted flowers, poison ivy, and natural creatures of comfort such as snakes, spiders, poison ivy, wild turkeys, and foxes, just to name a few. And we had the swamps, where alligators lived.

When I was three, my father died in an automobile accident. It was a new car and the steering column came apart the day he bought it. I remember standing at the head of his grave, confused and sad as they were putting him in the ground. I didn't understand why people had to go to sleep and never wake up. After that, my mom had to work all day to take care of my younger brother Jimmy and me, so we were mostly with Sister Mary.

She was a very unusual person, and everyone knew it. She had a garden where everything was huge. It was like something out of a fairytale. In later years, it reminded me of the Findhorn Garden in Scotland, which came to be known during the sixties for growing huge vegetables on a diet of love and prayer. As my brother and I pulled weeds for Sister Mary, she would sing and pray. Those vegetables were raised on songs like *Precious Lord*, in addition to the vibrations that she put into the soil as she tended it. The results were incredible. An ear of corn would be sixteen inches long. One leaf of collard greens might be two to three feet in length. Tomatoes were like grapefruits. Her garden was next to the road, so when people drove by they would often stop just to look or take pictures. She also had a magnificent flower garden. One of her favorite flowers was gladiolas, in all the different colors. And she tended the yard like a Zen master. It was raked every day, not just the garden but also the path you walked on. That was one of my jobs. There was never a Saturday when the yard wasn't raked unless there was a major hurricane, which happened every year.

Sister Mary was married to Baba James Rainey, and his family was well known in the ministry, back to the mid-1800s. Baba James' father, my great grandfather, lived just across the road. He was called "Father" and he was the first person on the Island to have a car. After his death, instead of handing his car down, they took it into the woods and burned it, asking God to take care of him. His grandfather, John Hays Rainey, had been a congressman, representing South Carolina. He was elected for two terms and is mentioned in the Congressional Globe as having started the mail system to Haiti. His name can be found in books about the reconstruction of the South, and he was given a little recognition when America had its bicentennial year celebration. The town of Georgetown, the county seat for Pawleys Island, put something in one of their parks in his name.

Sister Mary and Baba James worked very hard. They were a wonderful team. Everything was geared toward survival. Baba James had about three acres where he grew corn and watermelons, lima beans, black-eyed peas, and okra. One acre of corn was for the horse; the rest was for canning in the fall. That was the bulk of our food for the winter. We'd buy a sack of rice and a sack of cornmeal for grits, and other dry staples, but that was it. We had a peach tree and a pear tree, both of which produced lavish fruits. Sister Mary made wine out of them, and some of the corn went into making corn liquor, which was used for medicinal purposes.

My little brother Jimmy and I spent a lot of playtime together with our cousins. We'd go out into the swamps and find a tall tree that we'd climb in order to spot an even taller tree. Then we'd climb the bigger one; it would take most of a day. The trees stood so thick together around Pawleys Island that we could climb them and dive like monkeys from one to another. We'd be wading through pecans, ankle deep under wild nut trees, blackberry patches, every green thing you can imagine. We were always barefoot. This freedom was unforgettable.

On one of these adventures we both suddenly smelled apple blossoms, but we knew it couldn't be apple blossoms in the middle of the summer. No, it was that fearsome black whuppin' snake, which was famous for putting out this odor. Man, we took off running. I was running a few steps behind Jimmy. The snake chased us, whuppin' as it came. We ran and ran until we got to the sandy dirt road. The surface was hot, but we were okay by lifting our feet up and down. The snake had to turn around and go back because of the burning sand. And when we got home, Sister Mary would pull the ticks off Jimmy and me.

In the wintertime, Sister Mary and I would go to the creeks in the marshlands to get oysters and clams and spend the evening opening oysters around the fire. We'd put on old '78 records—Nat King Cole, waltz music, classical music—and we would wind up with maybe twenty quart jars of oysters and clams to sell in Georgetown.

In the summer, we'd swim a lot; Sister Mary always told us to do that for its healing power, the healing power of the Mother. I used to go about fifty yards off the coast, past the breaking waves, and body surf onto the beach. But I wasn't a good swimmer. When I was eleven, surfing in the ocean was my favorite thing, especially as the wind picked up and the waves grew higher and more powerful. One time I knew I should go back to the shore, but it felt so good to just hang out there that I decided to stay in the bliss. Suddenly my body was slipping down the front of a wave. I decided to ride it in instead of swimming further out, but then I realized my timing was off because of the wind; I was caught between the waves. I started stroking toward the shore as hard and fast as I could, but a wave came up behind me, and my body was dragged down and back by the strong undercurrent. I remember saying to myself, "You're not going to get out of this one."

The next moment I was observing my body spinning around in the ocean. Then I was rising up to the ocean surface; everything in my awareness was the ocean surface. Then I thought "land," and instantly land was in view, and my cousin was swimming hard toward me (or my body, I didn't know which). I looked down to view my body and all I could see was my right arm above the surface. "Why is he swimming so hard and fast?" I wondered. Then his hand grabbed my hand, and the next thing I was choking up salt water. He brought me to shore and yelled at me for being so crazy and disrespectful to the ocean, thinking that I knew what I was doing. I remembered Baba James' lesson, I was just a grain of sand on the beach with a speck of salt water—and nothing compared to the ocean. From that point on, I knew something; there was something else besides the body.

Church was at the center of our lives. On Saturday evenings, Sister Mary would heat water and my younger brother Jimmy and I would take a bath outside. Sister Mary and Baba James had their bath when it was dark. This was all so we'd be ready for Sunday, the big day.

Sunday morning began early for my brother and me. By nine o'clock we were at Sunday school, where we did Bible study with one of the Babas (deacons) or one of the Sisters (also deacons). After that we'd attend the regular service, and people came from all around. When Sister Mary came up to the church she was greeted by everyone. She was regarded as a very special person.

There was never a dull moment in our church—Old St. John's African Methodist Episcopal Church. It made the church in the movie *The Blues Brothers* look like elementary school. It was *the* community spot, a true sangha (community) that supported you. If a person's house burned down, it was at the church that they'd organize to help that person. No one had a lot of money, but everyone was rich.

The service always began with a prayer by one of the elder deacons. There was no microphone system, so everyone spoke with a voice that resonated throughout the building. Then the minister would invite someone special, a Sister or Baba, to do the opening prayer. That person would go up to the front, or if they were already up there sitting on either side of the altar, they would kneel down at their seat, and everyone else in the congregation would join them in kneeling. This was called "going to knee-bone college."

When that Sister or Baba began the prayer, you could feel the juice flowing and moving throughout the room.

Sometimes it had the appearance of fog with a shimmering light to it, and a warm sensation, which would penetrate your bones. It would make you feel bigger than the building you were in. Sometimes the Sister or Baba would do a little something with the tone of their voice, and that something would manifest into the taste of honey in your mouth. Just when you thought that prayer would never end, it did; twenty to sixty minutes just went up in smoke.

After that, the Elders in the congregation would be saying "*Yahman*, thank you, thank you, thank you, Jesus," and fanning themselves because they were all wet with sweat. Some of the young men would be grumbling and remarking with their under-voice about the energetic heat that was just turned up; they were sweating and wetting their freshly pressed shirts. It was interesting to feel the salt from your sweat mixing with the starch from your shirt. And the men would look at their male neighbors and shake their heads, and their wives would jab them in the ribs to remind them where they were.

At this point, magic began to happen. The Elders would forget their bodies' aches and pains, as another softer energy would arise. Some of them would be walking up and down the aisle to cool down, and even those with crutches or a walking stick would be getting help up the stairs to the church door and walking up and down the aisle, carrying-on, with no stick!

They had so much juice that no one would dare get in their way or try and get them to sit down. They would be saying, "Yes! Can you feel it?" and if the response wasn't loud enough, they would say it again, even louder: "Can you feel it?" The congregation would say "Yes!" and several people would stand up as they were touched deeply by that juice.

Sometimes the congregation would seem to be out of control, speaking in tongues, which is a babbling tone from deep within the body. It comes from the instinctual reptilian brain stem that I believe connects us with the cosmic juices. That juice is the flow of life, sometimes referred to as the Holy Spirit, *prana*, breath energy, ambrosia, or the breath of Ram, depending on your tradition.

15

The juice was flowing all over the place. Old Saint John's would just be rocking. This was my early introduction to the energy of community and the power of prayer.

3. VISA TO MYANMAR
(July 1999)

I woke up as the jumbo jet was descending from the clouds into the landscape of Asia and the city of Bangkok. This was the first time I laid my eyes on the emerald lushness of Asia since leaving Vietnam, thirty years before.

The airport was like any major airport. I did my shuffle to get through customs, which was a warm greeting into Thailand. When my body came into contact with the heat outside, I remembered a musical tune the Isley Brothers sang: *The Heat Is On.* The sun was scorching hot with the humidity making sweat come out of my ears.

I had only $2000 for my "tour of duty," but I needed to get a taxi, so I caught one of those three-wheeled vehicles half the size of a Volkswagen. It had no sides or windows, but a natural air-conditioning system that nourished me with humidity and sweltering heat.

I ended up in a motel in the *hood* for Westerners. This *hood* was a place that could make you feel at home with pancakes, cappuccino, milkshakes, French fries, movies, conversations, CNN, internet cafe, and a variety of places to hang, all the things that I did not want to get into. I was thinking about the monasteries that I wanted to visit in Bangkok and elsewhere in Thailand before heading to Myanmar.

I went to the Burmese Embassy to get my visa for Myanmar where I would start my year as a monk, but the head consul and I got into a confrontation. At one point I told him to be quiet so that I could ask a question; that changed the expression on his face. I just wanted to know the difference in price between a meditation and a tourist visa. He wanted to give me a tourist visa because it had a price, and the meditation visa did not. Not wanting to talk about the meditation visa and refusing to grant me one, he said he would be glad to grant me a tourist visa to fly to Yangon and return with a letter confirming my monastic training. That rascal had a smile on his face, because he

17

thought that he would make some money, but I refused his offer with a smile of my own. I decided to do some chillin' activities instead.

I walked down the street away from the embassy and greeted three men who were in a shop. I was going there to get a cool drink and these joyful men were buying a package of sticks; this got my curiosity going. We walked together and shared conversation.

I asked them, "What do you do?"

"We are administrators and our job is very boring. It requires little attention, so we stop and pick up some chewing sticks," they replied.

"I am trying to get a meditation visa for Myanmar."

They said, "That sounds great. Working on being calm can be healthy."

They were from India and on their way to work; I told them more about what I was up to, and they shared that they were Hindu practitioners. They opened the packet of sticks and each one put one piece into his mouth and began chewing. They turned toward me and asked, "Would you like to try?"

"What is it?"

"Very good for you."

"Yeah, good for what?"

"Relaxation, please take one."

I took one and started chewing. Whatever was in that wooden stick, it felt like I had just dropped some purple haze acid. Come on Jimi Hendrix; play those tunes. I heard music and noticed that a Hindu temple was just across the street, so I walked in. There was a statue there with several heads . . . whoa . . . no, not several heads . . . my mind was spinning.

I backed up to a pillar and slid down to the marble floor. It felt cool and solid, which was what I needed. Vertigo was kicking my butt, and I sat there for about one hour. Then I said to myself, "Okay, Ralph, this building sits on a corner, just get there and you will be able to get into a taxi." I got myself up, and I felt like I had a ten-week hangover from drinking.

I was able to get to the corner and into a taxi. Every time the driver stopped at a traffic light, I partially opened the door and vomited up my breakfast. He got me to my hotel and up into my room, where I passed out on my bed. I woke up the next morning with a mild headache, slowly stood up to check things out, and felt that everything was working all right. What a trip; who *were* those people?

I tried three times to get a visa for Myanmar within a two-week period, and each time I had "Denied" stamped on my passport. The woman at the embassy said I needed a letter of invitation from Myanmar and that a faxed copy, which was all I had, was not sufficient. So I made a few calls to America to have a conversation with Jack Kornfield, to help my chillin' time. I told him about the visa situation, and he said, "Welcome to the world of people messing with you. Keep smiling and be creative." It was a reminder to practice patience. I started to think I might need to fly to Myanmar for that letter and bring it back, just to get my visa to return to Myanmar; but first, I decided to make one more attempt. I had smoothed out the wrinkles on my visa paper back in my hotel room.

So here I was, stepping into the Embassy again, a frequent visitor to the staff by now. Concrete floor, dust from the foot traffic, three windows at the counter in the lobby but only two with people working at them. The room had benches attached to the floor and a few plastic chairs along the walls.

I happened to sit down next to a gentleman who had a briefcase and looked like a Westerner. We began talking, and I learned that he was trying to get a business visa (which is the most expensive, with the next level down being a tourist, followed by a meditation visa). He had visited Myanmar several times and had been making a very good profit from gems. The essence of his conversation was money, which I wanted to get away from because I had already surrendered into becoming a monastic, and in this particular lineage, money is not used by monks or nuns.

When they called my name, with a slight smile I approached the counter, ready to dance with whatever situation they wanted to give me. I showed the faxed letter again, and the officer read it as if this were the first time she had seen it; and she accepted it, even though it wasn't an original.

I was then invited to step into the consul's office. He was sitting behind a desk, and on top of his desk were at least eleven stacks of passports, with about fifteen to twenty per stack. Sitting in a chair in front of the desk, I could see him only from his shoulders on up! He looked at the fax, then my passport, and asked if I promised not to engage in any criminal or political activity or any activity other than monastic practice. That was easy. I would have needed a small team to do all that. So he granted my visa and said, "Enjoy your flight."

I stepped out of the building, got into a taxi, and was off to the hotel to pack and make my flight arrangements. The next morning after breakfast at my favorite spot—banana pancakes was their specialty and mine—I was off to the airport and feeling very good.

The flight to Myanmar was just over one hour; and there, again, I had to go through customs. I wondered, "What will this be like?" The customs officer here was dressed in a white uniform with big golden bars on his shoulders, and he asked for a certain paper I did not have. After fumbling through my clothes, I told him, "No, I don't have it." He reached into his pocket, pulled out a piece of paper, and instructed me to write my name and passport number on it.

After I gave it to him, he took a closer step toward me and I took a closer step toward him as he peered into my face. We were nose-to-nose, even though he was a little shorter, looking into the depth of each other's ocean with no words. Then he stepped back and so did I. He could see that I acknowledged him with respect for just being and he stepped aside. So I walked into the country of Myanmar, knowing that I had just stepped deep into the grace of Buddhism.

I got a taxi without difficulty and asked for the monastery of Chanmyay Sayadaw. As we were driving through the city of Yangon on our way to Chanmyay Yeiktha (yeiktha means meditation center), listening to the music of honking horns like most non-Western cities, I rolled the windows down to smell the city and let the sweet humidity wrap around my bones. The city's smell contained the aromas floating up from the open sewer mixed with the diesel of two-wheel cycles, coffee coming from the cafes, musty leaves piled along the street, and my own sweat.

Chanmyay is the name of a section of the city, but it is also a title that attracts the highest reverence in the Buddhist community. The word means peacefulness. It is interesting that every traditional culture has its way to acknowledge an elder. Of course there is no written test or oral exam. It's based on the observation of the community. On Pawleys Island, the revered elders were given the title Sister or Baba depending on gender. In the Thai Buddhist culture the equivalent is Luang Por. It is wonderful to know that this ancient way of acknowledging revered elders continues in the modern world.

I had initially met the abbot, U'Janaka Chanmyay Sayadaw, in the mid-seventies, when he came to America with two other Burmese monks, U'Silinanda and Mahasi Sayadaw (see appendix: Mahasi Sayadaw). We were at a meditation retreat, and I was having a problem with sitting posture. I would shift from attempting to sit with my legs crossed on the floor to sitting on a kneeling bench. I noticed that the monks were sitting on the floor with their legs crossed but with one knee up off the floor, so in the question and answer period, I questioned the sitting posture. One of the monks said that it was important to sit comfortably with crossed legs if you can. But I wasn't satisfied and kept asking, "Why is your knee up off the floor?"

After about three times, one of them said, "You will eventually get it."

"Get what?" I said. No response. It would be another ten years, sitting with many other esteemed meditation teachers, before I "got it." The important thing in meditation practice is not posture but "What am I doing in there?"

We eventually approached the monastery that was just off the street with a four-foot wall separating the street from the grounds. The open sewer was on the street side, and on the other side the grounds were shaded by fully-grown trees that looked like oak (but of a variety in this part of the world that I didn't know). These trees had thick green moss hanging down to help shade the dogs that were slowly moving back and forth from the cool shade to a sunny area on the grounds. Several monks dressed in maroon robes were walking around, mixing with laypeople in colorful tops or shirts and fabric wrapped around them. They were in flip-flops, walking attentively and in silence. I felt a sudden shift of quiet after getting out of the taxi.

In the administration building, I was greeted by the staff. They made me aware that U'Janaka Chanmyay Sayadaw would not arrive until next month, which would be July. I was relieved because I didn't want the abbot to see me with a heart and mind that was so discombobulated. I had almost a month to practice and get myself as much together as I could.

In the meantime, I was assigned to an area where non-Burmese practitioners and monastics lived. One was from Japan, others from South Africa, China, and Korea. There were a total of six of us from various countries.

As I settled in at the monastery, I didn't receive any meditation instruction, nor did I expect any. Anyone new to the practice of meditation would be in a world of trouble in this situation; though I am sure that it has happened to many Westerners—*Yahman!* I just looked around and tuned in to what was going on.

My living space was just a little bigger than the single bed inside it. The funny thing about this bed was that it did not have a mattress. I guess that this was so we would not get too comfortable, and certainly no one complained about not being comfortable. I strapped up my mosquito net and got myself ready to practice. I just wanted to *practice*; it was so exciting to be around people who just love to practice.

There were two meditation halls in another building, one on top of the other. Either of these rectangular halls could hold at least five hundred people. The hall below with marble floors was for the public, and the hall above with wood floors was for the monastics and guest residents. The monastics sat up front and we sat behind them. Each one of us had a mosquito net that was cylinder-shaped, six feet in height and about three feet in diameter. The meditation hall had ceiling fans to help with the mosquito population. There were no glass windows, just shutters, and they were mostly open.

Looking outside you could see the dogs hanging out. My eyes moved down the tree trunk admiring the emerald-colored moss that had its own texture and design of swirls, cone shapes, and miniature mountains. Then at the trunk of this tree I saw a huge rat, the size of a full-grown cat. It had a damp, grayish look that helped it blend in with the ground.

Myanmar is the mosquito kingdom. During the rainy season, the numbers and varieties are off the charts. So the point is not to get into mosquito repellant so much, but to get into the mosquitoes. Actually, I didn't have a choice. There were a lot more mosquitoes than I'd brought repellant for. Besides, I didn't want to spend my time inhaling repellant; I did enough of that years ago when I used substances to alter my consciousness.

There was ample space inside to sit, as well as walking meditation whenever we desired. Between sitting and walking, I was able to practice ten to twelve hours per day. The humidity was off the charts, I would guess 95 percent; sweat was coming out of my ears again. It was a good and sweet sweat, like being back home on the island, except that here there was no lemonade. I was working at not being so negative, which was one of my reasons for being here. It was good to be in this climate, around people who love to practice. It just didn't get any better than this.

When the mind is in a very difficult situation, like mosquitoes and humidity, it's easy for the mind to blunder into a hellish emotional state. I practiced balancing that energy with a super positive state, which was my love for the practice and being with people who share the same joy. I was a professional at training camp; this was my world.

My twenty-four-hour practice included getting up at two o'clock in the morning and washing up. We didn't have hot water and didn't want it, because of the humidity. Around three o'clock I would do my first walking practice to become more concentrated. Then, after an hour or so, I would do sitting practice, working with the sensation of the breath.

The primary breath technique at this monastery was feeling the sensation of the rising and falling of the chest. I would also include a little loving-kindness at the beginning and ending of my sitting period, directing kind phrases towards myself.

There are so many systems of loving-kindness practice, from the traditional Theravada practice (which the Buddha taught), along with Zen, Pure Land, and Tibetan varieties to the Christian ones; all other religions have some form of this practice. In fact, I believe the application of meditation itself is the cultivation of loving-kindness. We take time out of our lives for a few minutes to several hours to give skillful attention to the body and mind. With kindness we invoke chanting or singing, mantras or prayers, visualizations, or just breathing into our practices. When we are angry, we do various practices to gain balance of body, speech, and mind; when everything is going well, we continue to practice—and all because of love. The application of meditation practice should always have the intention of a loving and affectionate kindness to oneself.

At about six in the morning, I would do walking meditation until we were given permission by one of the monks to go and have our first meal. This lineage permits two meals per day instead of one as in some other monasteries. Whether it is one or two meals, food must be eaten between 6 a.m. and noon. We would go into the eating room slowly, walking in a single line. This room had at least thirty tables, and six people could sit at each table comfortably. Upon reaching my sitting place, I would kneel down and bow three times, and then sit cross-legged at a table that was about two feet high.

When I first arrived, I sat with both legs to one side, as the monks do in Thailand, when not in meditation. But now I was in Myanmar, where the tradition is stricter. A monk came up to me, squatted down, smiled, and looked at me as if I was a major problem—to him, myself, or to the tradition. He finally made a gesture with his arms by crossing them and pointed to the women who were also eating in a separate section of the same dining hall. I got that he wanted me to sit cross-legged, and that only women are permitted to sit with both legs to one side. Okay, let's find equanimity within this culture.

Each table would have at least ten to fifteen bowls of different kinds of food on it, and the kitchen was constantly bringing more food out. It reminded me of Thanksgiving, Christmas, or New Year's dinner in America. In other words, it was a feast, and that was just our first meal of the day. The second meal was served at eleven, and this quality of feeding repeated every day.

I began my mindfulness of eating, but almost immediately, another monk came up to me and said, "Slow down." I thought that I was eating slowly, but it wasn't slow enough. An internal war broke out in me when I tried to eat even slower, a war with my senses. In Buddhism, there are six basic sense doors: the eyes, ears, nose, mouth, touch, and mental images. Sense information was coming in through the doors of my eyes—shades of red, orange, white, green, yellow, and a few unrecognizable ones since I am color-blind. My nose was picking up the delicious smells of cooked food mixed with the aroma of spices. The other two doors were my taste buds and my mental activity. The food tasted so good, and my mental activity was saying, "Let's get some of this," and before it came into my mouth, it said, "Let's try some of that." To slow this process down, I had to struggle with my sensations, which were burning hot inside of me.

I took in a deep breath and intentionally slowed my body down. That worked, with the help of my secret mantra, "Be patient." That got me through the meal. Then I bowed three times to a photo of the abbot and his lineage, which goes all the way back to the Buddha.

After a short break to brush my teeth and clean myself up, we students were back in the meditation hall for another two hours of practicing. I always began my practice with walking meditation to cultivate some tranquility. When it felt right inside, a feeling of being filled, I would begin sitting meditation.

At eleven when we would have our second and final meal for the day, we students would be in line behind the monks, and always, the table was filled with food—another feast. How did I get hungry within a few hours? Was I burning that much energy in the practice? I would start throwing food into my mouth; and, again, a monk would come by and say, "Slow down." I would take a breath between every mouthful, put my eating utensil down, chew, swallow, and pick up my utensil for another mouthful of this delicious food. I was later informed by studying nutrition that it is so important to chew your food down to mush. This will give the brain both time and complete information to send the proper enzymes to the stomach. Otherwise, the body will have to deal with undigested food and will not gain the proper nutritional value from a meal such as this one, prepared with heartfelt kindness.

After completing my meal came that routine again—bowing, slowly returning to my room, brushing my teeth, and washing up. Then I would lie down for thirty to sixty minutes. Ah, my body needed that.

Early in the afternoon we were back in the meditation hall practicing until tea at about four. By now, it was so hot that sweat was pouring out of my skin like running water, and they would serve us soft drinks and water. The monks also had something green on their table that looked like green plums. It was said to be good for the digestion but was definitely an acquired taste.

In the evenings, we were reminded that this was the mosquito kingdom. In the rainy season, the mosquito population would increase at least a thousand times, but in the evening it already felt like I was walking around in a spider web. In the meditation hall, each of us had a mosquito net to practice under, and there were ceiling fans. I would practice until nine-thirty or ten and then retire to my wonderful hard bed. Believe me, it felt good to do lying practice, which at that point was like "dead man sleeping." Being so exhausted from the day, that bed felt really good, and of course I would be under my net.

After six weeks of this practice, the abbot returned from his teaching tour, and I was summoned for an interview in his two-story building. From the outside it appeared to be at least two thousand square feet of floor space, all marble. I was waiting for my turn outside in the sun, and the heat was seriously on. My light cotton shirt and the wrap-around cloth from my waist down felt like a winter coat. A western tee shirt would have felt like an electric blanket on "high." It was "hotter than the fourth of July," as Stevie Wonder would say.

Finally it was my turn to go inside. I had met this abbot in America about twenty years before, in California, and even then I had felt an abundance of respect for him. I liked the way he carried himself, his attitude toward people, his love for the Dharma, and how he carried it with so much pride. He knew Hindi, Sanskrit, English, Pali, and of course his own native Burmese language. He was a master of Buddhist psychology. And this would be the 53rd Rains Retreat he had supervised. But in the heat of the moment, my respect was taken over by mental states that were plotting ways to stay cool in this heat.

I was finally inside of his main greeting room, sitting on a cool marble floor. His room was air conditioned, and I said to myself, "Yeah, this is The Man." My mind was trying to figure out a way to get in here to sleep—"All right, come to the breath." He sat on a long couch with other monks who were opening and reading his mail. The abbot was talking to someone in front of me. I told myself how much I enjoyed being patient, because I didn't want this situation to end. That cool air felt *so* good.

At last it was my turn to go up and introduce myself to him. He sat at one end of the couch, with a coffee table in front of him. His legs couldn't touch the floor, so he had a six-inch bamboo stool to place his feet on. I guessed that the stool was made especially for him, because my size eleven feet would be too big to fit on it. I was kneeling down on the other side of the table, and he motioned for me to come toward the end of the table so that the element of space would be the only thing between us. I stood up and walked with my knees and torso bent over out of respect.

Throughout Asia, bowing is a sign of utmost respect. So as I got within two to three feet of him, I began my bow. He stuck his right hand out with palm down, as if he was fanning me. As my torso bent forward and my lower body began to go down on my knees, I started to sweat, and I mean seriously sweat, even though there was air-conditioning in there.

"Why does he want to do this to me?" I said to myself.

As my head got closer to his hand, it appeared that I was seeing something coming out of his hand, like a smoky light substance. By the time I was on my knees, I was pouring sweat. My body felt like it had just walked into a Cosmic Sauna.

Kneeling in front of him, I began to prostrate with my head going to the floor three times. He said with a deep voice, "Yes, that's right, bow. Now what is your story?" I knew he meant to ask about how I got in this body and ended up here.

I told him that I was born on Pawleys Island, South Carolina. I was surprised that he knew the state. After I told him my story about my childhood, the war, and how I came to meditation, he asked me what I would like to do. I asked him for permission to take robes and sit the Rains Retreat under his supervision. "Very well," he said, "Continue with your practice and someone will get in touch with you."

I bowed three times and walked outside where the temperature was much hotter. The temperature inside me felt cool as chocolate ice cream.

4. STUTTERING
(1950-1960)

I have told about the sunny side of life on Pawleys Island, but I also need to speak about the darker side.

A large part of my time as a child was spent in bed. A very sickly child, I was ill a lot. There was nothing unusual with my health, but I went through all the childhood sicknesses. Also, I had asthma. Sister Mary and Baba James had no concept of medicine or doctors; we used herbs. As a matter of fact, there was a house up the road that we called the hospital, because up in the attic there were medicines left over from the Civil War. Sister Mary would consult with a woman there who was an herbalist; all of my healing was through herbs and urine therapy. Of course, it didn't work as fast as medication. There were many times I would say, "Just let me die." I got tired of changing pajamas from sweating and drinking all these different kinds of teas such as sassafras, mugwort, chinaberry, moonshine, and many other kinds of snake-oils that were put together for me by this herbalist. Sister Mary would apply huge leaves to my chest to draw out the poison and wake me in the middle of the night to change the leaf, and I would see that it was all brown. The most interesting part about this was that it worked.

One time Sister Mary put me against an oak tree and drove a nail a foot or two above my head. She said when I passed that nail my fear about asthma would be gone. And she was right. I also had a severe speech impediment. Often, it was hard just to say a sentence, and I would pound my hand on something, just to get the words out, or I would cry. So I didn't talk much because it was so difficult to speak.

When fear hits the nervous system at a young age, our body, speech, and mind are altered. The body shakes, the mind has difficulty with sentence structure; and when you speak, the speech pattern is broken up like a scratched CD or record. The word for this is stuttering. When a person has been traumatized, stuttering is one of the many symptoms of post-traumatic stress disorder. Stuttering is a form of shell shock: you're in shock, and it goes deep into your bones.

The world around was mostly beautiful, but there was also violence. Sister Mary and Baba James would get into serious fights. At times Baba James would have to go to another house and stay a few nights until things cooled down. Sister Mary would mend her wounds because she spoke her mind. It is not easy now for women to voice their opinions; can you imagine what it was like fifty years ago? Out in the community, many times I would witness someone getting hit in the face so hard that teeth and blood were going in various directions.

This used to frighten me, but it was nothing compared with my fear of the white man. From my childhood perspective, it appeared that there were not many whites on Pawleys Island, but whatever they said was right. You had no one except God on your side. I heard many stories of a white woman not liking a black man for being on the planet, and making up a story so that black man would end up on the chain gang.

When talking to a white person, I would wet my pants, cry, and throw things on the floor, as I tried to get a word out of my mouth. When I grew older, I learned to control my urination, but the stuttering and shaking continued. Eventually I found a speech pathologist as well as using meditation to deal with it; but at the time, what helped were physical and mental activities like the Cub Scouts and later the Boy Scouts. Both offered me a way to be in nature.

I had a couple of jobs working for white people. The first was just to pick up little sticks, thousands and thousands of them, on the grounds of the air force base at Myrtle Beach. We got ten cents for a bushel! It took a long, long time to get a bushel. The foreman treated us like animals.

Then, when I was eleven, I worked at the King Bowling Alley. It was situated on a section of the beach that was for whites only, and we black folks did the majority of the labor. My cousin Lonnie Ford worked there, and he got me the job. The bowling alley did not have machines to re-set the pins when they were knocked down, and his job was to re-set the pins, for ten cents a game. He showed me all the fine points in pin setting, especially how to protect myself when that ball came down the alley hitting those pins. Sometimes kids would say something like: "Look at that nigger down there. Can you hit him?" But afterwards they would throw a nickel or a quarter down the gutter for my tip.

Mrs. King took me to and from work. One night, we were a few minutes late getting to work. As we drove up (I was sitting in the front passenger side), Mr. King with his huge overweight body walked up to the car to ask why we were late. Mrs. King began explaining, but before she could get her words out, he was hitting her. I was the only black person around. After he got through with her he rolled his big red eyes up to me and said, "Get your ass in there." I quickly went to work.

The next night when Mrs. King came over to pick me up, Sister Mary had told me what to do, and she was there waiting. I went out to the car and said that I was not ever going back to that bowling alley. We shared a deep silent gaze at each other, we both took a deep breath at the same time, and then she said, "I understand." I knew that Mr. King was going to go upside her head, but I did not want to experience being in that white hell again. Mr. King eventfully died from a heart attack.

Worse than that was the Ku Klux Klan, which spread a terror that touched us all. They caught one of my uncles and slit his ears like a pig. He was lucky because he didn't die. When they did kill people, they would throw them in the ocean. We heard that sometimes they skinned the black men they caught.

My sense of how the world works was formed by Sister Mary, and what I learned from her fit very naturally into my later spiritual development. I never had to face spiritual contradictions, and I believe it's because she prepared me for everything, from Vietnam to Insight Meditation. She was like some of the advanced teachers I would meet later in life, with that same peaceful concentration and confidence. She gave me my earliest lessons in what I now call mindfulness—experiencing life fully in every moment.

Mindfulness supports the heart, and the results are healing and sweet.

Sister Mary taught me compassion, especially when the chain gangs came by in the summertime to clean the road. This was pretty scary. You could hear them singing, and you could hear the sounds as they cut weeds. They'd come right up to the house, all Afro-Americans of course, except for one guy with sunglasses and a shotgun draped over his arm. Each man had a bush-axe, a long-handled axe.

My younger brother Jimmy and I would hide in the bushes and watch. All of a sudden, Sister Mary would walk out the front door with a pitcher of lemonade and a cup attached to it with a string. In her other hand she had a plate of sweetbread. It was like she was expecting them. The man with the gun would lock it in place and raise it disapprovingly, and Sister Mary would walk right past the man as if he didn't exist. She went to each man with a drink and some sweetbread. Her job was to console them. We saw all the respect and reverence she got. Sister Mary would basically forgive them for what they had done. Some of the men would have tears in their eyes.

This was compassion in action. She walked out of the house with food and drink, and she was completely focused on that moment. The guy with the gun might as well have not been there at all. He was invisible to her. Her practice of unconditional love over the years enabled her to walk up to each man and give what she wanted to give to him. Finally, she would walk up to the man with the gun and ask if he'd like some lemonade and some sweetbread. He always said no. He missed her blessing. Then the men would leave, someone would start up a tune, and the men would begin singing along and swinging their axes in unison. It was like a dance moving down the road. My brother and I always went out into the road where they had stood and shot marbles after they left.

Leaving Pawleys Island was traumatic. When I was thirteen, my mom married again, and my stepfather was in the military in Alabama, so Mom wanted us to move there. She spent a lot of time explaining the reason, but it did not make any sense to me. Moving to Alabama meant leaving everything I knew and loved, especially Sister Mary. I felt an ache in my chest for the first time, and my bones felt cold.

In a very short time I went from a secure and magical existence to a place I had never imagined—Montgomery, Alabama. This was the end of my childhood, and my introduction to the so-called *real world*. All of a sudden I lived in what they now call a *hood*. I couldn't believe it— houses were ten feet apart! And the kids were mean and often violent. They couldn't figure out who in the world I was. To this day, I wish we had never left the island. I've been around the world, and it seems as if everything important I've experienced happened on Pawleys Island. I realized that "Life is an experience of practicing to shine brighter because the dark can get darker."

In Montgomery, I went to an all-black school, George Washington Carver High School (they were all called that, or Booker T. Washington); then after a year we moved on to Bakersfield, California. Here, out of the blue, I was in an all-white school. That was when I first discovered that it wasn't just me who was afraid of white people; they were also afraid of me!

One day I was cornered in a bathroom by a bunch of guys who wanted to jump me. Luckily, some other kids came to my rescue and taught me there were certain places not to go. But still, the teachers would ridicule me, make fun of my stuttering, and so forth; and there were so many confrontations that I would start shaking. Even if no one was talking, I'd shake.

I didn't know it, but I was angry, and I took that feeling with me to Yokota, Japan, where we moved in 1963. There were maybe fifteen or twenty blacks in our new school, out of about eight hundred kids, and we were all Americans. A lot of the time I just tried to make myself invisible. I began playing sports—football and basketball—and was hoping for a career in sports. Scouts would come over from the States to watch the various high school teams, and it looked like a good ticket into college. Then one day at an inter-school tournament, the coach came into the locker room and said, "Steele, you're not suiting up." There had been a fight of some kind and he blamed me. Some kid got burned in the eye with a cigarette, and he said it was my fault.

I said, "Coach, I don't even smoke." He didn't believe me and said I couldn't play. I was shocked. I didn't know how to handle it, so I quit. Right there, I gave it all up.

Something else happened instead, an experience that I believe set me up for a lot of things that came later—like being able to handle racism and Vietnam, as well as being receptive to something as foreign as Buddhism. It was my exposure to the discipline of karate, through a very unusual and amazing teacher.

My first encounter with him was at the gym in Yokota, at the Air Force Base. I had been watching a basketball scrimmage among the servicemen, and I heard a loud shouting sound coming from one of the rooms way up at the top of the bleachers. I walked up to see what was going on, stood in the doorway, and observed several rows of men shouting as they threw punches.

I looked down for an instant and the next thing I knew the teacher had flown across all the rows and was standing in front of me. He had somehow, some way, sailed over to hit one of the students beside me with his bamboo stick. I couldn't believe it. How did he do that?

The answer was, he flew. He jumped high and tumbled over the rows and landed right in front of me. I was so stunned to see a human being do such a thing that I stayed until the class was finished, then asked him if I could join. He answered me through an interpreter, saying that I had to take judo first. I needed to learn how to fall. So that's what I did.

When I came back, he let me into the class, which I learned was called karate or kung fu (50 percent use of hands, 50 percent feet). My teacher was amazing. He would break a stack of clay roof tiles with one strike. There would be so many of them he needed a step ladder to get to the top and place a towel over that tile; and then, depending on his mood, he would either come down with his forehead, his elbow, or his hand. I knew that every tile was broken, because he made me clean it up . . . *Yahman!*

Sometimes he would get a few of us to try to lift him off the floor. He made himself so heavy, part of the ground, that we couldn't even budge his feet. After we let go of him, he would bend his knees slightly and go straight up in the air. Once I saw him kick the basketball rim, with his right leg kicking out from his right side, then settle back to the floor like a butterfly slowly coming down.

During one session, he called me over, slapping himself on the ass. "Steele!" I hurried over. He faced off at me.

I thought to myself, "Oh God, what now?" I went after him but of course the next moment I was on the floor. I was just amazed. He hit his ass again, and I got up and tried again. We kept going through this routine, and every time I would end up on the floor. After a few times—and he knew this was going to happen—I got raving mad and just charged at him. I was a football player so I tried to tackle him. Boom! I was on the floor again. If I hadn't taken judo and learned how to fall, I would have broken all my bones. I kept going for him, swinging like a wild man, but pretty soon I felt like giving up. He knew it was coming. He bowed. And I bowed. And from that moment on, I had a real teacher.

I saw him do the same thing later to another man, a weight lifter who looked like the Hulk. Each time this huge man would go gangbusters at this tiny teacher, he would end up high in the air, and the teacher would cradle his head as he came crashing down. In this simple way, my teacher broke down a man's ego, taught him to surrender, so that he could learn something new.

In meditation practice, this kind of surrender is what I call *keeping your sweet ass on the cushion.* It's not about becoming somebody special; it's about being opened. As Ayya Khema, a Vipassana teacher from Germany, says: "Meditation is being nobody and going nowhere."

My work with Sensei was like all-out training. I had to limp home sometimes. My mother asked me why I kept going back for more punishment. The reason? His kindness and his humility. I hadn't met anyone with those qualities since Sister Mary and Baba James. It was a mixture of true human feeling and discipline, and it has stuck with me ever since.

The most important thing about my training in Japan was not the physical part. I did become a very good athlete and a very strong man, much stronger than I am today. But the real training was in compassion. I had the privilege of attending the 1964 Summer Olympic Games in Japan. Mohammad Ali (then Cassius Clay) was knocking people out in the blink of an eye; Bob Hayes ran the hundred meters in ten seconds. The experience was all about love; it was about being in an ocean of love with people from around the world and experiencing the generosity of kindness, gratitude, respect, and curiosity—everything that goes with having a boundless heart. Sensei, my martial arts teacher, had a boundless heart.

I was pretty much a lethal weapon by the time I came back to the United States, but I had also learned to be gentle in a still way, and it had a calming effect.

I saw this soon after we got back to America. My step-father was now stationed in Kansas City; and one night I was driving home from a friend's house, a little after midnight, when I noticed a car was following me. I was about a mile from home, and it was a police car. I said to myself, "Oh, shit, I hope all my lights are working. Only eight more blocks, Ralph." I turned in sooner than I usually would and started driving through the neighborhood. He followed me. I got within two blocks of my house and he was still behind me. Suddenly I saw a headlight coming toward me. Then I was surrounded with cop cars. Lights all over, guns clicking, doors slamming.

"Don't move," I heard. "I'll shoot your ass, nigger."

One of them came over and asked what I was doing in this neighborhood. I said I was going home. They all started to laugh.

I said to myself, "Ralph, be calm and do not give these 'Boys in Blue' a reason to put your lights out."

An older cop came up to where I could see his face. He said, "Son, you got a driver's license?" I told him I had to reach in my pocket to get it.

He said, "Go ahead."

These guns weren't up in the air; they were on me so I moved very slowly. I gave him my license, and when the cop saw that my address was on the street where he was standing and that my home was visible with the front porch light on, he sort of relaxed, turned around, and returned to his car. Then he came back.

"Son, you can put your hands down," he said.

I didn't put my hands down. I just stayed there until they left—in a still way, looking at my home down the street. I realized then that the discipline of tending one's fire can be a nourishing and insightful process, which can also save one's life.

5. TAKING ROBES
(July 1999)

Those first mornings at the monastery of Chanmyay Sayadaw were so peaceful. It was one of those mornings when you could stick your tongue out and taste the mist in the air. As occasional vehicles went down the street, monks were practicing Bhavana. This includes the meditation practices of walking, sitting, chanting, and reading guidance literature; all this concluded with a soft-spoken discussion about the Dharma. I was settling into the deeper rhythms of my meditation.

Then, one morning someone came to me and handed me a fax: "Sister Mary is dying, you should call home." I felt my heart stop. Because of the time difference, I waited until later in the day to attempt a phone call.

In the evening, I went over to the building where the phone was. The assistant abbot was there, as he always was during that time of evening. He was about five feet four inches in height, with a large frame and a trim body. He walked with pride and dignity. He would have someone put out a chair for him in the courtyard. This was the time of day when the mosquitoes came out to party, and this monk would climb up in his solid wooden arm-chair and sit there, like a baby in a high chair, with one knee up and the other laid out to one side. He sat with no mosquito net with his *mala* in one hand and he chanted. His concentration was so powerful that unauthorized beings could not enter his space. The mosquitoes, monks, dogs, and laypeople all made a wide turn when flying or walking by him.

When darkness descended upon the evening, he would go inside and sit in another high chair, and laypeople from the community would come and ask him questions—about the Dharma, illnesses, family problems, or spiritual worries that we in America would take to a psychotherapist or life skills coach.

When I stepped into his energy field, he smiled with an inner smile, and I said to myself, "Sweet." Then I realized that it was just the two of us in the room. He couldn't speak English, so after bowing to him three times I pointed to the phone, and he gave me the okay by putting his right hand into the air with his palm facing me and turning it back and forth once.

Someone had already given me instructions for making a phone call to America. I got the international operator in China, which meant that my calls were being monitored. Then I was able to get through to Pawleys Island. Aunt Bertha, one of Sister Mary's daughters, answered the phone. "Just a minute, Ralph," she said. Just recently, Sister Mary had decided to move up the road into Aunt Bertha's house, to leave her body. At the age of ninety-four, she had out-lived four of her five children, and she was ready to go.

Then Barbara, who is now called Cheptu, picked up the phone. She is one of my fifty-plus cousins. Cheptu was in a special group of eight of us who were being groomed to become ministers of God. As a master of musicology, she helps people get in rhythm with their own true nature to make it easier to connect with the Divine. She has a heart bigger than the world and our lineage's smile that will melt your bones.

Cheptu told me, "Sister Mary finally stopped talking. She is in a coma but I will try and see if she can come around by mentioning your name." I waited and then I heard Sister Mary's voice. She had come back into being conscious, and we had a wonderful conversation. Toward the end of it I said "Bless you" and she responded "Thank you." I didn't know *that* was coming. All of my life up to that moment she had always said "Bless you" to me, and I would respond by saying "Thank you, ma'am."

At that exact moment, the phone operator cut us off. Man, I wanted to eat the phone or hit something with it, but I ended up making some kind of a wild gesture with the receiver in my hand. I looked toward the assistant abbot with rage and confusion at being cut off. He took his right hand and held it up and twisted it several times, with a smile on his face. He knew what was going on between the phone and me. That gesture meant to me several things at once: so be it, it's God's will, shit happens, let it go, let it be, life goes on, breathe.

I bowed three times and left the room. I don't know if that behavioral discipline came from Sister Mary, martial arts, police pointing guns at me, or all of these.

Thoughts and feelings were racing through my mind and heart, as if I were in a whirlpool. One was: "What should I do? I need to get on the next plane to America," then "No, I need to do my duty and take robes," then "No, I need to get some rest and work this out tomorrow." By the time I entertained that last thought, I was standing in front of my bed, so that's what I did.

At 2:30 a.m. I was doing my morning practice as usual. I began with turning up my desire to practice, and I took the concept of desire, which has an enormous amount of potency, and put my persistence behind it. I noticed that with the quality of my concentration, I could just let go and practice and keep the mental states, especially the emotional ones, at a distance where I couldn't see them but could sense that they were there. With a month of practice behind me, I could feel the adrenalin moving with the breath energy. I did not let the thought of "You need to go home" take over. Using the four skills of desire, persistence, intent, and wisdom gave me a format to proceed through the cauldron of my mind-state.

At seven, I went into the eating hall for my first meal, then with joy pulling me, back into the meditation hall, then back into the eating hall for my second meal, where that voice came into my ear again: "Slowly." After eating and brushing my teeth, I decided to go to Chanmyay and explain to him my dilemma. It just so happened that he was out for a walk, carrying a sun umbrella for shade. I was supposed to take robes in two days, yet as I bowed down on the stone path, my knee was screaming, "Get me out of here. Let's get on that damn plane."

He told me to wait a while and see what I would like to do, go home or take robes. I gave no response except to bow three times, because no response was necessary. I began to investigate my mental state.

41

"Ralph, you are on the other side of the planet, and it took two years to plan for this year."

"Yeah, so what? What would be the purpose of going home? Help her live longer?"

"No, I don't know how to do that. I just want to have another conversation with her."

"No, what needed to be said has been said. Besides, she came out of a coma to work that ninety-four-year-old body."

I thought of that five-minute telephone conversation when I said, "Bless you" and she said, "Thank you." What a moment. When Sister Mary and I had that final telephone exchange, it felt as if she was giving me the torch, the helm, to continue with the family ministry.

At the same time, I was thinking, "Well, I am now ready to die." My mom had died just twelve months before at the age of sixty-four, the result of having lived with an alcoholic husband. Now Sister Mary was leaving. The loss of my two favorite women, who had taken turns raising me, hit me hard. The force of my grief made me feel like not wanting to live any longer, but the thought of suicide never crossed my mind. In Vietnam, our company motto was, "Let's get the bloody job done." I took a breath and made the decision to stay and nourish my fire.

The next morning, his second day back, Chanmyay came to the meditation hall. I remember when he entered the hall. Most of the monks, nuns, and we lay practitioners were on the second floor, practicing and trying to add more quality minutes and mind moments to our session. I was at just over one hour of sitting practice, struggling with physical sensations, and was about to get up and do some walking. Walking practice is excellent for deepening concentration, cultivating tranquility, and promoting muscular movements so that your body fluids can oil the system to cope with any uncomfortable sensations. It's also good for waking up when drowsiness becomes over-whelming.

The meditation hall below us was for people not staying at the center. You could call it the public meditation hall. That day about six hundred people were down there, with another few hundred standing outside; and just before standing up to begin walking practice, I heard and felt movement downstairs.

Chanmyay was arriving. The ceiling fan above stopped, and everyone rolled up their meditation nets. Yes, there were no mosquitoes, and the once-barking dogs had stopped. I gazed out the windows and looked into the trees from the second floor. I could sense that late afternoon delight, lemonade time, with the setting sun. When I heard a few minutes of complete stillness, I knew that Chanmyay was coming into the hall. It felt like a mountain had settled within the hall.

Then I heard his deep voice resonating throughout the hall. That sound brought back memories of Old St. John's Church on Pawleys Island. The minister there didn't have a microphone, but his voice would explode in such a deep way that all thoughts would stop.

That's what was happening to me when Chanmyay first gave an invocation and blessing, and the people all chanted and carried on. I said to myself, "Kiss my bones!" I had never attended any Buddhist event in America like this. I understood why so many monks and nuns were up here. As he continued, my physical pain began to decrease; and when he gave a Dharma talk, in Burmese, well, all I knew was that two and a half hours had gone by.

The next day, during the first and second meal, everything seemed to move even smoother. The entire meditation center was like a smooth machine. After eating and going back to my room to clean up, I decided to go over to Chanmyay's residence and let him know that I had decided to take robes.

In Yangon, it was not easy to get Chanmyay's permission, because he wanted me to wait at least several more weeks, but that would be into the Rains Retreat. I had to convince him that I had mentally let go of my worldly possessions and clinging, especially the concern I had about Sister Mary. Another way of putting it was that I had to be ready to die. After my childhood years witnessing the Ku Klux Klan and the race riots at the time of Dr. Martin Luther King's death, and during my time as a soldier in the Vietnam War, I knew I had been trained in that before I was twenty-one. It was no issue for me to convince him that I was ready. Sister Mary's passing was much on my mind, but I needed to learn how to transform this grief into medicine, stay mindful, and let Sister Mary go. He listened to me, said yes, and I felt relieved.

Someone came to get me and took me downstairs, where I was introduced to a lady who had volunteered to be my "supporter." Every monk needs to have a supporter, a person who supports him throughout his monastic life, like an adopted spiritual parent. In the Theravada tradition, this act of generosity produces some of the highest merit one can accumulate. It lasts for lifetimes to come. One must understand that in this culture one's view is not from birth to death, but lifetimes.

My supporter is about five feet three inches tall with large bones. She is round in shape and her presence is soft. She would easily fall in the basket of Ma's. After her three prostrations, she said, "I look forward to taking care of you." One of the monks was translating. I responded with a smile.

I had a touching experience before taking robes. As I was walking through the crowded market place, a kid about eleven came up to me and held my right hand; the two of us walked several steps together. His only comment was, "We are brothers." He then looked up at me and smiled, let go of my hand, and slowly disappeared into the crowd. At his age I could not have wrapped my mind around that statement.

I went back up to the meditation hall to continue practicing, just as Chanmyay's Dharma talk was coming to an end. I continued sitting for a while, but could not stop the mental activity fueled by my taking robes the next day. So I got up and did walking meditation, which settled my mind until tea. What it came down to was, "My life as I know it will change tomorrow." Was I lighting a new fire or working on transforming this one?

Personally this was a very serious situation. I thought of the highly respectable and powerful Elders on Pawleys Island; I was about to enter into this ancient lineage. I was leaving my ordinary life. When you take on the title of monk, you are seen as more than just an ordinary person. Around the planet various titles are used: priest, sadhu, preacher, *madhi,* shaman, elder, *baba,* rabbi, sister, just to name a few.

Years before I had been close to this commitment; now here I was again. When I was in college working on my second major in religious studies, I would frequently visit the Catholic Camaldoli Hermitage in Big Sur during the 70s. There were around twenty monks in residence there. I took on Father Bernard as my adviser, as Father Bruno the Abbot was busy traveling back and forth to the Vatican. This was the 70s, the time of the Pentecostal movement; born-again Christians were also on the rise. The week of Thanksgiving, I decided to do a one-week retreat. I was considering two courses for my life at that time and needed to decide which way to go—getting married to the woman I had been living with, Sandy, or becoming a monk at this monastery in Big Sur. I had been having conversations about this with Father Bernard.

In the summer of 1998 the two of us were sitting on a bench on the monastery grounds. From our perch one thousand feet above the ocean on the Big Sur Coast, we both gazed at the Pacific Ocean horizon on a warm clear day.

"So you would like to become a Buddhist monk."

"Yes, Father."

"Buddha did a lot of good things for this world."

I was surprised to hear him say that and support my decision.

As we went into silence, I reflected on having been there on retreat in 1977. During that stay I went through the Stations of the Cross every day. One afternoon the monks invited me to have lunch with them. This was highly unusual; I guess they knew that I was contemplating taking robes there. Except for the monk reading from the Bible during the first half of lunch, we ate in silence. Anytime that I would think of what I wanted from the table, someone would pass it to me. I was very moved by this sense of community. After my meal I felt expansive. I felt very drawn to taking robes.

Father Bernard said that whatever decision I would make would be the right one; he said to be gentle inside—in other words, the decision would make itself. When I returned home, one night as I lay next to Sandy (whom I had met during my last year in the military with a stateside assignment), my mind was overwhelmed with a moon-colored light. I sat up in the bed, opened my eyes, and shook my head to try and make it go away. It eventually did. Sandy told me not to worry and that everything would be okay. Even though I still felt called to being a monk, I decided to marry her; we got married the following month.

Now I was embarking on the other road I had not taken when I married Sandy. The day had finally come for me to be a monk. I was at peace with myself. My partner, Sabine, had followed up with a letter confirming that she would be okay if I did not return; she understood how much I loved the practice. Sister Mary and I had made good healing medicine with our phone conversation. Yes, I was at peace with regard to leaving the world of Ralph Mitchell Michael Steele. This mental process of letting go is important because when taking robes, one's intention is for the remainder of your life in the body.

After my usual practice in the morning and getting both eating periods out of the way, it was about one o'clock. Two monks came to get me and took me to a chair placed outside. This chair was for me to sit in. With joy, I took advantage of the opportunity for the first time since arriving in Myanmar to sit in a chair. I had forgotten what it was like to sit in a chair and, most importantly, the desire to have one was missing. That "desire" is so powerful: if it were not for desire, we would not have been born.

It is so interesting to constantly be reminded that life in the body is mainly about training one's mind and, more precisely, one's perception. Our perception can be in the present, future, or past. Sitting in that chair was like having gone eleven days without washing and suddenly being invited to take a bath. The experience was beyond words and the sensation was pure bliss, absolutely divine. I also realized that this was the spot where the second senior monk sat every evening to do his mantra practices. It was the energy spot. Some energy spots on our planet are created by humans, some created by nature, and some are a combination of both. This particular spot was created by the assistant abbot of the monastery.

I remembered my initiation into church; we call it joining church, meaning you are now given recognition of moving from childhood into becoming a young man or woman in preparation for adult life. In the Christian tradition at Saint John's African Methodist Episcopal Church, this happens at the age of twelve. The preparation for that day was nightmarish. I had to not only remember the lines of a song but had to sing it with people looking and listening.

When the day finally came and they called my name, I had to go down to the front where all the Elders, the Sisters, and Babas hang out. These are people who knew me before I was born; they knew Sister Mary during the time my mom was born. Their love for the practice and worship of Jesus Christ was at the point in their life where they all exemplified the Holy Spirit. As I walked slowly down to the front, their voices sang out:

"Ooh, Lord, looky yonder dat's Sister Mary Rainey boy. Come on son. Now that you have been baptized, it is time for you to be graced by the Holy Spirit. Yes, Lord! Help us to guide this boy! Can I get an Amen? Amen! Amen! Amen!"

Just being down there, one could feel the juice. It was like standing inside a sauna with your clothes on. During the ceremony, the Elders came over, all shining like a car's headlights on high beam, and each put their hands on my head. It was like someone just turned the sweat machine in my body on high. It felt so deliciously good.

Oh yes, this was the spot. The monk wet my hair with water, and I noticed he had a double-edged razor blade with no handle. He just put the blade between his fingers, and I watched his hand coming toward my head. All of a sudden the heavenly bliss evaporated. My eyeballs rolled up to where I felt the razor was, and my curiosity was like a cat's. No way was he going to shave my head without some cream, soap, or something. The only something was water.

The monk held the razor blade in his hand and began to come across my head with it. The sound was like coarse sandpaper going against a wood surface, or sliding a cardboard box across concrete. Because of the intensity of the sound, I decided to focus my attention on the sensation of the sound as well as on my breath. The sound from the razor took me deep inside; it felt far away and non-obtrusive.

Sound meditation is a wonderful and important skill to have (see appendix: Sound Meditation). The first important point is having the appropriate view. I used to get annoyed because of certain sounds, especially when I wanted silence so that I could concentrate or relax. Not knowingly, I got caught up in the pleasure and pain principle. I was pushing away the sounds that I label as noise; simultaneously I was craving "silence," as this gave me pleasure. For several years this was an excellent exercise in feeding ignorance; I developed an attitude of resisting meditation when I felt it would be too noisy to practice. Ignorance is the primary cause of suffering. It took me many years to understand that silence is within, and there you can hear this universal hum if your listening skills are good. Silence is letting yourself feel, hear, and bathe in that universal hum.

This universal sound is peaceful. When I was a child, people would always ask me, "Why are you always smiling?" I could never explain. One of my favorite walks was on Pawleys Island Beach, looking at the thousands of seashells on the sparkly white sand beach, picking up the different sizes of seashells and listening to them.

The sensation of a razor shaving my head left my perception. It was just the sensation of the sound connected to the sound within. I opened my eyes and saw my supporter Daw Aye. I had been told she was an owner of two fish stores, one up north in the city of Mandalay and the other right here in Yangon. She and a friend of hers were holding a towel in front of me to catch my hair. Later I found out they do that with everyone, to keep the hair in case the person becomes enlightened.

I realized I was part of a long lineage; hundreds of thousands of people had gone through this process. Having that understanding and right view, I was able to drop in even deeper with the process of the breath. The sound and sensation of the razor became comforting, and my body became huge. I totally forgot I was sitting in a chair. After my haircut, my head was seriously bald and buzzing from the razor and water process and whatever else. When I looked into the handheld mirror they gave to me, I noticed that it had a dull shine, with steam coming off it.

Two monks came up to me with a set of robes that had been tailored for me. The three of us went to a private room.

"Did you wash?" one of the monks asked.

"Of course," I said and they smiled.

"Well here," they told me and handed me two pieces of fabric. I looked puzzled; one could fit over a king size bed and the other a single bed. The two of them stepped back and chuckled.

"Okay," I said. "Now I know why the two of you are here."

"Yes," they answered with a beautiful smile. "We have to dress you."

"So are you really from America?" they asked.

"Yes," I said.

"We have never seen a black person from that country so interested in Buddhism."

"Well, is something wrong with that?" I asked.

"Absolutely not. We thought all blacks were Christians."

"Is something wrong with Christ?"

One of the monks responded, "No, I first heard of him when I was a child. He was a great man who did a lot of good."

"Are you sure that you can do the Rains Retreat, three months of intensive meditation practice?" they wanted to know. Then they told me, "We are going to teach you how to be a monk."

Yahman.

We all continued to smile as they were dressing me. It felt like "family" being with them.

In some traditions you stitch your own robes, but in this tradition it is done for you. Putting my robes on was like wrapping a beautiful upper and lower cloth around me. The lower robe goes from the waist down, and the upper robe goes from the shoulder down to the ankles. You are allowed to have two sets, because you wear fresh robes every day. So every day you wash your robes.

It was time for the ceremony to begin. Including Chanmyay, twenty monks were present, which was the rule for the official taking of robes in Myanmar. I also noticed my supporter and about twenty to thirty other laypeople from the community. Again, it reminded me of when I first joined the church on Pawleys Island. I was twelve and many people attended from the community. All my ancestors were there with me in the room on that day as they were now. And because both Sister Mary and my mom had died recently, and within twelve months of each other, I strongly felt their presence during the ceremony too. Now here I was again, being initiated, and this time the ritual was being witnessed by Burmese monks and laypeople.

There were about seventy-five people there, and most of them I had never met before. At one point, Abbot Chanmyay gave me a name, *Pannananda,* which meant "wisdom." The chanting that was going on would make a dead person get up and dance, and since I'm connected to music that rocks my bones, I rocked back and forth just a little. I thought no one would notice, but Chanmyay did. He changed my name in the middle of the ceremony, from *Panna* to *Punnyananda,* meaning "someone bringing good qualities and generating good qualities."

After the ceremony I was told that Chanmyay had never changed anyone's name like that before.

"You must be an interesting individual; we are going to keep our eye on you," my fellow monks said.

That's a classic trigger kind of statement for American blacks, and I said, "You do that. You do just that." I had my robes on, and felt I could say just a little something. We smiled with the joy of beginning a new relationship.

The next day I was taken to a meditation center in the countryside—Hmawbi, a place closer to nature, like Pawleys Island. Ah, calmness.

6. VIETNAM WAR
(1969)

All veterans have their war stories, here is mine. I volunteered for the Vietnam War. I came from a long tradition of family in the military, and it came naturally for me to sign up directly after I graduated from high school.

I was knowledgeable about some electronics and was assigned to work in the avionics department. There were five or six of us in our unit, plus our commander, and our job was to make sure all the navigation and communication systems for the gunships were working—all the time, day and night.

Within weeks, I was wounded. It was just after midnight, a few days after the new moon, meaning it was dark and the stars lit up the sky. Suddenly, enemy rockets started coming in at our base. I jumped up and already knew what needed to be done. As a company we had to get all our aircraft into the air.

We had finished checking the equipment around nine or ten, but these systems were temperamental for many reasons. Maybe there was an open wire somewhere, caused by a mouse chewing on it, or a bullet grazing it, or the line sitting in some moisture. The problem could also be the radio, so we would always have a few extras in our jeep as we drove out to the flight line. However, this night presented us with more work because we needed to get the command console set up for our company commander. It was a unit that sat in the back behind the pilot and co-pilot's seat: it was about 125 pounds, four feet high, two feet wide and three feet long.

Mortar rockets were coming in and landing on the asphalt as we were attempting to load the console. The jeep was backed up to one side of the helicopter, which we referred to as a ship or chopper; I jumped out and quickly ran around to the other side in the dark of the night. The engine was not running. I went around to the tail, and as I turned the corner, something hit me and lifted me off my

51

feet onto my back. Seconds later small pieces of asphalt were raining down on me. One of those rockets had come down close.

I was taken to our company doctor. He stitched me up as I sat on a bench outside; he didn't know if I would be all right or not because I had been hit over my left eye. I had this huge bandage around my head for about two weeks, not knowing if I would ever be able to see again.

What a space to be in: "Don't know." There was nothing anyone could do. My duties were at a minimum. I just worked at staying focused, not wanting to entertain any kind of thoughts such as, "Will I have to continue with one eye or not?" When the medic eventually took the bandage off, he had to manually raise my eyelid, and a flood of light came in. It was bright. After a few minutes or so, I was able to look out into the world with that eye again.

One day we lost close to ten men in a firefight, and the commander asked for volunteers to train in door-gunning. I said okay. A guy named Michael trained me. The first thing he did was to take me into a room full of handguns and assorted semi-automatic and automatic weapons, and I picked an M-14 as backup for my M-60 and my M-16. Then we were off on our first flight. He got shot in the arm during one of our missions that day, and I remember moving over to his side of the ship as he was laying there, and picking up my M-14 to fire out his side of the ship, and suddenly it came out of my hands!

Our pilot elevated higher into the sky, and I realized my M-14 had just been shot right out of my hands. I tended to Michael, who was shot in the arm; it was a million-dollar wound, meaning that he got to go home. We dropped him off at a field hospital; and I helped carry him to the stretcher, passing other guys who were lying outside the door waiting their turns. I wondered why we got to be up front and later found out that the doctors were treating those who had a greater chance for survival first. I got back on my chopper with the two pilots waiting. They thanked me for being calm and alert during the entire process.

A lot of guys got killed in their first few weeks, and you quickly realized that you might live if you didn't make any mistakes. You didn't want to get too drunk, you didn't want to get too high, and you didn't want to be too much of a soldier or, for that matter, too little of a soldier. It was a fine line. I became obsessive, evaluating every reaction, every action. Like some of my older colleagues, I tried to pay attention to my intentions. I didn't want to end up in a body bag. This was probably my first experience of real mindfulness. Later, when Buddhism came along, I began to understand this more formally. But for now, I just tried to pay great attention to body, speech, and mind. It was a survival technique. There was no room for mistakes.

We had missions where we would bring supplies to our men on the ground. The ship was loaded with food and ammunition, and we knew we were a flying bomb if someone took a shot at us. But no one ever complained because we needed to get the supplies to our brothers. There were times of tremendous closeness, especially when flying night missions. We would get a call for help from a ground base that was being fired on. There would be two or three ships flying in formation. One would be a light ship, all nice and bright to draw fire, and the other ships had no lights. You get the picture. And sometimes we drew fire and sometimes not.

One of our missions took us into Cambodia where we joined at least a hundred other choppers to support thousands of ground troops. We spent four days in the longest firefight that I have ever been in. It was absolutely horrific; so many died. Leaving there and going back to our company base was as much of a joy as leaving Vietnam for home. Our commander gave us a day off, and that meant *party*—a fork-lift to pick up a few pallets of beer, our cook coming out with his best food, and some group (ladies dancing and singing) that was on the military entertainment circuit to entertain us. That was our stress reduction program.

In all of this, I must have killed people, but I never saw them die. Once we were asked to fire up this thick vegetation as target practice, and a few days later, our administration inside man told us that we had wiped out an entire village. B-52s had bombed the night before and missed the area. Shit! It took me several joints, two packs of cigarettes and half of a fifth of Johnny Walker before I was able to get to sleep after that. I didn't want to shoot at anyone, and of course I didn't want anyone to shoot at me.

It was the same racist world in Vietnam, but it was different because we were all in it together, black and white, and this changed our ways of seeing each other. One soldier, for example, had been raised as a racist. Where he came from, they actually thought black people had tails. When he saw a black soldier come out of the shower with no tail, he was almost in tears; he didn't know what to think. It was a big revelation to him. But he still couldn't shake the old habits. For him, it was still us and them.

One time, we were moving back to our base down south, after we'd been run off by Charlie (a name given to the opposition), and our first sergeant, whom we called "Top" because he was the top non-commissioned officer in our company, asked me if I would ride shotgun on a convoy headed down to reoccupy the base. I said "Sure." It felt better than being a door-gunner in a helicopter.

To my surprise, I was paired with that soldier. He was an excellent driver. We were driving a long flatbed, an eighteen-wheeler, just the two of us, because the convoy was ahead of us by two or three hours. I had my guns, two of them, an M-14 and an M-16. Everything else I had turned in. It was another hot day in Vietnam. We were frying. We didn't like each other, so there was no conversation. One time we stopped to buy some Coca Cola, a big risk. You didn't know when you touched a can if it was a bomb.

We drank about three or four cans of Coke. Then we knew we'd better get going. Something could happen. We were making sure no kids were coming close to us; that's how a lot of guys got killed. They'd strap a bomb to a kid. So we jumped back on the truck and smoked a joint together. We were both really nervous and we knew we shouldn't have stopped. Then, about dusk, we got to our turnoff and overshot it.

He told me to get out so he could back up, which he didn't know how to do. However, I wasn't about to do that. I told him to kiss my ass. There might be landmines; I wasn't going to go find out. We just sat there. I said, "My job is to ride shotgun." We just kept sitting there. No lights, it was too dangerous.

Finally he said "All right," and started to drive. He did a U-turn on this narrow road in the dark. The bed was tilted; it was amazing he could pull it off. He was very careful, very mindful. You get that way when you face death all the time.

Then we were headed back to our turnoff and gave each other the high five. In fact, we were so relieved that we started laughing. This was enemy territory and it was dusk; that's when it was most dangerous. We were still laughing when suddenly we heard gunshots. Oh, my God! I almost fired back, and then realized I shouldn't; it would give away our exact location. The guns had tracers. He floored it and for a while we felt really close to each other because, together, we were riding death.

Half an hour later we reached the base camp. We looked at each other one last time, didn't say anything, and never spoke again. What do you do with all this adrenalin?

My problem with heroin began in Vietnam when I was put in the hospital. The reason why I was in the hospital is embarrassing, though it didn't exactly seem that way at the time.

The only way to have sex was to pay for it; that's how it went down in my circle. For a lot of women who were indirectly connected to the war, it was a way to make large sums of money; and for the guys, it was a kind of paradise. Women of all descriptions and cultures were available. But, of course, we all got venereal disease.

I was very sexually active, which meant I was always getting infected, so it was decided that I should get circumcised. It was a hard decision, but I made it, or I think I made it. There was a whole ward of men who were there because of sexual problems, most of them to be circumcised. And every single one of them was a brother. We were all black. I don't know where the white men were. I didn't see any.

So there we were, all lying in our beds with injured penises. And there was an American nurse. I hadn't seen an American woman since I stepped off the plane. To prevent us getting erections, we were given this spray can, to keep it down. They issued it to us. You get the picture. And when this American nurse was walking around, you could hear the cans going off from every direction, hissing. Everybody was covering up and spraying as she walked around, without cracking a smile.

"How're you doing today, Mr. Steele?"

And she would reach down and grab your penis. She knew very well what she was doing. I would say, "Please don't do that, you don't know what you're doing to me." But she didn't care. She loved it. She wasn't black. She wasn't old and she wasn't ugly. You'd go through a can a day. In this ward the mental factor known as desire was out of control (see appendix: Desire).

At this time of my life, however, I was skillful in an unhealthy way. One evening we were all going to see a movie and the guys were saying to me, "Ralph, make sure you get a wheelchair."

I wondered, "Why should I get a wheelchair? I can walk just fine."

They said, "No, get a wheelchair."

So I requested a wheelchair and wheeled myself down the aisle. On the way to the movie area I passed by the room where a kid had been dying of malnutrition. I'd been talking to him and holding his left hand while he lay there with a stomach extended as though he were fully pregnant. His only response was a gentle squeeze. I talked about life as we soaked up the warmth and energy generating back and forth through our hands.

But now he was gone. A nurse walked by. We had seen each other on the ward throughout the days. "Where is he?" I asked her.

She stopped and said with a broken voice, "He is dead." And then she continued walking to attend to her duties. I took a few moments to wish him well and thank him for being there.

Meanwhile, the rest of us were going to the movies. I found a parking place and the movie started. Pretty soon somebody passed me a film canister. It was filled with white powder. There was a small spoon. I had watched the others snort from it, so I did the same thing. It came around twice.

The next thing I remember was early the next morning. I was lying in my bed.

That was the first time I ever used heroin. We used to call it "Riding the Horse," which was a phrase off one of the recordings of the Godfather of Soul, James Brown. From that point on instead of doing a lot of drinking on the days we weren't flying the helicopter, I would just smoke marijuana and snort heroin. We had our own medical staff so we could always conjure up a way for them to test the stuff for us. For my last few months in Vietnam, that was the pattern. It wasn't a daily thing, maybe two or three times a week. I felt stable. I didn't give it much thought. I definitely never considered myself to be an addict. Heroin and alcohol were part of the coping process. I had no idea it could go any further than that. These drugs helped keep me sane. It was an unskillful way of self-management.

At the end of my tour I went up to Saigon. And Saigon was scary. You didn't know what was going on. Out where I had been, in some sense you knew. But Saigon was wide open. You could easily get killed.

All I had left was my M-16. The police stopped me and wanted to take it. I wouldn't give it up. So they told me to at least take the clip out, but as soon as they left I put it back in. I had never been in Saigon and I didn't know what I was getting into.

I met some Korean soldiers—rock soldiers, we called them. They took me downstairs to this tiny club. It was like a very little room, and you couldn't see because of all the blue hazy smoke. When you looked closer, you'd see old *papa-sans*, with their beards, smoking long pipes. It was opium. They were just sitting there. Someone passed the pipe to me and soon I was so high I couldn't think straight; I had to get *out* and find some air.

The *papa-sans* were looking at me with beady eyes, smiling. I walked back upstairs and got into a taxicab. The driver started talking to me, trying to see if I'd get him some cases of Coca Cola. He told me he owned a hotel. I could have a nice hot shower, a woman; all he wanted was some Coca Cola. I said to myself, "Why not? Why not?"

What goes around comes around. If you put good intentions out there, you will attract good intentions. It's a natural law of our universe. But who is going to teach us how to become a good human being? I came to understand later that this was what Siddhartha was researching with his "body, speech, and mind," to become a Buddha.

We drove to the military base market and I bought him ten or fifteen cases of Coca Cola. In broad daylight, they just loaded the cases into the car; no one seemed to care. The driver was really happy. He drove me up to a building and said, "See, this is my hotel. Come on in!"

Yeah, sure. I was really apprehensive about going inside. I took my gun off of safety. These guys came up and started to take the Coke. I followed him. Another GI was walking out, so I kept going. We went upstairs. This was a man's dream. There were all kinds of women. All kinds.

The driver said, "Pick."

I said, "You, you, you."

"No, no, no, no. Just one."

So I picked one. We went to this room. It had hot running water and clean sheets. I hadn't slept in clean sheets since I left the States a year earlier. She and I played around Saigon for a few days. It was a delightful situation, the ultimate fantasy.

Two days later, I left for home. As we walked up the steps to board the plane, they were loading bodies into the baggage compartment. When the wheels left the ground, simultaneously there was a loud cheer. It was the kind of cheer where tears came out of our eyes. This was for real!

Back at Fort Dix, New Jersey, my knees hit the airport concrete and I bent down and kissed it. A lot of other guys did the same thing. Then we went inside the airport, and the first thing we saw was a woman in a miniskirt. Man, we'd missed out on a lot of things, like fashion.

In the taxi on the way to the airport for the next leg of our homecoming, we heard a sudden loud noise from a construction site. Bang, we wanted to hit the ground. The doors of the cab flew open, scaring the hell out of the driver. Then we realized it must have been a car or something, and everyone started to laugh. None of us realized that we were experiencing post-traumatic stress disorder; we had just been activated and experienced a "flashback."

When I got on the plane for Kansas City, the sweats started. I was shaking; I didn't know what was going on. A doctor on the plane thought that maybe I had malaria. When we landed I was in pretty bad shape, but I managed to get myself to my mother's house. I thought I'd just get some sleep and then report to my home base.

The next morning the sound of my mother walking down the stairs woke me. In an instant I was on my feet, alert, and careful. I was in another zone. The way I got out of bed, I was ready for combat. She was startled and I was startled. She said, "You're not the son I raised. I'm going to have to get to know you all over again."

My parents went to work and I was supposed to go over to the base to get some money. Also, I was thinking about seeing a doctor because of the shakes on the plane. But like a good soldier, I decided to get a haircut first. The trouble was, I knew the area was racist. I knew it. I'd been here before but I was now twenty, and a lot more confident. I think I wanted to test things. So I drove over to this barbershop.

There were three guys waiting and two barbers. I sat down. The barber said, "Can I help you?" When he said that, I knew something was wrong. This wasn't going to work out. I told him I was there to get a haircut.

"We don't cut your kind of hair," said the barber.

When the other guys heard that, they were struck. One of them said, "If you don't cut his hair, you don't cut mine." Those three guys, white of course, walked out. I didn't say anything; I was just being cool. I got back in the car. But by the time I got home I was shaking like crazy. I was thinking about going back over there and driving my car through the window. But I knew I would end up in jail. I didn't want to go to jail. This was Kansas City. During the Martin Luther King riots the "Boys in Blue" shot and killed many people with skin color darker than theirs.

You learn through meditation that a certain level of pain will always arise to wake you up to the fact that everything is impermanent. Though I didn't understand it at the time, this was happening to me in Kansas City. In Vietnam, the racism had been manageable. There was a stalemate between the races. But everyone had told me to watch out when I got home. It would not be the same. Just because I had been in a war didn't change anything.

I called my mom at work. I told her what happened and she got me to calm down. After a while I went over to Richard Gebaur Air Force Base and got some cash. Then I went straight to the liquor store. I went home and got drunk to where I could go to sleep.

For the next few days I hung around the house. I tried to look up some friends. A few were in jail while some were dead. Then I left and went to Georgia for my next military assignment—a company that repaired aviation equipment. But I was shaking all the time, and I would experience shock quite often. Sometimes it would knock me off the bench.

They said they didn't know what was wrong with me. The Army psychiatrist gave me a test called the MMPI, a ridiculous response to my problem. One of the questions was, "Have you ever had sexual feelings toward your mother?" This really pissed me off. I threw my pen at the wall and left. I went into town to a bar, and there was a brother at the bar, a civilian, and I told him my story, about the shakes and all. He put it very simply: "I know what's wrong with you. You got the *jones*."

As soon as he said that a light went on in my head. I knew the word *jones* but never connected it with myself. I was an addict. I was withdrawing from heroin. The fire was burning out of control within me. I needed structure, rehabilitation, something totally different. The most effective rehabilitation is in a calm atmosphere.

Since my practice of Buddhism became a pivotal part of my rehabilitation, I will jump ahead in my story here in order to share how I've integrated my experiences as a war veteran into my life as a Buddhist practitioner and teacher.

During the years following my return from Myanmar, a Vietnam Agent Orange Relief and Responsibility Campaign was created in support of everyone involved: the victims, their parents, soldiers, and civilians who served in that war.

I was invited to their international conference in Hanoi in 2006, and again in 2011, and I was surprised to experience the thousands of victims of that terrible chemical that I was involved in spraying. The movie classic *The Night of the Living Dead* is like a beauty pageant compared to what I saw among the Agent Orange victims. Take all, and I mean *all*, the various forms of cancer and make that part of the experience. It has been a diagnosis that has been systemic for generations in Vietnam.

An American team of five, including me, was invited to have dinner at a Vietnamese veteran's home. There were two other Vietnamese veterans present. While we were sitting at the table, one of the Vietnamese asked, "Did you get into any combat?"

I replied. "Not much. I was a door-gunner for six months."

We both laughed. I inquired what he did.

He replied, "Infantry, like most of us." We both laughed again, then poured each other drinks. Some flight co-ordinates, which referenced a geographic location, came out of my mouth.

The Vietnamese man replied, "Is that along the border of Cambodia and Vietnam?"

I could see the sparkle and moistness in his eyes as we gazed deeper into each other's eyes. I could feel tears in my eyes, as I remembered a four-day firefight. He shared that he and his brother had been in that same firefight, and then he pointed to an altar as he mentioned his brother; no words were necessary. He lost his brother during that battle.

We were nineteen or twenty years of age then and in our fifties now, working at tending our fires. Our conversation got everyone's attention. All of us got up and went to the Buddhist altar with the picture of our friend's brother and quietly stood there, breathing together. In the end, we all bowed to the altar.

At the 50th anniversary of the spraying of Agent Orange, in 2011, sponsored by the Vietnam Association for Victims of Agent Orange, for the first time there were victims, from the U.S.A. and from other countries, whose fathers had done a tour of duty in Vietnam. I gave a talk entitled "Acknowledging What Has Been Done, Preparing the Ground to Move Forward" (see appendix: Agent Orange and Forgiveness).

War is gross, and it is part of being human; it has been going on since we came into existence. My ancestors were soldiers. We all have freedom because soldiers gave their lives. I really do not know if it could have happened any other way. However, because of the advancement of consciousness, global leaders are slowly beginning to talk before killing.

7. HMAWBI
(July 1999)

After taking on my robes, I was taken to Hmawbi (mow-bee), one of seven country centers attached to Chanmyay Sayadaw's monastery. This particular center, about one hour from Yangon, was for "Westerners" and any Burmese who wanted to practice with Westerners. I was going there for my first *vassa*, or Rains Retreat.

The drive was beautiful, on an open truck with benches in the back. The view included roads with potholes, acreage with banana trees, rice fields, fields with various farm vegetables, and people working in them. You could smell that deep mustiness coming from the black dirt in the air. It was midmorning and the sunlight was burning the morning mist.

The area where this center is located reminded me of my childhood home. The roads and streets were soft dirt, unpaved; the homes were set up in close proximity and on stilts. Hmawbi would be the equivalent of a country suburban neighborhood in America, only with more of a natural feeling. I could feel the presence of Sister Mary all around me; it was a joyful feeling with deep calm, an inner sound that registered about five or six on an earthquake Richter scale.

I felt that I was ready to face and experience anything. It was a feeling of being very fragile, but at the same time having the sensation of great strength and courage. I felt fragile because of the appreciation of living in a body with the uncertainty of when death would occur. There was also some grief, as I worked through my relationship with Sister Mary and her being gone from her body. My grief began with sadness and transitioned into a force of energy moving through my body like never before. I wondered if this was the energy that flows with the continuum of life throughout our universe.

8. RAINS RETREAT
(July 1999)

We don't say, "Hell is bad and heaven is good"
or "Get rid of hell and just seek heaven," but
we encourage ourselves to develop an open
heart and open mind to heaven, to hell, to
everything. Because only then can we realize
that no matter what comes along, we're always
standing at the center of the world in the
middle of sacred space, and everything that
comes into that circle and exists with us there
has come to teach us what we need to know.

Pema Chodron:
Awakening Loving-Kindness

Our monastic hours were as crazy as crazy can be; there was only one beautiful person in charge, and that was myself. No one ever rebelled about the schedule, because this was just what we did.

From 6 to 10 p.m. one practices the training of one's heart/mind. This is called *bhavana* in Pali or "meditation" in English. It is interesting to note that the words "meditation," "medicine," and "medical" all have the same Latin root word "med-" which means healing. From 10 p.m. to 2 a.m. one is allowed to lie down to rest. From 2 to 5 a.m. one is in *bhavana* or meditation. Alms round, which I will discuss in more detail later, begins at 5 a.m. From 6 a.m. to noon one is allowed to eat and do various work activities. From noon to 4 p.m. one continues with work activities and some *bhavana*. Tea is usually at 4 p.m. and afterward there is chanting and perhaps a Dharma talk or discussion. All of my monastic life on retreat is *bhavana*, which means hanging out with people who have integrity, reading literature about the Dharma, verbal or silent contemplation, and enjoying my day with every breath.

My solitary practice at Hmawbi was from 6 p.m. to 4 a.m., though sometimes I would lie down from 10 p.m. to 2 a.m. During the night I would have several interruptions, and all of these deepened my practice. In this chapter, I will share with you some of the things that interrupted my practice.

Rain: It would start like the rain in Seattle, coming down in tiny droplets and very steady. I would be lying down and I would start to hear the sound like a train in the distance. As the sound got closer, it changed into ten thousand horses, and as it continued to get closer, the horses would change into ten thousand elephants. The droplets were huge. If I was in bed, I would jump out, get onto my knees, bow three times, cross my legs and go into *bhavana*. Before getting into bed, my back, knees, legs, and neck would have been on fire with pain from practicing throughout the day, but the sound of those ten thousand elephants made me forget that I had a body. I became very present in the moment, soaking in the grace brought up by those elephants. This interruption by the rain's rhythm would happen every day during the three-month cycle, and I would be in *bhavana* a large part of each night. I was dancing the only dance there is.

Sometimes, the sound of the rain, the elephant rain, would remind me of being in Vietnam as a soldier, lying in bed and hearing the sound of bombs being dropped by the B-52s. In the beginning it would be like very faint footsteps coming toward me, but then the bombs got closer, and the sound got louder and stronger. Then the earth would shake, and I would be overcome with fear that they had made a mistake and bombs would be dropped on us. By the time I got one foot or perhaps several steps away from my bed, the sound would stop, the bombing would cease.

The sound of the rain brought back those memories, and I would notice them; but because of the concentration, strength, and wisdom that I had developed from practicing so much, I could choose a more skillful view and see it as an object of meditation to work with. It feels wonderful to abandon bad qualities and cultivate good qualities. I would get up out of my little bed, quickly cross my legs, and listen to the sound of the rain as it got closer and louder.

Instead of stopping like the bombs, it would rain on top of my *kuti* (living quarters) so loud that I could put my fingers next to my ears and pop them, but only feel the sensation, not hear any sound. In other words, the sound was absolutely overwhelming, and it was the most pleasing sensation for meditation practice. I could sit for hours in what would appear to be an altered state. I was very present.

Roaches: One night, I went to bed at about ten o'clock. It had been a long day and I was very tired. At about eleven-thirty, I was awakened by a sound as if someone was eating potato chips, but it sounded very faint. I thought I was dreaming but when I opened my eyes the sound was still there. I moved my head and the sound stopped, so I closed my eyes again. The sound started back up, and this time not only did I open my eyes, but I also turned on my flashlight. Again the sound stopped. I looked under the bed and under my altar table but couldn't find anything. I stood silent in the room but could not hear anything. I was trying very hard not to get upset because one needs to be very careful getting in and out of the mosquito net so that a mosquito will not get caught inside the net.

After getting back into the bed, the sound came up again. This time I tried my best to determine where the sound was coming from—the altar to my left? I carefully got out of bed again and with my torch began looking all over the altar. Finally, at the back of my altar, I made eye contact with a cockroach the size of a fifty-cent piece. I thought, "How can I get it out of here without causing any harm?"

I had a mosquito-catching net about twelve inches in diameter, shaped like a butterfly net. After several attempts I caught this roach (it felt like a rock in the net) and took it out on the porch and tossed it toward the edge, which was close to the ground. It flared up with its wings, as if it was sticking its tongue out at me or saying some unkind words such as, "Go sit on it."

The next night, I heard the same sound and instantly knew it was that roach again. It was about one in the morning and I was very tired, but that sound of potato chips woke me up. It took about thirty minutes to catch this roach again. This time I walked off the porch and tossed it about thirty feet away toward some bushes.

The next night, at about eleven o'clock, I got under the mosquito net and in a few minutes I heard that sound again. I already had my small net in my hand. I tried my best to restrain myself and mindfully got out of the bed. I began to look around the table and under the table. "Can I find it?" I had never thought of looking on top of the table, but this time I did, and there it was under my ginseng tea bags. Not only did I catch it, I found out where the noise was coming from. That roach was nibbling on my tea bags!

This time we went for a walk down the street to a streetlight. There was a ditch next to the light, and when I looked down toward the ditch I didn't see anything there except some small shrubs. With a smile I dropped this roach down into the ditch, and it crawled underneath one of those shrubs. Then I noticed a small iguana come out of the darkness into the light, and instantly it went under the shrub and ate the roach. I was blown away and became depressed because I had killed something. I had broken the rule of non-harming and could not sleep the rest of the night.

For the next few days, I included loving-kindness meditation toward the roach in my practice. It was interesting to note that the thought of killing had never come across my mind during my dance with this roach. I actually was in deep grief and surprised about my feelings toward it.

Four days later, at around ten o'clock, I got under my mosquito net and had already turned the light off. I began my lying meditation with my torch next to me, and after a few minutes of settling in something hit me on my head. I quickly turned my torch on but didn't see anything. I got up and turned on the room light and got back under the mosquito net.

In the upper part of the net there were five small roaches about the size of a dime; these were the offspring of that first roach. They began to dive-bomb my head, and they made me realize that I had killed their mother and they were pissed off. I caught them one by one, took them outside, and threw them under another *kuti* for shelter. Was that the right thing to do? Was that a skillful thing to put those roaches under someone else's *kuti*? Was I causing harm? Really, I didn't know, I wasn't totally clear about my actions. In the end, I decided that all I did was to continue my cycle of suffering. Learning to be "awake" is serious work. I went back to my *kuti*, bowed three times, and began sitting practice until it was time to go on my alms round.

Cobra: Next to my *kuti* was another *kuti* where two nuns from Malaysia were living. In this tradition, one nun could not live next to a monk, however two nuns could live next to a monk. The dining room was about fifty yards away, and this was a perfect place for me to do walking meditation. It would take me forty-five minutes to an hour to walk to the dining room.

One day as I was returning, I turned left instead of right, to take a look at the abbot's *kuti*, and I met a nun walking back from the dining room. She was looking down and walking very slowly, as if moving in slow motion. She turned right and began to walk in front of my *kuti*. She got almost to the end, where there was a banana tree. It caught my attention because one of the leaves began to bend down toward the ground.

As I watched, a four-to-six-foot-long snake fell off the leaf. The snake began to move across her path and stopped right in front of her. At that point, she was mindfully walking about fifteen feet from the snake. The snake began to rise up at least three or four feet, and I said to myself, "This is not just a snake, it's a cobra." What to do? If I disturbed the nun and she saw the snake, it might take weeks for her to settle down again. Never noticing it, she continued to mindfully walk toward the snake. The cobra lowered itself to the ground, continued its journey across her path, and went underneath her *kuti*. I never got to open my mouth, but my heart was beating faster. I had observed the movie and exercised discernment.

I began to understand that "right action" comes from the practice of restraint in terms of taking refuge in one's own shelter, observing and assimilating with our "six sense-doors," and deciding the appropriate thing to do in that situation. That was a wonderful wake-up call for me, because I could understand that the moment presents us with the entire cosmos, whether we are paying attention or not. I was beginning to understand the nobility of right action.

Ants: I believe that there are more varieties of ants in Myanmar than anyplace else in the world. I encountered tiny red ants, tiny black ants, gray ants, ants with fur on their backs, large black and red ants about the size of a dime, and all the other sizes between tiny and large. There were hundreds if not thousands of them. In America, I would sometimes come across a path of ants, and usually it would be just one lane going in one direction. In Myanmar, I never saw just one lane of ants. There would be anywhere from four to eight lanes. Imagine a chalk line on a football field or tennis court. That's how wide the path of ants would be.

Being stung by one of these ants is like having a needle stuck in your body and simultaneously being burned by that needle. And every additional sting heightened the intensity of the sensation. So when we went out on alms round, I would try to be extremely careful where I stepped, because I was barefoot.

Now, one would think that after a good rain there would be no ants, and there weren't any ants to be seen on the path because, as we all know, ants have an aversion to water. So I might be relieved after a good rain—and everything would be okay until my feet touched a blade of grass. Those wonderful creatures would camp out underneath blades of grass, not on the ground but attached to the bottom of the leaf, waiting for me to come and play with them.

One morning as a group of monks and I were walking in the neighborhood, we accidentally stepped on thousands of red ants. By the time we knew anything, they were up to our knees, and we were lifting our knees up waist high. People were about ten yards away from us, waiting to give us food, and the men quickly came over and began to brush the ants off our legs with their hands. I had two sensations at the same time: the ants and the feeling of a man's hand rubbing on my legs. One monk turned to me and said, "I never had a man brush my legs before."

Mosquitoes: In Myanmar, mosquitoes are never out of season because they mostly have open sewer systems in the cities and the countryside. During the rainy season the mosquito population peaks, and Hmawbi is a breeding ground. During my alms round I could feel the mosquitoes under my robes, and the only thing I could do was practice appropriate attention, pay attention to my bowl, and walk. After returning to my *kuti*, I would take off my robes, which were wet from the rain, and my butt would feel very bumpy. I often had thirty to fifty bumps from mosquito bites. I had to get used to it because it became a very common blessing. I was giving an offering of generosity—*dana* is the Pali word—for the mosquitoes. Because I was so serious with my practice, the attitude of generosity helped me to embrace the conditions. Generosity is a wonderful tool to get through the difficulties of the practice.

My *kuti* had windows with screens; by keeping a towel across the bottom of the outside door and washroom door, I could decrease the population of mosquitoes coming inside. I had trained myself to feel the touch of a mosquito on my face or hand. Then I would turn on the light to see them. One night, after catching one in my mosquito-catching net, I decided to open the net in such a way that I could take a closer look at this tiny thing. I realized that I was looking at its belly movement, and this reminded me that we all have a body to be responsible for. There were three of them that night, and it took at least an hour to catch them all. That night, I got only two hours of rest before getting up to do sitting practice.

The toughest time with mosquitoes was when we shaved our heads every two weeks on the new moon and full moon. A shiny, bald head meant party time for mosquitoes, and during the first few days after shaving, I tried my best to remain inside.

Interviews: I had an individual interview every other day with my Abbot, U'Janaka. The monk next in line for the interview would be doing walking meditation. Sometimes my own walking meditation would be up to thirty minutes, and then it would be my turn to go inside. As soon as a monk (who was coming out of his interview) was outside the door, I would begin slowly walking in. It would take four to six steps to get inside, and it was incredible how mindful I could be during that process. I would mindfully take out my sitting cloth and put it on the floor in front of me and slowly prostrate three times, representing the triple gem. The abbot would be sitting in a chair, and one of his most senior monks would be sitting on the floor next to him. Both of them spoke English very well. The abbot was a man who was deeply experienced and knew the nature of the mind; it was an honor to be in his presence.

One time I was not following the instructions: I did not share that I was doing a Hindu practice of chanting the Hanuman Chalisa, which I had been introduced to at the Hanuman Temple in Taos, New Mexico. It is composed of 108 lines, a hymn to our love of God. One of the many results of chanting the *chalisa* (a class of prayers) is the development of a concentrated mind. I did not look content at the beginning of the interview with U'Janaka after bowing, and I was not.

U'Janaka turned to U'Kamisura, "What you think is going on?"

U'Kamisura said, "He is seriously concentrated."

U'Janaka responded, "But he lacks mindfulness. This makes the nervous system overloaded."

"Yes, and that can cause various kinds of body sensations, such as itching, swelling, hot/cold, sensations of something crawling on you, shaking, cramps, aches, skin rashes."

U'Janaka added, "Also, it causes agitation in the mind, mood swings, depression, difficulty in memory, attachment to situations, anger, impatience, fear, difficulty with following through with your intentions, such as not putting your robes on correctly."

They both turned their heads toward me and asked, "Have you been experiencing some of these dispositions?" They both had slight smiles on their faces.

Feeling busted, I said, more to myself, "Yes, I have been experiencing crawling sensations. I stopped the practice of chanting the *chalisas* for now."

"Yes, you have been doing another kind of practice, which is okay. However, you need to balance it with mindfulness," said U'Janaka.

From then on I would try my best to stay with the program.

I would begin by sharing my state of mind/heart at that time, how my body had been during my last sitting, walking, standing, and lying practice. U'Janaka would give me guidance, instructions, and clarification on how I viewed the world, and then I would work with that for the next two days. Even though I would find myself being rebellious at times, I would just note it. Sometimes I would make statements regarding his instructions or clarifications about my view, and the two of them would quickly analyze out loud my intention.

U'Janaka always seemed to know my intentions. Often, he referred to the Four Noble Truths: stress or suffering, the cause of stress, stopping stress, and cultivating a path that is continuously free of stress. Looking through the lens of the Four Noble Truths helped me become more skillful with my inner and outer communications. At the end of the interview, I would bow three times, slowly rise up, pick up my sitting cloth, and mindfully step out of the room. I would go to my *kuti*, briefly write down my thoughts regarding the interview, and then go into *bhavana*, beginning with sitting practice for one hour.

There would be days when my abbot U'Janaka could not make the one-hour trip from the city monastery because of heavy rain the night before. Then I would not have an interview that day. Instead, I would arrange to have an interview with the abbot of the country monastery. He could not speak any English, but he was always delighted when I requested an interview with him.

One day he was requested by U'Janaka to go into the city to meet with him. I happened to be in the monastery office when the phone call came. As he waited for his ride, he began to do walking meditation practice. After about thirty minutes, he began to chant, and continued walking. His driver drove up to his *kuti*, and he got into the car. I was sweeping outside then, and I purposely spent more time in the driveway sweeping the leaves so that I could notice everything.

As the car began to drive down the driveway, I positioned myself so I could be on the passenger side. He rolled down the window as he got closer to me and I noticed this luminous being sitting in the car. He turned his head toward me and said a few mantras as a nice wave of sweet juice flowed through my body. I noticed that his body was so bright that it was difficult to see the color of his skin; however, I knew that his skin tone was darker than mine. I said to myself, "I would love to have some instruction from this person."

I observed another situation with him, during the *Patimokkha*; a monk is selected by the abbot to chant the 227 monastic percepts that make up the Code of Conduct. This special ceremony for monastics would happen only every full moon and new moon. The chant is from memory of several hundred pages, and the recitation takes one to three hours. When the assigned monk would begin chanting, one of the senior monks would have a book to follow the chant, and this country abbot would correct the monk who was chanting without looking at the book. I thought that was pretty cool.

My interviews with the abbot of Hmawbi Monastery were very rich and precious. Throughout my three-month Rains Retreat, I had an interview pretty much every other day, so I had good guidance, especially when I was moving through my hell realms.

Pain: There was a period of time when I didn't want to leave my *kuti*, not even to go on alms round. My desire to eat began to decrease; I just wanted to practice. I had never been in a situation like this before—not having any desire for food. I was also going through a lot of pain, anger, and rage. During my sitting and walking periods, the rage and pain were so intense that my eyes would run water like a waterfall. The Trappist monk Thomas Merton called his experience "the dark night of the soul." I call it a dark night in hell. I had to learn how to embrace my shadow.

One night the rain was roaring hard for several hours. I wanted to keep my awareness in my body and remain aware of the sensations, which went from hot twisting steel to pine needles exploding. There was a point when I opened my eyes and yelled out several times, "Please let me die." I was stiff and tight with my words, and my body added that to the tightness already there. Eventually I collapsed for a few hours and was awakened by a cold sweat. After three prostrations, I got up and did walking practice for a few hours.

The pain in my back and my left leg was like a hot sharp knife cutting through my flesh, and I asked my supporter to help. She sent me support, a man who gave me rubdowns with oils that I had. We would talk when he visited, and he told me that he was a policeman who was considering becoming a monk. He was surprised that I came from America, and most important that I was an African-American Buddhist. He said that he thought that all African-Americans were Christians because when he had the opportunity to watch a sports video—basketball, football, baseball, boxing—and they interviewed the winner, if that person was an African-American, the first thing they said was, "I thank God; I thank Jesus Christ."

So he was honored to see that I was practicing a tradition that he was born into. As he worked on me, I became aware that my body felt like a piece of steel. He said I looked like Mike Tyson, the champion boxer. That surprised me. I didn't think I looked like Mike Tyson, but I did realize that I was feeling a lot of rage. He said he liked being a policeman because of the toughness and fear that came with it. He did eventually become a monk, but he disrobed after a few weeks because it was too difficult.

After several days, my strength came back, and I began to go on alms round again. My back was still very painful. Sitting cross-legged and standing seemed to be the worst or most intense, and often these postures would bring me to tears. But it was also wonderful. I felt joy in my pain, because it gave me a deeper understanding of how a mind state could shift my entire reality.

I had no idea what I had done until after my return home to America almost a year later. My friend David Caldwell, an orthopedic surgeon, ordered an x-ray of my back and saw that I had ruptured both a lumbar (L-5) and a sacral disk (S-1); the latter was completely gone. His remark was, "You know the process. We can fuse those vertebrae together or you can do body maintenance." I chose the latter and continued work on being humble.

Alms in the Rain: In this tradition all food "must" be *given* to you. You could be standing under a mango tree with mangos lying on the ground, but you are not allowed to pick them up to eat. Most of the people were farmers or supported the farmers by working in the fields. They were living day by day. Food was just as precious as anything else and, as a matter of fact, rice was referred to as the "mother of pearl." This was a high-level exchange: generosity coming from them and blessings coming from us.

Going on alms round is a very sacred process. It begins with group practice at 2 a.m., usually with chanting together for one hour, then sitting *bhavana* for another two hours. Meditation is a process of cleansing and training one's mind and heart, and this cleansing practice before going on alms round is like washing your hands before eating your meal. As monks we are required to be thoroughly clean when we present ourselves to the public. We create a protected area in and around us and try not to be attached to any unskillful mental states. If we are clean, we can become like a bar of soap for those we come in contact with; they can wash up with the energy medicine.

At the end of our meditation session, we would put on our outer robes, dressing up like something out of a leading fashion magazine, ready to go stepping. On alms round, you wear no shoes, no raincoat, no poncho, no mud boots, and no mosquito repellant. You have no umbrella. All you have is your robes and your begging bowl.

We would start around 5 a.m., and because this was the rainy season, it would of course be raining. I do not mean raining lightly. The water would be coming down in sheets, and each drop felt like a bucket of water. You could notice small lakes forming right in front of you. And before we left, I would stand in the dark on my porch, very nice and dry, listening to the loud noise of the rain. My thoughts would turn to all the reasons for not going out into the rain: flu, cold, pneumonia, death, and stupidity. Other thoughts would be: I'm hungry, I could eat a horse, and everything in the kitchen.

It was always interesting to notice how one mental state would take over from another. Then I would breathe mindfully and rise above or let go of both mental states and understand that alms round was about *dana*, the practice of generosity. We give blessings and the community gives nourishment for our bodies.

I took a step off of the porch. Somewhere between the second and the fourth step I would be soaked to my skin. I would join the other monks and begin this timeless walk. Twenty-five hundred years ago the Buddha and hundreds of thousands of monks in different areas of Asia would be doing the same thing, knowing that the cold and wetness that came with the rain would dissipate.

As we passed by homes, we would hear people up at that time of the morning doing their morning chants. I assumed neighbors had gathered together into one home to practice. By the time we got to our village, thirty minutes to an hour had passed, depending on which village was our destination for that day. It would be daylight, but the rain would be going strong. The most amazing thing is that people would be waiting for us in this heavy-duty rain, and that would bring tears to my eyes. To be a part of this act of generosity was just unbelievable. We would receive food from a whole range of people, from the poor to the very wealthy. What came into our bowls ranged from baked flies or gecko to crab soufflé. We received food for the body, and they received food for the heart.

For people to be out here in the rain with cooked food, waiting for the monks sometimes as early as 4:30 a.m. means—well, you can figure that out. Most homes didn't have electricity, so that meant going to bed early and getting up early. That's the rhythm we had on the island. After several days of going on alms round, I was able to step up to the plate with utmost pride and dignity. I was tending my fire.

We would stop in front of those people waiting for us one by one, and they would have such pleasant smiles. Their act of giving made me want to bow down and give thanks, whereas they were the ones bowing down to give thanks after placing the food in our bowls. That would be their blessing for the day. Their generosity made me feel at home.

One day, we were walking through a neighborhood that we frequently visited for alms. The homes were mostly built of straw and wood, their front yards well-kept with various flowers and shrubs. There was a little ditch coming from each house to a bigger ditch that went down both sides of the road. The water in the ditch was never aesthetically pleasing to me, and I always had negative or unskillful mental states toward it, such as, "How disgusting, the city should put in pipes; the government is so stupid," and other thoughts that were forbidden to say.

As we stepped onto this road, people would come out of their houses with food to offer us. During the act of giving, my perception was supposed to be confined to my bowl, and the bowl had two symbolic meanings. One was a representation of the head of the Buddha, which definitely added a different level of respect toward the bowl. When you slept, the bowl should always be at your head and not your feet. Secondly, your bowl represented the lining of your stomach, which added another dimension to how we were to take care of and guard our bowl.

I also kept my awareness on where I placed my feet, especially since we could not wear shoes while doing alms round, and I paid attention to my breath. I came to realize that skillfulness is working at performing one's duties the best we can. Every now and then, one of the monks would give me a tip on how to lean forward, or how to remove the cover from my begging bowl, or what to do with my eyes, or being careful not to make skin contact, standing upright, and how to give a verbal or non-verbal blessing. Those moments of exchange took generosity to the highest level because two humans were interacting with the utmost kindness, love, compassion, respect, and support.

As I went toward one individual, I lifted the lid from my bowl, and my lid just rolled out of my hand onto the ground and down into the ditch. It was an embarrassing moment, but it served me right for being so mindless. I was so stunned that I just stood there as a few of the laypeople went down to the ditch and retrieved my lid. The neighborhood tea stand was a few feet away, and one of the women picked up a teakettle and poured hot water onto my lid, then gave it to a man to give back to me. I continued my journey down the street doing alms but remained stunned from the experience.

Then we came upon a wagon that was parked, with no horse or animal connected to it, and it had a casket on it, draped with flowers. Someone had died during the night. People were across the road, standing around having a conversation. Since I was the head monk (at the head of the line) during the alms round, I stopped and chanted a few prayers. This quickly drew attention from the neighbors, so I stopped chanting and continued my alms. I had a few moments thinking, "When will it be my turn to lay my body down? Until that moment comes, I'll try to live each moment as fully as I can."

The dead body lying there in that casket created stillness, an order in the atmosphere. It was in my mind, that one day I would die and life would continue without me. On Pawleys Island when my great-grandfather died, his body was there for everyone to come and pay their respects. It took a day at least for the mortuary to come and take him away. In fact, one day would have been a short time: it normally took several days. Even though the funeral home was African-American, there was always a story about a run-in with the police, or the KKK not letting them across the bridge.

On our alms round, we would go by an old woman's house, and we would get as close to the gate as we could, so that she would not have far to walk. She would slowly come out of her front door, walk down the three steps from her front porch onto the walkway toward the gate, and she would place food into my alms bowl. Her hands would be shaking and trembling but she would not touch the bowl, which would have been disrespectful. One morning we went by and she didn't come out; we later found out that she had died.

At another house, a woman came out to give us food, and just before we left, a younger woman came out. She walked as if she was drunk, but we found out later that she was dying of cancer. Her mother had to help her back inside the house. The generosity of these people was off the charts. Here they are dying and their biggest concern is about giving. The Buddha said that *dana* or generosity is the highest protection: If beings knew, as I know, the results of giving and sharing, they would not eat without having given, nor would the stain of selfishness overcome their minds. Even if it were their last bite, their last mouthful, they would not eat without having shared, if there were someone to receive their gift. (Itivuttaka 26.)

At one point on our rounds, we would come around to a café on the corner (one time I heard the sound of music, and it was the tune *Let's Get It On* by Marvin Gaye, a Motown singer and songwriter). The building was set up in such a way that if you blew too hard it would fall down. I smelled the spices of the food coming from the kitchen. People were sitting outside at small tables that were about two feet high; most of the tables were from crates, and the stools were even smaller, but it worked for people their size. The entire floor inside was of sand.

During my childhood years on the island, we would go into a shop like this and get a "Jonnycay Cookie," which was a big round cookie about eight to twelve inches in diameter. Being in this environment made me feel more comfortable, and I slowly began to forget that I was in a foreign country.

We would stop out in front and someone would come out and give alms to us. As monks, we couldn't look around to scan the scene, but I had already scanned while walking in this direction, an old habit for me as an African-American and for anyone trained to be aware of danger. Mostly it was women and a few young men who came forward to give alms. They would take off their shoes as a sign of respect before putting food into our bowls. When we walked by a school, it was always a delight to hear the voices of children playing.

After getting back to the monastery, we had a choice of giving the overflow food to the kitchen to support them in serving the second meal, or give it away. There was a family living about fifty yards from where I was staying, and they had very little to get by on. They had two children around the ages of five and seven, a boy and girl, and I would give them most of my food. It was such a regular thing that they always looked for me to come.

I would then return to my *kuti*, set my bowl down, wash my feet, and arrange my place to eat. I would bow three times and do a blessing chant to all those who gave me food, and to those without food, reminding myself that this food was for my body, not for pleasure, although it looked and smelled very good, and I was always extremely hungry.

After eating, I would give the leftovers to a young dog that always showed up when I was eating. At night he began sleeping on my porch. Here dogs are treated with respect. Dead dogs are common on the American roads, but I never saw a dead dog in Myanmar. Most temples have lots of dogs because they know they will be taken care of.

Hmawbi dogs are kept outside the house and they roam free. Rarely are they left behind locked gates or fenced-in yards, as in America. They bark, of course, but not as in Germany where, if dogs bark consistently, neighbors call the police. In Hmawbi, the sound of dogs had a wonderful orchestration.

At night they are mostly quiet, but around 4:00 a.m., when the monastery rings the first bell, it all changes. Bell? What bell? This was not the normal object that one would call a bell. This object is a log twenty feet long and two feet in diameter. Most of the inside is hollow; a six-or-more-foot cable is attached to one end of this log, so it hangs about two to three feet above ground, vertically. The other end of the cable is attached to a tree or something very high. The mallet is a stick that's about four feet in length and two to four inches wide. The sound echoes with a deep resonance, and a wildlife person might think it was a bull elk or moose.

A small country town like Hmawbi, with a population of forty-to-sixty thousand, has at least twenty-five Buddhist monasteries. At four, when the bells ring, all these dogs start barking for about a minute. Then the dogs start talking to each other for another twenty to thirty minutes.

It was an amazing experience to observe the dogs interact with each other. One day I witnessed the most amazing dog talk as I was practicing on my porch. This very small male dog (I will call him Littlebit) was attempting to play with a female dog three to four times his size. As they were playing, another dog the same size as the female came up and growled Littlebit away. Littlebit barked back, but he knew he wasn't a match. So Littlebit went under and around fences until he had found two dogs the same size as the one that ran him away from his playmate. It was in the early afternoon, nice and hot, and these dogs were taking a nap, staying out of the sun. Littlebit started barking at these sleeping dogs, woke them up, and the three of them came back over to the big dog that had run Littlebit off. The two friends growled and snapped at the big dog until he left the scene. Then Littlebit went back to playing with his girlfriend while his two friends found a spot nearby and went back to sleep.

That dog scene stimulated my mind to the arising of various mental qualities. It is said that in all living things there is a spirit or life force, a body in the body, a light body, God. If this is true, no wonder that "connection" with another body, including humans, can result in a sensation of being very alive. I believe that it is true, which is one more reason for us to take good care of each other.

The concept that we are all one is mostly expressed in poetry and folktale. I recall a folktale about how we all came to this planet and realized that there were too many of us. Our ancestors decided that half of us would live in the water and the other half live out of the water, and both sides agreed not to forget about the other. If only we remembered! *Yahman.*

Ending the Rains Retreat: At the end of the retreat, thirty of us from our monastery went to the main monastery. The monks from several other monasteries came to pay respects to our abbot, so in all we were about three hundred monks. The laypeople lined up to give us offerings: toothpaste, tooth-brushes, soap, new robes, flashlights, batteries, and other items. The line was about a half block in length. Instead of the laypeople looking like a store, we looked like a store. We each received ten to twenty items, and I was thinking, "What am I going to do with all of this?" As I was the first African-American to practice at this monastery, I was always up front. This made my practice of mindfulness relentless.

When I got back to my *kuti*, I found I had eight tooth-brushes, twelve boxes of soap powder, and three robes. The robes had to be given away, because there are rules with regard to having several sets of robes. Several of us were in this position, and a more senior Western monk suggested that we go with him to a small monastery to give our robes and any other items to the monks living there. It was a wonderful, pleasant, and relaxed experience to walk to that monastery. It was the first time we were given permission to take a walk, other than our walking meditations. We walked through rice fields, noticing the beauty of the fields, the sky and the clouds. We walked through a small village, where at least thirty kids were playing while adults sat or stood in conversation. They all acknowledged us as we passed by.

When we reached the monastery, the monks greeted us; they had such joy and love radiating from them. They, too, had just completed the Rains Retreat. This monastery was very small and it didn't have much. I really felt at home. And I think they picked up that I felt at home, because they asked me to stay; they didn't want me to leave. And it was difficult for me to leave. They were solid in their devotion and so kind and generous.

9. INSIGHT
(1970s)

When I left the army to live in Spokane, Washington, in 1970, I was clean. Many vets were junkies when the war ended, and they tried to get us all on methadone, but I didn't want that. I remember during one of our Monday morning company meetings, the commander told us about a rehabilitation program and how, if anyone signed up, it would be kept in the strictest confidence. Yeah, right. Those who did come forward ended up losing their rank, which was a hardship for their families, because they lost pay. I wonder why none of the white guys came forward.

I had a lot of will power and I made my own program: heavy duty working out, running, dieting, and meditation as I remembered it from Japan. I also went to the base chapel on Sundays, where I was the only non-commissioned officer. I would sit quietly in the back. Just being in an environment where something bigger than myself was being acknowledged felt nourishing for my system. This was my organic methadone and it worked. Of course, I was also motivated; I wanted to be able to get a job, which was hard enough in America for a person of color during those times. It had only been twelve years since Dr. Martin Luther King had been assassinated. Also, most importantly, I didn't want my mother to see me as a junkie.

After getting out I applied for jobs, but it didn't take me long to realize that I didn't have the necessary training. So I went to live with my mother and stepfather in Spokane, Washington, and enrolled in community college. I thought, "If I can go to war, I should be able to go to a college and get a degree." So I did and that's where I discovered that I had an interest in humanistic psychology.

The winters were intense and very cold. The clouds would come over and hang out for a few months. During the summer months it was unbelievably beautiful. There was a smoky blue haze that animated the lush ponderosa trees. It is said that within a one-hundred-mile radius, Spokane has more lakes than any other city in the United States.

However, by the time my bones had defrosted in the summer months, winter would come around again. So, after two years and the completion of my associate of arts degree, I headed down to California.

Uncle Luther, my stepfather's cousin, lived in San Francisco, and I stopped by the general hospital to visit with him. I had always admired him from our visits during my teens before we moved to Japan. He was an accomplished person. He had been a Tuskegee Airman and was the first person of color to work in the California State Attorney General's office. He had recently returned from living in Tanzania, Africa, to undergo eye surgery.

So, here I was in his hospital room, observing him walking around, asking me questions about what I had been up to. He was supposed to be totally blind, but he walked easily around the room, and I thought this was odd. I told him the story of my life as a soldier and a college student, and how I was looking for a university to continue my studies. He was quiet for a while, and then said, "Santa Cruz, you should look into the University of California at Santa Cruz." I had never heard of it, but I said, "Okay. Thank you."

After I left, I called his wife, Aunt Joy, and told her that Uncle Luther's eyes were getting better. She interrupted me and said, "Ralph, he is blind." It took me a few years to figure out that his other eye, known to some as the third eye, was wide open. This phenomenon is when you can see clearly into your present surroundings without using your eyeballs. *Yahman.*

I found out that I needed to be a California resident to go to the University of California, so I moved to Salinas and waited a year. I worked a job with Firestone in Salinas and got married for the first time, to Sophrania (Sandy) Walker from Savannah, Georgia. We met in her hometown during my final tour of military duty, maintained contact after I got out of the military, and began living together when I moved to California. She was tall and slender with silky black hair. Her dark brown eyes sparkled and her high cheekbones showcased a definitive ebony sheen. The wedding was in

Carmel, California, and the minister just happened to be from South Carolina, my home state.

That marriage was an emotionally abusive relationship, with the abuse initiated by me. The stress of war had taken a toll on my nervous system and my heart. More importantly, I grew up in an abusive society, which nurtured and trained my nervous system to have a post-traumatic stress disorder. White men abused black men, which seeded black men to become abusive to their loved ones and the community. This was a male hierarchy where white men perceived themselves as being dominant. During my childhood years, women were restricted to the kitchen, bedroom, church, quilting group, and fields. In that seven-year marriage, I was still carrying some of those old and destructive views about women; those views destroyed my marriage. I take responsibility for that.

Coming home from Vietnam had been the opposite of a welcome; if you were a person of color, it was not only coming back to a racist society, but also a society that didn't want to deal with you. Post-traumatic stress disorder was new to the healthcare system as a diagnosis, and the doctors did not know how to deal with it. All they offered were medications that I couldn't take because of the side effects. So I had to work harder on managing my stress. I smoked marijuana for a while, but it only slowed me down.

The University of California, Santa Cruz, UCSC, or Uncle Charlie's Summer Camp, as some called it, was a popular campus. Students were transferring from Harvard to become a banana slug; yes, that was our mascot, a huge banana with legs and tentacles, sometimes with reading glasses, or a copy of *The Republic* by Plato. There was a student body of five thousand, no major competitive sports, a sailing club, and two recreational facilities. Sounds like a summer camp to me.

It was a very special place—all embracing and experimental. The grading system was "pass or fail with a narrative evaluation." It had high rates for dropping out and transferring to other undergraduate schools (a larger number of students than on any of the other eight UC campuses moved on and completed graduate degrees elsewhere). There were eight women to every man, so it was a very feminine place. I believe the Vietnam War contributed to this situation. Also, female divorcees would move down from the Bay Area to go back to school and start a new life. The sixties were very much alive. All the white guys had long hair and the women wore long paisley dresses. There was a nudist colony on campus, and sometimes women came to class topless. No, it did not disrupt the class but it did disrupt me! Eventually, the Chancellor of the university came down from Berkeley to shut the nudist colony down.

Discovering Buddhism: I never guessed I would meet some lifelong teachers in Santa Cruz. The first was Jan Willis, an African-American woman of caramel skin tone and Afro hair that expanded almost to her shoulders. She had a voice as gentle as a butterfly, yet it could rattle your bones. Jan is a precious diamond, an excellent teacher. I was studying Religious Studies, and she was the only black American in the department. After studying various religious groups and cultures (Pygmies, Aztec, Mayans, Incas, Catholics, South American Indians, Protestants and Celts), I signed up for a course on Buddhism and Jan Willis was the teacher.

She was born in the state of Alabama, in a segregated community like myself. I lost my father because of the Ku Klux Klan, and she had her experience with them burning a cross in her family's front yard. She also protested during the civil rights movement. Then she went to India where she was introduced to *bhakti* yoga, or singing love songs to God, and eventually met her Tibetan teacher Lama Thubten Yeshe.

So here I was, my head fully blown up from completing a degree at community college, stepping into a Buddhist studies course. And here Jan was at the door, slamming a book into my hands, saying, "Give me a paper on this book by the end of the week." I quickly replied, "No problem," and I was up nights until two and three o'clock, pushing everything aside to give this book my full attention. It was the Diamond Sutra, which contains the essence of Buddhism and how everything is an illusion except illusion. Life is like a flash of lighting. My studies with Jan were like that, book after book. She filled my head with academics; her courses were difficult. I would fall asleep with my head on the books at the library.

I was simultaneously going down to the Palo Alto VA Hospital to deal with my flashbacks. Flashbacks from Vietnam were overwhelming me. I frequently argued with my wife and was smoking pot to try and calm my nerves. My stuttering was getting out of control; communication was getting very difficult. Just the thought of the prescription drugs that the VA wanted to give me activated sensations associated with doing heroin and what recovering alcoholics called a "dry drunk." I preferred marijuana, even though it made my mind dull and gave me hunger sensations, which made it difficult to concentrate.

Then Jan Willis left to finish up her dissertation, and her teacher Lama Yeshe came to take her place. My dear friend Randy Solick and his wife, Robbie, had studied with this Lama for several years, and they said I should take him a flower on the first occasion we met. My response was, "I don't give men flowers, not unless they are dead." I was nervous about meeting this Lama. My knowledge of such teachers as Lama Milarepa and Lama Naropa came from my studies and I was wondering: "Will he be like that? Will he have that juice, that sharpness of mind, that brilliance?"

Lama Yeshe had fled to India from Tibet during the Chinese invasion, and I had never seen or met a spiritual person from that part of the planet. Robbie Solick's friend Stan had offered the Lama a room to stay in while he was in Santa Cruz, and it was in Stan's place in the campus housing that we met. He was rolling around on the floor with Robbie and Randy's two girls as if they had all been friends for many years. The joy and playfulness were just bubbling out of the three of them. He was wrapped in an orange sheet-like robe but when I glanced closer, I noticed that it was intricately stitched. He looked so natural, not fancy at all. I had never seen a priest or minister act childlike in their uniform. I was impressed, but I refused to give him flowers. I just couldn't bring myself to do something like that.

When we were introduced a smile came across his face that blinded me; it reminded me of my Elders at home. So much light came out of his eyes it seemed to cover his face and blind my vision. It was like driving a car at night and you are already straining your eyes because of the oncoming headlights and then all of a sudden the high beam is turned on. I was stunned, speechless, and partially breathless for a few moments. After regaining my focus I noticed that he looked like someone I had known, though I knew that I had never met this person.

I was awestruck by his gentleness and playfulness. I wondered if this was what it's like being with someone who had experienced awakening. It felt that I was with a special person and his presence created joy in me. From that experience I knew that everything would work out for the best. Which is the same phrase Sister Mary would use in two words, *"Yahman."* I later found out that Yeshe means wisdom and absorption.

The following morning, I walked across the campus to his first class. The Santa Cruz campus is about a thousand feet above the city of Santa Cruz, and it is covered with redwood trees with rolling green grass nestled between them. There was a morning mist that day; the fog was situated in such way that you couldn't see the ocean. Like a blanket of clouds, you had the feeling that you could just walk down the hillside and out onto the clouds.

The classroom was like an auditorium, and I entered through one of the top doors; the seating goes down from there towards the lecturer. All of a sudden, I had stepped into a field of energy that stopped me in my tracks. It felt as if the air was dense; my body had tingling sensations all over it. I stepped backward a few steps until I was outside this energy field; then I stuck my arm into it, putting my arm straight out in front of me several times. It was an unbelievable experience. Down below, Lama Thubten Yeshe sat on a platform without a chair. I thought, "How odd."

His head was bold and big; he was a big man, with large bones. He was wearing what looked like the same orange saffron robes, but there was also a layer of yellow. Black Americans called it "mellow yellow" during those years when bright colors were fashionable. He looked at me and smiled, and I knew that he knew that I was blown away by that energy field.

The energy felt like being in a room where a hot shower is running. I could feel the warm, misty sensation all over my body. My initial feeling of this energy sensation occurred at my church on Pawleys Island. The result of this sensation was a feeling of being very, very alert in a comfortable way. I slowly found a seat and began to listen to this brother rap about awareness and concentration. This was my first teaching of the Dharma.

As I matured more with the theory and methodology of the Buddhist teachings, I came to the realization that the energy field I walked into was his presence. Hello, Lama Thubten Yeshe. Hello, Tibetan Buddhism. And many, many thanks to Jan who completed her dissertation and was offered a faculty position at three major American Universities. She went on to become the first female chair of the Department of Religion at Wesleyan University.

His Holiness: His Holiness, the 14th Dalai Lama came to our campus to give a talk. I had read about him, but this was just a cognitive process in my mind, it had no base in experience. The most astonishing thing was that he was supposed to be the same being in his fourteenth body. At that time in my life, it was difficult for me to wrap my mind around such a concept. My family had participated in an African Methodist Episcopal Church for more than one hundred years, as ministers and deacons. I came from generations of organized Christian Religion, with Bible readings at home and certain clothing, shoes that were worn only on Sundays at church. That the 14th Dalai Lama was in body number fourteen was a challenge for me. It was weird and difficult to grasp that life continues after the death of the body.

When I was a child watching my dad's body being lowered into the ground, I thought that was it; death is lights out. When I asked Mom why they were putting him into the ground, she said, "He has gone to sleep." But in my studies, I was hearing that life is a continuum, and the body is a temporary abode. When I thought about it, I *knew* there was something else. I had experienced it that day as a child when I nearly drowned and had my first out-of-body experience. Still, it was a challenge to grasp.

I was also beginning to realize that I was responsible for my body, and I needed to learn to be present in it, so I could look after it. This would be one of many important insights that came out of my early meditation experiences. Being present is the biggest job. You may think you are present, but through practice you realize that the process of presence can be hugely increased; the fog dissipates in the sunshine, and the clarity rises to another level of mindfulness. Not working at being present in the body leaves your emotions in charge, and this can create a tremendous amount of suffering.

His Holiness was to present himself in an open forest green meadow. The grass looked freshly cut, it gave the appearance of a green carpet that was inviting. Walking on it made you want to take off your shoes; it would send off a vibration quality that made you want to let the leaf of the grass that sprouted out of the mother earth massage the bottom of your feet. About five hundred people were there, and as far as I could see, I was the only African-American or person of color. This made me highly visible. Maybe I wasn't looked at like a brother from another planet, but I felt like one.

The sun was high up in a very clear blue sky. It was about twelve-thirty and His Holiness was scheduled to arrive at noon. Sweat was already running down my face and I was thinking, "Is it worth a sweat to see this brother? He better be somebody different."

It was about two o'clock when his train of cars arrived on the meadow. I had no idea what he looked like. Among the several cars there was a black Cadillac limousine. People who knew him were running alongside his limo chanting with joy, some in tears.

The stage had an orange parachute for the top, so that His Holiness could chill a little from the sun. As I stood there looking across the stage, I could see the top of the limousine, and the tops of heads, some bald and some with hair; and the heads came around the stage and turned into faces. The clothing was orange robes and suits with neckties; one of each walked up onto the stage. I assumed the one in robes was "the man."

I was tight and upset because he was in the shade and I had to hold my hand above my eyes because of the brightness of the sun. He walked up on the stage with that bright orange cloth wrapped around his body, a color that means caution in America, slow down, be aware, and look out! During the hunting season people are advised to wear orange when walking in the woods, and most everyone knows about the orange barrels along construction sites on the highways. So I found it interesting that he would wear a color that captured my attention.

I noticed his hand as it touched the railing along the steps. It had a bright look to it, as if a light was underneath his skin, like someone sweating, but he wasn't sweating. His shoes and socks were black. If his socks had been white, he would have lost points with me. His appearance was very natural and yet it was definitely not ordinary. His head looked as if it just had a spit-shine job, and his posture reflected humbleness and kindness.

A campus official took the microphone and welcomed everyone. He was wearing a white shirt and tie, which were totally out of context. At that time on the campus you were instantly designated as abnormal if you wore a white shirt and tie. Still, that person did have a joyful stiffness about him as he introduced his guest. Then His Holiness walked to the microphone, with his head slightly bent, and when he got there, he slowly lifted his head to the looking-you-in-the-face position. I was about fifty yards from the stage and I felt as if he was in my face.

I will never forget the first words that came out of his mouth. He said, "You know it's not a coincidence that the sun is directly above and behind me, and you are out there having to squint your eyes in order to see me." After that statement he had all of my attention! The silence that was already around us became deafening to me. My heart was beating loudly in my ears; I was attached to his presence.

He talked as if he knew me. I had never heard anyone take charge of the situation like that, unless it was on the island in church. What a wake-up call! I knew something was different about this brother. He was different from anyone I had ever met.

And the energy! Five or ten minutes into his talk, a wave of energy came over us, and it definitely came from his direction. People around me were saying, "ah," "oh," "hmm," as His Holiness's ocean of energy touched them.

After he left, I walked off into the meadow; I had the feeling of having just finished my usual five to fifteen-mile run. I was absolutely floating; it felt as if my body had zero weight.

Baptismal Ceremony: Not long after, the 16th Karmapa, head of the Kagyu lineage of Tibetan Buddhism, came to town, and I took my first Buddhist vows, which I refer to as being baptized. Sixteenth meant that he had lived in sixteen bodies—I was starting to get used to that idea.

The Karmapa embraced everything, including one's dark side. In his travels around America, he picked up people from the streets who were attracted to him. I heard about one person who was packing a fully-loaded gun that could take your limbs off with one shot, and the Karmapa asked him to travel with him, gun and all. So this person said "Why not?" Within a few months he not only disposed of his fire-stick, but he had become an ardent practitioner.

When it was my turn to go up and receive his blessing, I was chanting a mantra quietly when I felt my rosary in my pocket getting warm. I reached in and grabbed it. As I came closer to the Karmapa, it became warmer and the next thing I noticed was a tray next to the Karmapa with people putting various small objects on it and, without thinking, I put my rosary on that tray, and I felt so relaxed. I received his blessing and was given a spiritual name. With regard to that tray, I found out that he used those objects for special ceremonies back in his home monastery in India.

The next day I was among a select small group to have a personal interview with him. It was interesting that all of his translators were Oxford trained. There were eleven of us with him; we all had our questions written down so that we could maintain some composure. One of the questions was how long he planned on staying on this plane of existence.

He told us the year and month he would leave his body, and when that time came he said he would be gone. What an introduction into the practice. I had no idea where it would lead me. However, meditation practice immediately supported me in my efforts to stop smoking.

A Softer Lineage: I was starting to feel connected with Buddhist thinking and practice, and I went on retreats with several Tibetan teachers, but I was also interested in Zen. I remembered reading a set of instructions in Suzuki Roshi's book *Zen Mind, Beginner's Mind: Informal Talks on Zen Meditation and Practice* on correcting one's posture; every time I read it I noticed another detail about how I was sitting, or wasn't.

So I began to sit with a group led by a Zen teacher named Kobun Chino Roshi, who led a Zendo in Santa Cruz, California. The experience was like this: I would be sitting in the Zendo (correctly, I thought) waiting for the teacher, and after about forty minutes he would come in, wearing his black robe. As he walked past you, he would reach down and move some part of your body, like your finger. And everything would change. I learned from this that how you sit in meditation has a big impact on your state of mind; sitting correctly can greatly enhance concentration.

I appreciated this, but at the same time I was put off by it. I didn't want to wear a robe, which I thought of as a "uniform," because of all my time in the military. And the practice was very regimented, very strict. During a retreat, you walked together, bowed together and ate together. And that began to push my buttons. I had just moved away from the controlled world of the military; I had left my uniform in a closet in Georgia. They said that Soto Zen was soft, but I never found anything soft in it, except for people's voices.

I needed something less harsh, a softer lineage. That's when I met Stephen Levine and Vipassana meditation. It all happened because of a visiting professor from England, a Catholic nun who was teaching a death and dying course at Santa Clara University, my graduate school. Her name was Sister Patrice, and I liked her because of the way she handled the cross on her body. As she moved her hand to the traditional points on the body, she would say, "Vanilla,

Chocolate, Strawberry," instead of "In the name of the Father, Son, Holy Spirit." To me this was inspiring. She could bring everything down to earth by relating a sacred ritual to ice cream flavors.

The person she wanted me to meet was Stephen Levine. He lived in Santa Cruz, so I called him up and we had lunch in the park. We sat together on a bench eating our lunch. I was wearing a pair of jeans with a few holes, a wrinkled shirt, and sandals; while he wore a pair of drawstring pants, a wrinkled shirt, sandals, and a beard that needed some serious grooming. We were dressed in the style of the community. His voice was gentle, and to me he was weird, until a bird flew within an arm's distance of him and he tossed it some breadcrumbs. I was awe-struck at how gentle and kind he was, and I said to myself, "I can learn something from this dude." I knew what kindness and gentleness were, but I had mostly deleted them along the way. I felt that this man could help me remember.

As a result of our conversation, he said I could come to one of his meditation classes. I told him I couldn't sit cross-legged, and he said, "Fine, bring a folding chair." So I went to his class. I was the only person of color, and that was okay. I decided I could work on making myself comfortable being the only person of color.

In that class, he asked one of the participants in the sitting group if he wanted to say a few words. This was a man with a beard and a real kindness about him. He seemed to know what he was doing. He was comfortable with who he was or should I say within his skin? Listening to this bearded brother made me feel that I was sitting under an oak tree with one of my Elders back home on the island.

After he spoke, I got up to shake his hand and thank the bearded guest. I also thanked Stephen, and said I would consider coming back again. On my way out the door, I turned to someone else and asked the name of the person who had talked. It seemed that the whole room turned around and looked at me, as if the earth stood still for a few seconds. With a soft smile, he told me that the man's name was Ram Dass!

I later found out that the building was The Hanuman Tape Library, a place dedicated to the Hindu Monkey God, Hanuman, where I later received instructions in various meditation practices and chanting (from another group).

My wife Sandy never joined me or asked any questions. She had her own practice of tending her fire, which is speaking in tongues, an ancient tradition going back to our ancestors. She took me to a church that someone told her about in the San Francisco Bay Area. There we all would take turns speaking in tongues, rolling on the floor totally out of control while others would make sure our bodies would not hit any objects. The result was like taking acid laced with ecstasy, peyote, and ayahuasca—all with no side effects! A lot of blacks from the South could speak in tongues; I do not know why. However, I was exploring outside the Christian lineage.

At Stephen's sitting group, I became interested in a woman named Danna. Her body was lucid like liquid glass, with the edges not defined. She would just sit there and continue to play in that meditation state by rocking from side to side and making a sweet sound with her voice. I kept my distance because I didn't want to give mixed messages with regards to sensuality, but my curiosity was high with regard to learning more about "meditation." Every now and then, I would ask her a question, and eventually got a private interview. She shared some yoga postures, and said to practice, practice, and practice. Perhaps that phrase was her transmission to me, because I still use it for others and myself. Danna worked in prison, teaching meditation. She had a bright light, but eventually she put a gun to her own head and turned her light off.

I continued to be in Stephen's guided meditation group. I hadn't done anything like this since my martial arts experience in Japan. I thought to myself: this is a real teacher. I knew I'd keep up the practice. He held a weekly sitting group and at least once a month he led a weekend retreat. We moved from the Tape Library because we needed more space, and it became a dance moving from one building to another for a while. What I loved was that this practice gave me an actual high; the adrenalin reminded me of being in Vietnam. The difference was that instead of being destructive, it was constructive. I was a self-rehabilitated heroin addict, and suddenly I had a new kind of high. No drug could touch it.

Stephen's book *A Gradual Awakening* came out of the meditations and talks I attended with Stephen in the mid-seventies. A decade later, I started a driving-while-intoxicated treatment program in Santa Fe; I used his book as a textbook. It is so clear and concise that I was able to use it with a diverse group of people: Hispanics, Jews, Native Americans, and white Americans. Stephen was one of the first to interpret Buddhism for a diverse American culture. I had people with ten, twelve, even nineteen convictions and, in some cases, Stephen's book turned them around.

We were practicing American Vipassana in the Theravada tradition, and it's interesting that all the Vipassana teachers were Jews, just the way it happened. Jack Kornfield, Joseph Goldstein, Sharon Salzberg, and Jacqueline Schwartz-Mandell were the people to bring this practice to America. They found that it was impossible to teach it in the format given in the Asian monasteries. The Dharma had to be translated in an American way. They didn't change the Dharma, they changed the format and presentation for a different culture.

The word Theravada means "The Way of the Elders" or "The Old Way." Theravadin Buddhists try to straighten out the discourse in order to keep it pure. The Tibetans have all kinds of rituals they've added onto the original teachings, which is excellent, but Theravada stays focused on the original source. I think this is why this particular school of Buddhism is so small and, to some, so boring.

Stephen's topic was not the traditional teaching in the Buddhist Canon, yet it seemed like the essence of what the Buddha was about. The Buddha taught one thing and one thing only: that there is suffering in our lives and that we must understand the causes of our suffering—and know how to stop it by cultivating skills, techniques, and wisdom to the point where there is no clinging, no attachment, and no residue of desire.

Another very important teacher I met at this time was Jack Kornfield. He was teaching a retreat in the Santa Cruz redwoods; I remember a moment when I was gazing and I heard this voice saying, "Be mindful of what you're doing." I turned around and here was this little skinny guy. At that time, if he turned sideways, you could hardly see him. He was like a martial arts guy.

Stephen joined Jack and Joseph Goldstein in teaching at one of their retreats. They brought some Theravadin monks from Myanmar: U'Silananda Sayadaw and U'Janaka Sayadaw. Venerable Mahasi Sayadaw was present at another retreat. Sayadaw means meditation master. I had no idea that meditation practice could produce such quality men.

We had interviews during the retreats, for ten minutes each and I interviewed with U'Silananda Sayadaw. He strongly reminded me of my grandfather, Baba James. His skin color was very light, like my grandfather's. I trusted him. I began asking questions about the practice and he responded. The dance continued with questions and then something happened—yeah, I went into an unconscious zone and don't remember what happened except that suddenly I heard a "ding"! He had a timer, set for ten minutes. A little while later, it went "ding" again, and he said, "Mmm, thirty minutes."

Later I visited him in Daly City, just outside of San Francisco, and during my last visit he gave me a manuscript of talks on Buddhism and told me to study it. I used to open it up and read a page or two, but it didn't make any sense. Six months later, I had read only a chapter. I felt I was slowly starting to get it, but I had to push myself. I realized that the reading had to be done in connection with practice! It would take me close to a decade to get through that book.

I did my first week-long Vipassana retreat with Jack Kornfield and Jacqueline Schwartz-Mandell. There were about one hundred people in attendance, and I was the only person of color in the room. Jacqueline came from South Carolina, like me, and we talked about the beauty of walking up and down on the beaches in the area of Pawleys Island— the beauty of hundreds of seashells, dried starfish, and seaweeds that Mother Ocean would bring to the beach. The sparkling white sand talked to you when you walked barefoot across it. I told Jacqueline how you could only walk so far on that beach before there would be a sign "White People Only." She made a similar comment about the same beach, except the sign said, "Colored People Only." She was very straightforward and gentle. She felt strongly about diversity, and eventually left the Vipassana teaching group because of inequality for women. Today, largely because of her, there are more women Vipassana teachers than in any other Buddhist lineage.

In the Buddha's teachings there is a phrase, "May All Beings Be Free from Oppression." I thought it was an important phrase to work with. I noticed that just saying this phrase to myself gave me a sensation of letting go of heaviness, followed by a sensation of lightness in my body. I realized that this acknowledgement helped me disengage from that particular mental quality of oppressiveness; it seemed to change the chemical, cellular, muscular, and nervous processes of my body.

Stephen talked a lot about "conscious living and conscious dying." We all know about death from an intellectual understanding, he would say; however, it's a deeper experience when someone you know dies, or if you have a personal near-death experience, or you live with a terminal illness. He said death was a great teacher and we should always keep it on the table. If death were on the table in our meditation practice, then thoughts, various mental states, and physical discomfort would all be gone.

The topic of death can either get you so activated that you need to take some kind of mind-altering substance to calm the nerves, or this topic can elevate you into an absorption level of concentration that shuts down your doors of sensation. You don't know what happened in that meditation until after the fact. Death as an object of meditation is an ancient tool or skill. Awareness of death fosters mindfulness of your inner and outer environment; it can create healing, growth, and balance.

Back on Pawleys Island, when somebody died we'd have a wake. The room where the casket lay was filled with the scent of roses. Baba James died when he was just fifty-seven. He choked on something he ate and got sick. Sister Mary went to make up the bed while he sat in a chair. When she came back into the room, it was just his body sitting in a chair; his spirit just took off. After the funeral we left for home. As my mother and I were leaving, we blew the car horn at Sister Mary, who was waving from the porch. Suddenly the horn blew from Baba James' car that was parked alongside the house. I said, "Mom, somebody blew that horn."

She said, "No."

But years later I asked Sister Mary and she said, "Yeah, that car horn blew. Baba James was still here. He wasn't goin' nowhere." There were times after that when this huge white crane would come into her yard and hang out for a few minutes. She told me it had come every morning after Baba James died.

Stephen led death and dying groups, and at one of these at a hospital in Santa Cruz, he asked: "Has anyone had a brush with death by almost drowning?" It just so happened that seven out of ten raised their hands. I was remembering when, as an eleven-year-old, I almost drowned swimming off Pawleys Island. When we compared experiences at Stephen's group, our common experience was that there was no physical pain going out, but discomfort in coming back in.

Through Stephen, I met Sogyal Rinpoche, a Tibetan teacher. He gave a talk at the Hanuman Tape Library where I frequently went for evening talks and meditation. I ended up studying with him for the next four years. He never shared any sadness in his teachings—what was the fuss? Death was just a dance of the continuum of life. It took a while for my Western mind to assimilate his teachings.

Sogyal, Dr. Elisabeth Kubler-Ross, Stephen Levine, and Ram Dass were all offering death and dying retreats at that time, and it was a lot of work to keep up with everyone. However, I believe that participating in those retreats helped me get a superior grade point average and a scholarship to graduate school. The downside was that I lost my first wife. I walked out on her, and that was a bad, bad thing to do. When you live with someone you love, you help your partner face her demons and she helps you face yours. I was not yet mature enough for that.

I ended up living in the house Stephen taught in. Fifty to a hundred people came to the sittings. They were all over the house, including the porch and terraces, interested to hear his talk, or just to enjoy the juice, with everyone getting toasted from sitting.

I attended many weekend retreats; there was a core group of us "death groupies" who always showed up. We were his experimental project. Most of the techniques we practiced ended up in Stephen's book, *Who Dies?: An Investigation of Conscious Living and Conscious Dying*; they were new and they were great. Stephen would guide us in dying meditation practices called "letting-go," and every time, several of us in the room would find ourselves out of our bodies, not knowing how to get back in. Stephen would come around and softly tap us down the spine, which created an echo in the body, like sonar helping us to come home. Meanwhile, as a former drug addict, I was becoming a meditation addict.

The frequency of waking up in a cold sweat had decreased, but the activation of my nervous system and my dark mental states related to my time in Vietnam were still there. However, there was a difference now in my reaction toward those mental states: instead of keeping them inside me, I would talk about them to my cousin Lonny, who was a retired Sergeant Major. He was like an experienced psycho-therapist, and talking with him eased the pain. My post-traumatic stress disorder decreased. I felt that I was riding the tiger instead of running from the tiger.

My body was becoming calmer, and my shakes were less frequent. It felt like some excellent honey had been injected into my nervous system. I didn't know that it would take a few more decades to fully mature, but it felt wonderful to be moving in a wise and healthy direction. My speech also was getting better. I had more confidence in speaking up and challenging my teachers in the Religious Studies depart-ment. Perhaps that was one of the reasons I received Board Honors when I graduated. I believe this helped me to get into graduate school.

Sandy and I had an interview with the Vice President of Santa Clara University, Father O'Donnell. We walked in his office dressed semi-formal and sat across the desk from Father who was wearing his black uniform with white collar.

He asked, "Where were you born?"

"Pawleys Island, South Carolina."

"Pawleys Island? Mmm . . ."

"Yes." I proceeded to give him a brief description of the island.

He sat with his hands on the desk. With a smile he asked Sandy, "Where is your birth home?"

She answered with pride in her voice, "Savannah, Georgia."

There was a moment of silence. Father turned back to me, "I looked over your academic records and you received board honors from the Religious Studies Department at UCSC."

"Yes, Father."

"Now you would like to study marriage and family therapy?"

"Yes, Father."

"I have always been a nigger lover," he said with kindness. "Well, Santa Clara can at least support you with a scholarship."

Sandy and I looked at each other with warm smiles. Father remained seated in his swivel desk chair, turned to his left to his typewriter, and asked, "What's the cost of that program?"

I fumbled through my notes and told him the cost. Father typed my scholarship check. After giving me the check, we all stood up, and before shaking our hands, he reached around behind him and pulled out a bottle of wine. "This is from our winery. Enjoy."

After graduating from Santa Clara University, I drove up to Spokane to visit my mother and stepfather. I was not in a good space, because of the separation from my wife. On Pawleys Island, divorce had been unacceptable. No one ever got a divorce; they just stopped living together. Some of the men had two households or more (at my Uncle's funeral three of his five wives were there), but no one got divorced. I was feeling a huge hole in my chest.

My stepfather, George Wheeler, was finishing up his twenty-year Air Force experience; we had a war connection because our paths had crossed in Vietnam. I remember visiting him at Bien Hoa Air Force Base, and we ended up playing a family card game called Pinochle. There were four of us and I was playing against him. Well, he played his first perfect game with me and afterwards he said, "I had to come across the ocean to give you a 'woppin.'" We had a wonderful, special time together. The experience was insightful because it helped me understand how valuable, priceless, loving, and healing the present moment can be.

Up in the Northwest, I assisted in coordinating most of Stephen Levine's and some of Ram Dass's retreats. I was often the bell-ringer, a volunteer position that meant I had to wake up early in the morning. I'll never forget one morning I rang the bell and heard a person say, "Lord, you sent a nigger to wake me up!" Now that phrase sounded seriously racist, not like Father O'Donnell back at Santa Clara. I was thinking, "Should I shoot him or give him a mercy beating?" The situation offered me incredible insight; just because this is a wonderful spiritual practice, it does not mean people stop being asses or are magically released from their neuroses. After all, I am in America, where the cultural concept of Black vs. White has been around since the very beginning of our country. How ignorant of me to think that everyone is kind just because they are attending a mindfulness retreat!

Because of my practice, I took a breath and continued walking. Was I being a do-gooder? No. I was using my practice to work with my experience of that comment and not react while continuing on with my duties. I had been in Vietnam; I'd seen a lot of people die, and from that perspective, I realized I should wish kindness for this person, rather than argue with him.

During this time, I continued studying with Tibetan teachers. I had the good fortune to spend time with some of the great teachers—for example, Kalu Rinpoche. People would come to him to pay their respects and take pictures. He always had a sense of playfulness about him—a wad of candy in his mouth—he would have fun playing with his *dorje*, a spiritual object used in ceremony, and weaving his head around as he sat on his seat. And then the next person would come to pay respects and he would just stop moving; stillness would take over the room. Only I knew he had that wad of candy in his mouth. I would experience that same stillness in the room with other saints.

He taught us that practice is about everything: joy, playfulness, walking, talking, sitting around, laying down, being serious. It took years for me to understand that formal practice happens twenty-four-seven. This is how unskillful behavior patterns are broken and how one develops depth and consistency in one's practice.

The abbot of Portland was the young Lama Lodu who came up to me and said, "So you like Tibetan practice?"

"Of course, Lama," I answered with my hands together.

"You sit on the floor cross-legged pretty good."

"Thank you."

I realized that he had never seen a black American practitioner. Tibetan practice is equivalent to the upper level of University graduate school. I said, "Okay, I am on board." He responded with a slight, intense, warm smile on his face.

A young kid in robes about the age of twelve walked up to the Lama. They spoke Tibetan and the kid went away. As I continued sitting with my hands in prayer position, the Lama turned to me and told me that the kid was a Tulku, meaning that he was a Lama in his last life. Mmm . . . *Yahman.* I gave the Lama my meditation beads or *mala*; he took it and said some mantras and gave it back. He was pleased that I would be traveling with him and many others down to California.

Sometime in the late seventies or early eighties, we traveled with Kalu Rinpoche down to the San Francisco Bay area where he gave one of many teachings on White Tara in an old building in Golden Gate Park. The room was small, with perhaps a hundred people. He was exhausted after the ceremony; two young Lamas escorted him out of the room, each one of them under a shoulder. Kalu Rinpoche was using them for walking support. They walked right past me and I could see that his body was smoky white. I started to sweat. Could this really be true or was I imagining his body looked like that? If it was true, then where did all that heat come from? Why was I feeling so stoned out of my mind? No, I wasn't indulging in any stimulants.

Kalu Rinpoche was giving talks and ceremonies around the Bay Area to prepare for the second Kalachakra ceremony in North America. It was a four-day ceremony and said to bring the highest blessings in the Tibetan traditions. Eight hundred people gathered at the Japan Center in San Francisco. I was able to rent a room two blocks away. I thought that was a lot of people, and it was, but nowadays thousands participate in the Kalachakra ceremony. At the end of each day, we practitioners would stumble out of the building; I would be tired and limping with all the body aches from practicing since early morning. As I approached the exit, I turned around and looked back up on the stage. Kalu would look as if he was just warming up.

He'd be up there with his *mala* beads in one hand and his *dorje* in the other, chanting and rocking his body back and forth. Sogyal Rinpoche and at least a dozen other monks would be below him, scrambling around, trying not to run into one another as they transitioned into another phase of this unbelievable ceremony.

Kalu was a living example of consistency in the practice. It didn't matter where he was or what he was doing, what we call formal practice or just living, he was absolutely aware and mindful of what was happening in and around him. I think that this was one of the many reasons he was called the modern day Milarepa, and the only person at that time who could give the Milarepa initiation. As a young man, Milarepa could be sized up with any rascals today, but he developed consistency in his practice and eventually became saintly before leaving his body more than a thousand years ago.

Consistency in practice is just as important as, or even more important than, the breath. Now that's a big statement, but this is how our mind and body are trained. If it weren't for consistency, I don't think we would have elders, great singers such as Mahalia Jackson, Jessye Norman, Barbra Streisand, or Aretha Franklin, and that's just naming a few. Consistency is what stimulates, cultivates, and brings out the master within the master. It takes consistency to be exceptionally bad or to be exceptionally good. If men refer to another man as "a good chap," then it is understood that this gentlemen has been consistent and is exceptional at what he does.

10. SUNLUN
(October-December 1999)

After completing my first Rains Retreat with U'Janaka Sayadaw at the Hmawbi Monastery in Myanmar, I was advised by my senior monks to keep practicing. When you are doing sitting practice fourteen to eighteen hours per day, it is not good to take too long of a break, they said. Consistency is what cultivates growth.

Jack Kornfield, who was once a forest monk himself, had introduced me to the Sunlun meditation practice several years before; and I had found it to be very rewarding. It is an advanced breath meditation.

I have always had a fascination with the breath. Asthma was my cousin as a child, and though it went away when I entered early adulthood, it decided to come back during my fifties. I personally believe that the chemical Agent Orange that I sprayed in Vietnam was a major contributing factor to its return. From talking with other veterans of that war, I know that some of the symptoms are only now surfacing, twenty to thirty years later.

The Buddha gave sixteen basic ways to breathe, based on the Four Foundations of Mindfulness. Larry Rosenberg, an Elder and teacher in America, talks about this eloquently in his book, *Breath by Breath: The Liberating Practice of Insight Meditation* (see appendix: Breath Meditation Methods). From that beginning, one can go into many other qualities of the breath, a fair number of them inexpressible with language.

The Sunlun instructions are very simple. For the first forty-five to sixty minutes you breathe very fast, as if you were running. You can begin in a standing posture and then go into sitting breath meditation; or you begin in the sitting posture and, after a period of time, transition into letting the body breathe at its own rate. In the second part, you sit for two hours or three hours or however long you choose.

The primary purpose of the fast breathing is to cultivate concentration and cleanse the wind channels of the body.

While the breath is moving extremely fast in and out of the nostrils, you focus totally on the sensations of the breath in that area. The second part is to learn how to work with the cultivated breath energies for further refinement. This leads one into the dance of Shiva, a Hindu god. In other words, one is dancing with God or the Dharma or the Cosmos—whatever cultural language you choose—and that's an absolutely beautiful thing to do (see appendix for further instructions: Sunlun Meditation).

I had put the word out that I wanted to explore more deeply this breath of fire practice. One day a woman who was familiar with the Vipassana meditation taught in America approached me and said, "I know the monastery that would be good for you." This woman was a colorfully dressed Burmese with soft features; looking into her eyes was like looking at a star.

She said that the abbot spoke excellent English and was a disciple of Sunlun Sayadaw, the founding father of the Sunlun way of Buddhist Vipassana Meditation, who had died in 1953. He was also a student of Ledi Sayadaw, the most influential teacher in Myanmar in the twentieth century. She also told me that the abbot's most senior monk spoke English very well and knew Buddhist psychology. I felt comfortable with her and what she had to share. She then told me something else that really got my attention. She said that when Sunlun Sayadaw died, they did not bury or alter his body in any way; he was still present without a living body. It was one of those statements that you hear, but it doesn't register. My response was, "Okay." It wasn't that I did not believe her; I just wanted to experience it myself. I recalled reading about sadhus, holy people in India, who had died hundreds of years ago and their bodies were still intact. Some of my Tibetan teachers had shared the same information. It has been said that the body will teach us everything we need to know. Someone showed me a photograph of a monk who was full of light. I later found that this was a twelfth-century monk in China but the photo was taken in the '90s. Life is a mystery and it seemed that I was on my way to experience some of it.

I had three days left, so I decided to do some body maintenance. I investigated around town and found a man who did Chinese massage. I didn't know what Chinese massage was, so I spent a little more time researching it and found that it is a method that works with the nervous system. I made arrangements to have a treatment. My back pain had been getting more intense. This man was short and slender, and I didn't think he was big and strong enough to work on my body; but I decided to go with him, and his hands on me felt like a vice grip. The pain he inflicted on me was intense, but it helped to decrease the intensity of the pain in my back and the sciatic nerve pain down my left leg.

Then word got to me that my main abbot (the person who gave me permission to take robes) had someone who gave him massages daily. So I sought this person out and had him do some more work on my back. My body began to feel better with each treatment, and the pain was down to a manageable level. I even felt good enough to go to the bookstore where I purchased *The Great Chronicle Of Buddhas*, which is an eleven-volume set. I also went by Mahasi Sayadaw's monastery and purchased thirty of his books that were written in English. The Insight Meditation Society in Barre, Massachusetts, was founded on Mahasi Sayadaw's philosophy.

The day finally came for me to move to the Sunlun monastery. As I was preparing to leave, U'Kamisura, the senior monk for Westerners, came up and said, "You look nervous."

I said, "Wonderful. I am nursing my body and am about to go into another intensive practice."

He smiled and responded, "Hey, all the practices are intense. Have you forgotten about the first Noble Truth? There is an immense amount of suffering in the world, but none like what we carry inside. Be joyful that we have an opportunity to work on it in our lifetime."

"Okay, okay, okay," I thought, "but what about this fear and uneasiness that I am feeling?"

A taxi came to pick me up. A senior monk I had come to be very close to was there, and just before I got in the taxi, he gave me his sitting cloth. It was a heartfelt moment just as the taxi drove away.

After arriving at the monastery, I went to the abbot to pay my respects. He understood English, but he didn't hear too well even though he had a hearing aid, so I communicated by writing on a chalkboard. He advised one of the laypeople serving as an attendant for the monastery to escort me to my *kuti*, and as we walked toward this building, I saw that my *kuti* was the size of a college dorm, with three floors and no elevators! It looked newly constructed: the floors were of teakwood and the beds had a piece of plywood as their mattress. I had a corner room with windows on two of the four walls, which gave me a lot of daylight.

My window looked out onto a *stupa*, a sacred building that is also called a *pagoda* or *chedi*. These three words come from the three great Buddhist cultures—*stupa* from Sanskrit, *pagoda* from Chinese, and *chedi* from Pali. Those buildings all have a square footprint that rises up into a round shape and eventually to a point at the top. This design is based on sacred beliefs and ancient geometric patterns and has been looked upon for centuries as very auspicious. I would spend hours doing walking meditation around this *stupa*. The process was peaceful and serene—a level of tranquility which was beyond words. Being around those buildings was like standing next to a gentle fan blowing warm air. Just standing in the room looking out, I could feel the juice as it moved through my bones.

The washrooms were down the hall, and I realized that we had solar hot water. The panels were on the roof where we put our lines up to hang our robes to dry. Having hot water was a luxury; I had almost forgotten that it existed because there hadn't been any at the other monasteries I attended. They gave me a booklet explaining the Sunlun meditation practice. It was about twenty pages long and it contained all that was ever written about the practice. I had to return it within two hours and they warned me not to get too attached to the text. Breath practice is about "practice" and taking your experience to help you get to the next stage, which includes going nowhere or being nobody.

There is a story that once Naropa, the great Indian teacher from the eleventh century, was studying at a monastery, and a *deva* (a *superhuman* in traditional Buddhist cosmology), appeared to him and said, "If you want to know the way, drop those books and practice, practice, practice." He went out to search for his teacher and eventually found Tilopa. That's perhaps why Suzuki Roshi, the founder of the San Francisco Zen Center, had his students practice for several years before he ever gave them something to read. We tend to get attached to belief systems and the written word. It can hinder one's practice for years.

For my first sitting session, the same attendant came to my room and respectfully escorted me to the meditation hall. He said that it is very important that we be there on time. I noticed he had this inner smile. It felt like I was going to "get smoked," an expression I used in sports with regard to losing.

Pain brings the fire element in the body alive. Sometimes the pain in my back was so intense that it seemed that having a jackhammer or a branding iron pressed into my back would have been more comfortable. So from viewing that smile on his face, I knew that hell was coming, and I needed to try and make sure that only the unskillful parts of me would go up in smoke.

I was the only Westerner at the monastery, but there was a group of about sixty visitors from Hong Kong and the rest were Burmese. As I was walking down the stairs, I met the gentlemen from Hong Kong. As they were walking, they were making a fascinating sound through the nose, breathing very fast, as if getting pumped up for a game or serious confrontation. I would call that getting one's intention moving in the right direction, with extreme motivation. The sound in the stairwell of them breathing generated a chill through my bones, like the sounds at a Nascar racetrack in America. To put it simply, it was loud. Does hell exist in a monastery? No, but it exists within us and I needed to remind myself of that. It is so easy to create suffering for ourselves. I wondered how often in twenty-four hours I entertained negative thoughts. It was good that these gentlemen were pumping themselves up. It was a way to cultivate right concentration that is so important for practice. In my earlier years of meditation practice, I sat twice and sometimes three times a day for two years, practicing four to six hours per day. It was the concentration that supported me.

The meditation hall was huge; it could hold anywhere from three to five hundred people. There were between eighty and a hundred of us for this sitting session, which made it look like the place was empty. Women sat on one side and men on the other. The fifteen to twenty monks sat up front. I was sitting up front next to one of the entrances.

U'Vinaya Sayadaw, the abbot, came up and asked me, "Which country are you from?"

I said "America."

He said in a deep voice, "Three days. I will give you three days."

One of the monks from Hong Kong said to me that most people from America last one to three days, because the practice is too difficult for them. I was ready to get into this breath practice and was glad that I had already been introduced to it.

U'Vinaya began the session by giving a Dharma talk. Then we chanted from the text. Chanting is such a wonderful expression in working with sound and the breath. It is also a way to cultivate concentration and to produce tranquility and healing qualities. Afterwards we started breathing very fast, as if we were running uphill. The sound of everyone making this effort was invigorating. It felt as if my lungs were the size of a ship, definitely bigger than my body. My breathing felt supported and motivated. As I was breathing this way, I thought of Sufis chanting and breathing like this. Certain sects of Indian yoga practitioners refer to this process as the "Bhastrika Yoga" of the Hindu god Agni. In Africa it has its own reference, for this is a universal process. No one can own the wind or any element. The intense breathing went on for forty-five minutes; then the bell rang. They had one of those Big Ben clocks that had a disturbing ring.

In the second part of the session, we transitioned into letting the body breathe naturally for another forty-five minutes. The sudden silence in the room was amazing. My body was so full with breath energy that it was difficult to distinguish the surface of the body from the breath energy. I had to open my eyes to see where my body was. In technical terms, this space that I was in might have been related to infinite space with regard to *jhana* meditation. *Jhana* is a Pali word that means absorption. But I didn't come here to dance with concepts that can become huge obstacles to practice. First things first; for me, the first thing was to try and perfect the practice.

One hour and thirty minutes later, Big Ben did its thing again. I was so soaked with sweat that it looked as if I had just stepped out of a swimming pool. The straw mat that I was sitting on was also soaked with an impression of my rear end.

I looked around the room and realized that this is a family monastery. Moms had their children with them. They practiced just like us and sat the same amount of time, a minimum of an hour and a half. As I was seriously struggling through my sitting session, the eight to twelve-year-old children sat like rocks, looking as soft as a puff of white cloud in a clear blue sky.

Later, as we walked out of the meditation hall, two kids pointed their fingers at me and pulled on their mother's arm because sweat was pouring off me like beads of water rolling down a car windshield. They didn't have one bead of sweat coming off either of them. The well-dressed mother looked as if she was ready to go to a social gathering, with jewelry and makeup. Everyone seemed to be shining with light: eyes, skin, and the energy field around them. I was so frustrated.

My abbot advised me to go and have a conversation with a colonel who was the commander of a tank brigade. We had a wonderful time talking about practice. He said that if you can do the Sunlun practice, one of many meditation applications, you could do anything. We agreed that the most important point is to condition oneself to be consistent. After one of the Sunlun two to three-hour sitting meditations, I looked over to where he was sitting. You could clearly see a liquid-like bubble around him; when he moved, there was gentleness in his body, like a dancer subtly stepping across the floor. As a former soldier it was a good feeling for me to be practicing with at least a hundred military personnel, male and female.

We would have three meditation sessions per day: in the morning, early afternoon, and early evening. Some of the practitioners would sit from one session until the next, and that could be four to six hours. They would get up and walk a little bit before the next session.

After eleven days had passed, in one of the sitting sessions U'Vinaya sat down right next to me, looked at me, and began to give me instructions. He was right inside my head when an image appeared in my consciousness.

I said to myself, "How wonderful."

And he said, "Don't go there."

He then guided me through a sitting session. I had never been given instructions like that before. He was giving me information about what my body was unconsciously doing. The feedback was priceless. It was a great aid in managing my pain because the intensity was so unbearable. I couldn't distinguish the sweat from my tears. I said to myself, "I have been in this hell before." It felt familiar to the Rains Retreat. The difference was in my perception, because this time I said to myself, "I'm going to cultivate a little bit more kindness toward myself."

Not being mindful of the subtle, unintentional body tension had caused me painful stress. Now, seeing the nature of the body as it is gave me insight into reducing the tension. It was like playing and tuning a musical instrument, which was my body, my feelings, the condition of my mind, and my various mental states. When the sitting session was over, I opened my eyes and U'Vinaya was gone. It felt like I had sat for only a few minutes, but almost two hours had passed.

The laypeople would sit in meditation in various kinds of sitting postures. Some would sit with their legs crossed, with one knee eight to ten inches off the floor. Some would sit with their legs crossed, with both knees three to twelve inches off the floor. Some would sit with both legs folded under them, with their feet on the left or right side. The most fascinating thing about these postures is that they would sit for several hours. The floor was made of wood, and we sat on a straw mat, the kind of mat people would use to wipe their feet on back in America, although I think that these were at least twice as thick.

As the days passed by, I began to fall in love with this crazy and magical breath practice. I was getting to be pretty good at it. During one of the sitting periods, the abbot came up to me and asked me to stand up. He began to walk me around, pointing out people so that I would notice their various breathing dispositions. This was a revelation to me. I was able to notice how the breath energies moved through the bodies of different people. I saw various kinds of breath energy around people. I never saw any two with the exact same pattern of breath energy. He said, "Get to know these energies if you want to be a teacher."

In the courtyard I had a conversation with some of the people from Hong Kong and realized that most of them had some form of cancer, diagnosed one to five years ago. They commented on how much the breath practice had helped them manage their lives. The most common remark in their conversation was about how the breathing practice prevented their cancer from spreading. Some of them had been retreating here once a year for the past five years. They practiced weekly in their sitting group back in Hong Kong, as well as sitting alone every day. They had integrated this practice into their lives: it had helped them to decrease or even stop their various medications, sleep well and get through their daily activities. This was a living example of this cancer group tending their fire.

The courtyard was filled with statues, most of them behind a locked iron gate so they wouldn't be vandalized. It is sad to know that this kind of vandalism happens around the world. The statues were representations of *devas* in human-like form: a male and female couple to protect farmers, a female to protect the ocean, and a family of *devas* to support family life. Standing on top of one of the buildings was a statue that represented the king of the *devas* (Sakka).

With all this diversity, could this monastery exist in America? I thought people would perhaps burn it down because America is a strong Christian culture, which is wonderful, but it is not inclusive. It would be many years before the American sangha accepted that we do not have to leave our respective religions to practice Buddhism. Our elders have told us that when introducing a new practice from one culture into another, changes always have to be made. I got it that the essence of Buddhism is about understanding how nature works. We can destroy all the buildings, statues, decors, and whatever else, but nature is still there. When I say nature, it also includes our planet, solar system, galaxy, and so on. *Yahman.*

As the days and weeks passed, my meditation practice deepened. I was accommodating the various sensations and working at not getting so attached to absorption or anything else. One evening I was invited to be a part of a ceremony in the courtyard. Everything was decorated with Christmas lights and other ornaments. There were about fifty to seventy-five people including ten to twenty monks. There was a large comfortable chair sitting in the courtyard at the bottom of the steps facing the pagoda; we were also facing in that direction. One of the senior monks whispered into my ear, "This is a very special moment, and only people who were invited are here, including you."

U'Vinaya Sayadaw came out and sat in the chair. The door was opened, and we all could look in and see the two statues. U'Vinaya began to talk to the statue of Sunlun Sayadaw. As he talked, you could feel the molecules in the air change, becoming more dense and misty. Everything became still and quiet, even the frogs. The conversation lasted for about one hour. At the end we turned toward each other and didn't say anything, just appreciated the precious moment and how wonderful it was to be a part of this community.

I went back to my room on the third floor and found a frog in my room. I caught him and decided to open the window. I held him in my hand and stroked his back, then moved my hand out of the window. He leaped out of my palm and glided down towards the ditch a hundred feet below. It was incredible. I had never seen anything like that, a flying frog. Because the moon was full, I could see it all quite clearly. By the time I closed the window, this frog had quickly orchestrated many other frogs in a wonderful concert. Those tunes danced with me in my meditation for a few hours.

The next day, the monks and co-abbot invited me to be a part of the Sunlun Intensive, a ten-day meditation that happens once a year in the month of December. It would begin in two weeks at their monastery in the country, and people from all over Myanmar would be coming. My practice was beginning to flow pretty well, so I accepted the invitation.

This intensive is always at the country monastery southeast of Mandalay and north of Bagan, at the base of Mount Popa. It seems that most of the major monasteries in Yangon have at least one monastery in the country. The climate is cool. This is a big difference in climate as compared to living in the city and in southern Myanmar.

Because I was born in what felt like the tropics, the average temperature was in the high eighties, with the humidity just as high, if not higher, and two miles walking distance from the Atlantic Ocean seemed like nothing. For this reason, I was more aware that the tropical-type climate is especially noticeable before and after a sitting session. My body and mind were more attuned to the elements, maybe because of the hurricanes and thunderstorms. After all, this is what our bodies are made of and getting to know how the elements move in our bodies can be tremendously helpful for the nature of stress and suffering.

During this ten-day intensive, the population would include fifty to seventy-five monks, fifty nuns, and about four hundred laypeople from various parts of the country. Some of the monks had visible tattoos on their arms and they smoked cigarettes. The primary part of the precepts that they practiced was meditation, and they did it very well.

Our daily schedule would include getting up at three o'clock in the morning, and I would get to do my favorite practice, walking meditation. The temperature at that time of day was usually in the 50° Fahrenheit range, which added another good reason for walking; it was the only heating system accessible to me. It was a way of keeping the fire inside going.

The first sitting session was from seven to nine in the morning. In a group of about two hundred for the morning session, there would always be at least twenty-five people who would sit for more than two hours, and as we moved from the morning to the afternoon and evening meditation periods, that number would increase. It felt good to be in there with everyone for a sitting meditation together.

After my first sitting period, I would go and wash my robes. I was lucky to have two sets of robes, both made from a thin cotton fabric, so that they would dry in a short amount of time. Because of the humidity, I needed to change robes at the completion of each sitting. After washing and changing robes, I would go and lay my bones down because the back pain would become very intense. Lying down provides the least resistance for the back. After thirty minutes of this, the pain intensity would decrease. Pain is a wonderful teacher. Some people say "no pain, no gain." However, I had realized from sitting the Rains Retreat that I had way too much aggression toward my pain.

Around 10:30 a.m., someone would come and get us to go eat our only meal for the day. This was a very special time, the only opportunity when all the monks gathered together. Our ages ranged from early twenties to early eighties, and there were some profound individuals among us who had obtained extraordinary levels from practicing. Understanding and experiencing different individuals in their various levels of practice gave me motivation and supported my practice. This gave meaning to the Theravadin lineage, which is the way of the elders. Eating like this also gave a new meaning to making community. We ate together and enjoyed being with one another.

This was a different way of respecting "noble silence." Instead of absolute silence unless you needed something, it was a silence that had respect for the tone and volume of communication. For example, when eating, no one ever raised his voice or said something loud. Communication was precise and brief. This was an enlightening experience because it led the way to practicing right and wise speech, which is part of The Eightfold Path in the Four Noble Truths. Right speech can be one of the most difficult parts of practice. If we think about it, wrong speech is what leads to disturbing emotions and conflict with oneself and with others. We felt so good and warm with one another after eating.

After my meal I would take my bones for a walk. The walk was so enjoyable, having the smell of incense coming from the small tea shops and fruit stands that were along the roadside. I could smell the fragrance of the newly turned earth coming from the farm fields. There was a variety of smells coming from nature and the community of homes in the area; I didn't have a clue what the next smell would be. Because of that, my focus was attentive, thus increasing concentration and tranquility.

It was important to adjust to the subtlety of various fragrances, because it encouraged me in adjusting to the breath. When practicing sitting meditation, the breath qualities constantly change from coarse to smooth. I have noticed that being attuned to these qualities supports one's awareness in maintaining equanimity. Developing this skill helps in the process of letting go and changing the course of desire (see appendix: Desire).

Upon returning from my walk, I would lay my bones down again or engage in a conversation with some monks or laypersons. Around mid-afternoon, I would get ready to wash up. I needed to wait until the water got warm, and the temperature of the air heated up to its maximum for the day. This was important for me because of my love for heat. The building I used was called a washroom. It had a roof made of tin, walls of stone, and a concrete floor. I would disrobe to my lower robes and take a bucket of water and pour it over my lower robes and body. One of the precepts is to never totally disrobe, so as not to arouse *devas* or other disembodied beings, ghosts, or lost souls. Even though it was the warmest part of the day, the coolness of the water refreshed my senses.

After going through this process I would go back inside my room to stretch and do yogic breath exercises to warm up. There are so many kinds of yogic breath work. There is

121

the alternate nostril breathing, connected in and out breath awareness, breath-of-fire or Sunlun breath, and breath through the body in a systematic way. These are just a few of the breath practices. One needs to spend time working with these breath combinations, noticing the effects they have on the body. Anyone with just a little athletic ability knows that the speed of the breath turns up the fire element. Depending on one's temperament, one of these processes is more effective than the others.

I knew if I didn't breathe and bring my awareness to the proper point of concentration, and apply the appropriate quality of insight, pain would destroy me. This was why I needed the proper amount of concentration. It helped me not to let fear come and take control of me. Was I turning meditation into a technique? No, I was applying a level of mindfulness that was supported by wisdom. I became more skillful at utilizing the breath and breath energies, which brought enjoyment and excitement into my practice.

From two until four in the afternoon we would have the second sitting period. Then I would take another walk, this time a longer one; I knew that this would eliminate subtle aches and thus lead to a pleasurable feeling by the time it was finished. Even though I walked this road throughout this ten-day intensive, every walk was as if it were my first time. I looked forward to experiencing whatever there was to experience. Being aware of the touch of my heel as it came down, feeling the sensations that rippled up that particular leg, and tracking the foot that was in the rear to the front for the next experience of touch. In certain cultures this form of mindful walking would be called stepping.

Stepping is a phrase that was cultivated in the African-American culture. It was more than just your normal way of walking. One's walk had one's own signature to it, and of course some tried to copy-cat others. Most importantly, stepping wasn't a dull-looking walk when observed. It has a noticeable rhythm and a joyful feeling to it. It looks and feels as if you are dancing with nature . . . *Yahman.*

I knew that walking was the best thing for my bones, especially in the management of my pain. At about six o'clock, I would walk back onto the monastery grounds.

There was about one hour before the next and final group sitting session of the day. I remember during my early years of doing meditation retreats, my entire world seemed to consist of anxiety, restlessness, and fear. My mind would think of only the worst-case scenario. By the time I was ready to go into a meditation session I was tense and depressed. It took some time to realize that we are the owner, the cause of our actions, and we are responsible for our actions.

So I brought mindfulness and wisdom to knowing that there was one hour before the next sitting period. I went to my lying meditation spot and entertained myself with yoga. Yoga is such a powerful exercise: it should have been required in my high school physical education classes. I don't think physical education is a requirement in high school anymore. I guess it will be left up to the individual to gain an understanding of the importance of having a healthy body. I remember that after getting into yoga, my visits to the chiropractor decreased to zero. I don't know of a course, video, or book that can teach you about your body as well as yoga. Yoga, to me, means a combination of the breath and the body, so that one can dance with grace.

It was time for the final sitting period for the day. It was dusk, the sun was setting, and the birds and bees were settling into quietness. Nature was transitioning into evening. The evening meditation had a larger population because it included people who had been working during the day. The meditation hall would swell from four hundred to six hundred people. You could feel the increase of energy in the room. Those who were practicing with us during the day knew that this population increase or energy increase was like a rocket booster in their practice. So a lot of us looked forward to this session.

I would sit my bones in the middle of the front row, instead of at the end, because it was also feeding time for the mosquitoes. I needed to be mindful instead of fearful of the mosquitoes. Sitting in the middle gave me more of a position in which I would not get my blood sucked. There were ceiling fans which created movement, and that was important. Mosquitoes' bodies are at a level of lightness that a small air current for them is like a sixty-mile-per-hour wind to us. This was a good thing for all of us and especially me. It didn't take long to get used to those out of control mosquitoes smacking me in the face, but with the wind current, they would just keep going. I got comfortable into my sitting posture, and kindly said to myself, "Let's get it on."

During this session, the power of concentration balanced with insight was at a level that I had only heard about. Experiencing it was beyond wonderful and pleasurable. I would just put my perception on a mental quality or physical sensation, and it was gone before the next in-breath. For a while I just had fun with doing target practice, shooting all the unskillful qualities off my screen with my perception. I had forgotten that I had a back that was in disagreement with the rest of my body. So I went down and took a look at it. It was like going deep sea diving, finding the object and looking at it from all the possible views that one can imagine. Working with pain is such a delicate issue; implementing the wrong action cultivates more suffering. It's made me appreciate the Noble Truths, especially the first two: suffering and the cause of my suffering.

It was magical to know that six hundred people were in the room practicing with me, and the only way I would know that was to open my eyes. Otherwise I was just in an ocean of energy. The meditation intensive became the most amazing thing I have ever done for myself. I developed a deeper relationship with myself, and it is most difficult to put into words.

I was able to experience energy flowing in various directions throughout my body, even what felt like pools of energy in my head, chest, and pelvis. My feet were vibrating; I knew that I could only feel this vibration because I was in a physical body. How blessed we are! I could see other people's energy bodies as well, something that I had never been able to do before. I was awed and humbled by all this—who and what are we?

A student to me is someone who is ready to receive. I recall when the abbot went over to a Western monk and sat down next to him to begin giving him instructions while he was in meditation. That was the same way he had given me instructions. During one point of the instructions, the monk came out of meditation and asked a question.

He asked, "Why should I do something like that?"

The abbot got up and walked away, and he never came back.

A few days later, that monk came up to me and asked, "How come he stopped coming over to me?"

I said, "You are still working on training your mind so that you can receive instructions with an open heart." I noticed from his facial features that he thought I was joking or kidding around. I continued, "You don't have to get all worked up about it, and if you have a pressing question then go into that building and ask him."

There was a group of about forty to fifty people inside asking questions. I walked over to the door and tried not to be too noticeable as I listened. The abbot did address his question, but he never gave him individual instructions again. He always had something to say to the abbot, making sure that he always had the last word. It was clear that he was not willing to realize that his sense of self was a major obstacle for him.

That process gave me insight into the meaning of respect, especially having respect for elders. Also, it gave me insight into the reason for having 227 precepts. Those precepts were mainly to give our sense of self some instructions. Those instructions were about getting that damn sense of self out of the way so that the sun could shine. I could see how this I, me, self, mine, Bozo, dude, nutcase, and all the other words that cultivate a self could get me into serious trouble with pain, just continuing the cycle of suffering. I realized each abbot has a different style of teaching, which was something that I have never experienced in the Western Vipassana world. I am not talking about their personality but the presentation of the teaching.

After the Sunlun Intensive, we all returned to the monastery in Yangon. It was already one month past the original time that I was supposed to leave for Thailand, but it wasn't easy to leave this monastery. I went in to the abbot's interview room for my final interview with him, and this time it was just the two of us instead of a group of people. He shared with me the various states of a deep concentration with stories and insight into what to do with them. Working with the Four Noble Truths and not understanding them would be a waste of time and effort, he said; it would be better to spend that time cultivating concentration.

Insight into the patterns of our mental qualities is so important in discerning what is skillful as opposed to unskillful. He shared a story about a layperson who had acquired such good concentration and insight into the nature of causality that he could do almost anything. He could go down to the bottom of the ocean and practice there or he could listen to conversations on the other side of the planet. That was encouraging.

Finally, U'Vinaya Sayadaw gave me permission to teach in America. I bowed to him three times and walked out the door. I now had assurance that I was immersed in the Buddhist culture.

11. SADHU ON THE ROAD
(November 1999)

My supporter assigned me a tour guide. As you remember, we were given a supporter upon taking robes. My supporter Daw Aye volunteered, liked all supporters, to take care of my monastic life. She lived in northern Myanmar but came two or three times per month, because she had several monks who were in her care. This level of *dana* or generosity is remarkable, but this is how it works in the Theravada tradition (more about Daw Aye in a few chapters when I get up north). Daw Aye assigned my tour guide to me around the time of my ordination.

My guide's name was Aung Khine Moe, he was in his twenties, his fingernails were about an inch long, and his hair fell down to the middle of his back. He said he let his fingernails grow long because he was studying to become a classical guitarist. When I connected with him this time, he said he was very busy, but he would help me.

My guide and I talked about *The Great Chronicle Of Buddhas*. I did not know until I read it that Siddhartha was not the only Buddha. We were talking about the expansion and collapsing of this universe many times over. Yes, science has confirmed that our universe expands and collapses; there are many other universes as well.

Even after the Rains Retreat, I felt that my guide didn't see me as a monk, and most importantly didn't see me as part of his culture. I realize this was my perspective; perhaps he was just doing his job of protecting and taking good care of me. However, it is always important to me to try my best to become part of anyone's culture, especially if I am spending a period of time there. I understood that Daw Aye thought I needed a language translator; however, I just wanted to dive into this beautiful culture and swim on my own.

I said, "Just put me on the bus, and I will take care of everything else." I really wanted to go on a journey alone.

While waiting for the bus I noticed a monk who was carrying a different kind of monk bag. Instead of the usual-issue bag that was the same color as our robes, he had a bag that a sadhu, a holy person, would carry in India. I had never been to India, but I had seen lots of those bags on people who had spent time in India. It was colorful, with wonderful designs and tassels hanging from it. Who was this guy? I noticed that he was offering candy to the kids playing in the lot where the buses came and went. He gave it to them and pointed in a direction as if to say, "Go someplace else and play." There were several groups of kids playing. When my guide completed his bow, I gave him some candy to give to that monk.

I was surprised that this monk got on the same bus and sat right next to me, in the front seat behind the driver. Monks usually sit in this seat, so that in case there's an auto accident, we will be the first ones to go through the windshield, and hopefully save everyone else.

I had my begging bowl in my hand, and he kindly took it out of my hand and placed it on a shelf in front of us. I realized that he could not speak any English, and of course I could not speak Burmese. Still, he began speaking to me, and I found myself listening and listening, and I began to listen with my heart. I felt that he wanted to know where I was going. I told him that I was going to visit the Golden Rock. He smiled.

Back in America a year or so previously, I was with two Vipassana meditation teachers, Guy and Sally Clough-Armstrong, in their home. As Guy shared his monastic stories, I asked about the Golden Rock that had been talked about in the meditation gossip community, a nickname for the Burmese name Kyaiktiyo Pagoda (meaning pagoda upon a hermit's head). Guy mentioned that he had been there and showed me a picture. Seeing that huge boulder sitting on the edge of a cliff made no sense; the view in the photo defied basic logic. How could that be? As soon as I saw that photo I felt I needed to hike up to this most amazing rock.

As the bus continued on, we had this incredible conversation about life and practice. He was speaking Burmese and I was speaking English, telling him where I was from. It was most unusual, this deeper kind of listening. I had always thought that there is a universal language, but to actually experience it one needs to listen beyond words. He wanted to know where else I planned on going. I replied that I planned to visit Pa-Auk Sayadaw. This was the abbot that all the western monks were talking about during my Rains Retreat.

The expression on his face changed. I realized that he wasn't pleased with my statement. From that point on, he was silent until the bus stopped; then he turned to me, and with a slight smile and a gentle bow of his head, got off the bus and was gone. That was strange.

Another ten miles down the road, the bus arrived at the base of the mountain, and we all got off. I got on another bus that took me further up the mountain, but eventually the road ended and everyone had to get off and continue on foot. There were shops here, with places to stay, and places to eat. It was a small village. I looked around, saw the road that went up the mountain, and began to walk toward it. A person came up to me and offered to carry my backpack; he was already carrying a huge basket that was almost as big as his body (and looked like a backpack itself, even though it could hold three to six backpacks). Together we began to walk the windy path up the mountain.

We eventually came to a weigh station and checkpoint where people needed to pay a fee to continue on. The man wanted to see my papers, so I went inside the building and showed my identification as a monk; and then I was allowed to pass through. I wondered why they had stopped me like that; I guessed they usually never saw a Burmese monk over six feet in height.

We finally got to the mesa, the top of this mountain, and it was an incredible site. I could see for miles and miles and miles, 360 degrees. The elevation was about a thousand feet above sea level. There was a monastery, hundreds of gift shops, and sacred places for people to practice *bhavana*—and a huge rock painted gold.

The Sunlun Monastery has a building up there that was donated by the community, and this is where I was headed—but first I needed to find it. I asked around and eventually someone pointed me to the building. I found the building manager and told him I came from the Sunlun Monastery. He told me to go up to the top floor, and I walked up the stairs to a penthouse view. The walls of this room had tinted glass on all four sides . . . *Yahman!*

As I looked around I saw a *puja* with a Buddha on it, along with a photo of Sunlun Sayadaw. There was a terrace surrounding the room, and I walked out to hang a line for my robes and enjoy the fresh air. The view was very beautiful with mountains, rivers, waterways, and farmland reflecting shades of blues and greens with a little smoke resulting from the heat. The temperature here was a cool thirty degrees lower than down below. I found that I missed the sweet sweat down there.

After getting myself settled in, I went for a walk around the mesa, which was the size of several football fields. Eventually I met an elderly person who spoke English and was easy to talk to. We talked about a lot of different things. Then I got on the subject of the Golden Rock. He smiled and his face lit up like the full moon and the air between us suddenly became warm.

"Let me tell you a story," he said. "During my childhood years, my mother used to bring me up here. You could lie on the ground next to that rock—this was before it was painted—and look under it to the other side. It wasn't touching the ground, just floating about one or two inches off the ground. I saw people pushing on the rock, and it moved, and when they took their hands off, it would come back to its original position."

"One person could do this?" I asked.

"Yes!"

He said that when he was in his twenties, they began painting the rock gold and put a small *stupa* on top with some relics of the Buddha in it. He said over the years the rock began to touch the ground, but not much. "If you look at it now," he said, "you can see that it's not touching the bottom too much."

We went to look at the rock. It was a boulder about fifteen feet high and eleven feet wide that sits on a slope at a 25° angle and does not roll down. Below was a one-hundred-foot drop to a huge space where people gather to practice *bhavana*. There were steps off to the side of the rock that got you down to this place. I took a walk down there to check it out. What a powerful feeling! At first my thoughts went a little crazy, like the rock would roll down and turn my body into a pancake.

I remembered an experience I had at a week-long Vipassana meditation retreat in America. I had been sitting with my eyes closed. The floor was carpeted, and I was on a *zafu*, a meditation cushion. It was perhaps the fourth or fifth day of the retreat, and as I was sitting, thoughts began to arise that I was flying. Then sensations began to overwhelm me, and my thoughts turned into various kinds of fearful states, such as, "What will other people think about this? Is this really happening? No, I can't allow this to happen. Be calm. Shit!"

As the sensation of flying got stronger, sweat was beginning to trickle down my face. I slowly removed my right hand from my lap toward the carpet on the floor. Then I grabbed hold of the carpet with my fingers and held on until the end of the sitting period when I heard the bell ring. Slowly, I opened my eyes and looked down at my wet shirt, and the carpet with my body still on it. What a relief. I was too afraid to share that with any of my teachers because I didn't want them to think . . . what?—whatever my projections were with regard to how people might see me.

Sitting under that huge rock, I said to myself, "If it's for me to become a pancake, then let it be." I settled down, and the juice and the sensations were off the charts. It was good practice; I didn't know the front of my body from the back, or if I was upside down. I was in a timeless zone.

After about one and a half hours, I walked back up to the top. The rock obviously was the central theme in my heart. I noticed that there was a narrow footbridge to the rock and a ledge for people to go and make their pilgrimage. The ledge went one-quarter of the way around the rock and was just wide enough for two people to walk by each other. There was a person standing at the entrance with a bandana wrapped around his head and an ageless face. Stationed there, he acknowledged with a humble head gesture those who walked by; he was obviously the gate-keeper.

I slowly walked across the bridge toward this huge rock. It felt like the walk of eternity. This was the most powerful walking meditation I have ever experienced. As I approached, the gatekeeper saw me coming and immediately stopped all foot traffic going and coming from the rock. Cool energy was all around my body. I felt like I could just step off and walk on thin air. Back at the Sunlun Monastery I had heard the monks talk about people being able to fly through the air, but I decided not to take it to that level.

After getting to the rock, I got on to my knees, my face just a few inches from the rock, and felt the massiveness and presence of this thing. I began to ask myself, "What is this?" I slowly leaned forward with the intention of placing my third eye against the rock. Wow! It felt like putting my finger into an electric outlet. My entire body was buzzing. There is no drug in existence that could get you to this kind of high with so much clarity.

I walked back among the tourists and other monks and came across a group of people sitting on a platform. Most of them were women and children, but there was also a monk who was looking at me. The smile coming off his face was so bright that I couldn't see his face, so I walked toward him. It was the sadhu/monk with the colorful bag I had met on the bus.

As he was speaking to me in Burmese, I looked around and realized that all of these people were connected to him in some way. He looked to be the oldest of the bunch. One of the men came forward and began acting as an interpreter. He said that he was getting ready to begin a trip that he does once a year with his family, and he invited me to join him on this journey. I said, "Okay." He said that he would pick me up at five-thirty the next morning at the front entrance, which was about a five to ten-minute walk from where I was sleeping.

He walked around a little with me, as the sun was getting ready to set on the horizon. He gestured me over to the rock. There was an area that had a marble floor with a knee-high railing around it. It was for monks only. Three monks could sit and practice, with a view looking directly at the rock, the landscape, and the horizon far off as the background. He sat and began to do mantra practice and I followed.

Sunrise and sunset are wonderful times to practice. Culturally, this is universal since ancient times. With regard to praying, sunset is when the mail person comes and picks up the message that one is offering up. There are a lot of vibrational shifts going on at this time of day. As movement slows down, sounds transform and birds become quiet. Crickets, geckos, and thousands of other nocturnal beings come alive; tigers and so many other animals come to the water for drinking and feeding. Certain fish come to the surface to eat and mosquitoes come out to feed. Our natural light moves into darkness, heat to coolness, and dryness to dampness. The best part is that since our bodies are from these elements, there is an incredibly subtle process going on within. When one notices it, the body becomes very alive.

The two of us sat there and practiced as the sun dropped down over the horizon. We ended our mantra practice and I began breath meditation practice. Again, I didn't know which way was up or down, back or front. I remembered once drinking some moonshine that was seasoned with cherry that my uncle had saved for me. I couldn't feel my body afterward. This was the same feeling and then some. My perception of space was infinite, and then there was nothing, just nothing.

Eventually I felt some type of moving sensation, which awakened me into another dimension. I realized that the movement was behind me. I wasn't sure if it was moving, it just felt different. I began to feel a stream of breath at my nostrils. I engaged with that stream and my breath became deeper and my body became alive with a tingling. When I opened my eyes, I saw Christmas lights surrounded by darkness. And then I saw the rock. Whoa! I took another deep breath, slowly turned my head around, and almost shit in my robes. There were at least sixty to eighty people sitting behind me. I turned back and took another breath. "Okay you can do this." I calmed myself down to ground zero and moved my eyes only to the right. The monk was gone. I got up, bowed three times, and walked back to where I was staying.

The next morning the sadhu/monk with the colorful bag was standing by a vehicle the size of a dump truck waiting for me. The two of us got into the truck and the driver drove down to that small town at the bottom of the mountain. Here, we stopped to pick up the other passengers, who had been staying at a hotel.

The driver put several sacks of rice in the back for people to sit and lean against, and we all got in. There were about twenty of us. One of the children had novice's robes on; he must have been ten, which is the minimum age. Three of us along with the driver were up front in the cab, and the kids took turns sitting in our laps. Everyone else was sitting in the back as we drove off down the country road.

There was a roadblock about every ten miles, with soldiers checking identification. When the soldiers saw two monks up front with the little one, there were no questions. They just waved us on. I had the right skin tone for a Burmese; so as long as I didn't stand up or talk at these checkpoints, everything was all right.

We were traveling in Mon state, which is in southern Myanmar. The countryside of Mon is beautiful. There were huge trees that looked like oaks. You could smell that musty wood with its mysterious fragrance. We passed several bus-sized ceramic statutes, and one was a cool-looking Buddha wearing dark sunglasses, why not? The others had bandanas on.

I thought, "This is so cool," because my monastery practice had been so serious, and I was realizing that I should relax more and find that balance or equanimity between being too uptight and too relaxed. That was going to take some work! Equanimity comes from practice, practice, and practice. For example, I needed to be more mindful of the upper part of my torso in various postures, making adjustments with my muscular system when it was too soft or too tight. As the practice continues, you learn the difference of when you are too soft or too tight. You learn to feel when the body is in balance with the gravitational field.

In that moment the mind is peaceful and the speech is soft. The practice of yoga and its body movements support this process. Yoga is a wonderful preparation for meditation practice.

We stopped to get some refreshments at a small store where they did just one thing: they made sugar cane juice and served it on ice in a mug. It was that sweet juice. They had a manual juice press, and it was served in a glass beer-style mug. With the heat cooking my bones, I imagined drinking a cold one and the two of us sat down outside and let the sugar take us for a ride. I shared with the sadhu/monk about my difficulties during the Rains Retreat in Hmawbi.

Through his interpreter, he said "What difficulties?"

I responded, "I refused to move during a sitting meditation and blew a disc in my back."

"Now I know why God sent you to me."

He must have seen the expression on my face or noticed my surprise when he used the word God. He said that you can use Buddha or God if you know what the meaning is and with this he opened his hand and paused.

He continued, "You created your own misery by making a stupid decision of not moving your body. Even though you have been practicing meditation for many decades does not mean you are awakened."

I gazed into his eyes and it felt as though I was floating on the ocean.

Pointing to my heart, he told me, "Meditation practice is only an application—and you—are the source of inspiration." He smiled and then I smiled.

He said, "Yes, keep smiling. Someone or something took your smile away and you have to put it back." His words shocked my bones. I thanked him by putting my hands together and we returned to the truck. I looked at everyone on the back of the truck and they were all smiling.

We eventually arrived at the monastery, our original destination when he took me on the bus; all I knew was that I was at a monastery in Myanmar. Monks do not say good-bye, because we know on one level of consciousness there is nowhere to go. We just stood there for a few moments, soaking up the present moment. It was about dusk; I watched the sadhu/monk with the colorful bag and his family drive off into the night. My teachings from him were practice, practice, more practice—*and enjoy.*

12. IN THE PRESENCE OF GRACE:
THAMANYA SAYADAW
(November 1999)

A Western monk walked up to me and said, "Are you here to see Thamanya?"

I said, "If he is the abbot, yes."

Even though it was getting dark, I could see that the monk's face looked soft with excitement. He asked me what country I came from. He told me he was from India. And when I expressed surprise at this, he responded, "Yes! For the past ten years I have been coming here for two weeks to two months." He told me that he had an import/export business in India. I was impressed that he came all the way from India for these retreats. He told me that Thamanya would not be available until the next morning and that I could check in up top where the monks were.

I turned and began walking up the very steep hill to the monastery building. The steps went up and up. I put myself into this one-pointed groove, took one step at a time, and stopped looking up.

It is so interesting where the mind goes when placed in a situation that requires utmost persistence. Certain mental qualities were causing a distraction in me as I walked up those steps, such as, "Why on earth did mankind design something like this? Haven't they heard about escalators? What about a cable car or perhaps a tramway? I am going to have to change my robes if I ever get up there."

The sun had just gone down, and the temperature felt like it was moving to a nice cool 85° F. I became aware of my monastic robes as a person walked by me on his way up with the reverence reserved for monks. I stopped, took a breath, made a vow not to give those mental qualities any attention, and moved on up.

At the top, I went into one of several buildings. There were monks all over the place, a hundred or more, and it took a while to find a space big enough for my body to lie down for the night. That's right, no beds, just floor space—

and no one was complaining! I walked up to a monk sitting behind a table. He was big with very dark skin; like most everyone there, he was darker than me and I was thinking about skin color. I remembered seeing people in Russia and thinking that suddenly I didn't know what "white" was. African-Americans use the term "black" to describe our race, but compared to some other cultures, we're not even close. I realized that the words black and white are more related to a concept than a color.

This monk was chewing on a betel nut and spitting into a spittoon. The betel nut, when chewed on, creates this deep red juice. There is something in that juice that makes you feel that you've been drinking moonshine mixed with a little purple haze, the acid Jimi Hendrix sang a tune about. There are some betel nuts that do not have this moonshine effect but the redness is still alive. The spittoon was a few feet from him and already half full. Even with just the small lantern on his table, you could see that red slush fly through the air into the spittoon. I could imagine the sadhu/monk with the colorful bag smiling at me, as he told me, "You not only need to step out of the square, but into the circle and outside of that as well." Being in this community of monastics was truly letting go with no strings attached.

Next to the lantern on the table was a ledger book. He wrote down my name and identification in that book. I saw the moon twinkling in his eye, and there he went again, turning his head, and red lightning coming out of his mouth. His skin complexion was dark purple with a glow all around him. He pointed to an area in the room that indicated my spot for the rest of the night.

I went over to that spot, sat facing the wall, practiced with a few breaths, found tranquility and lay down. A monk across from me asked me my name in English. I sat back up and noticed that several other monks had their eyes on me as well. They gathered around, and all of us made a circle.

The questions began, mostly about America. "What is it like being black in America? Are you happy there? Do people treat you well?" To properly answer those questions would take the rest of my sleep time. It was 9 p.m., but these questions were most unusual and they were very sincere. The monks went through my bag; the only item of interest was my driver's license. That gave them a good laugh. It was then about 2 a.m., and I slept for one hour.

After that I was awake and refreshed. I got up and walked around the sleeping monks until I eventually found another monk who told me, "I couldn't sleep either." We talked about sleeping and practicing at this time of the night. Both of us agreed that awareness does not sleep because it is not the body. The body rests only to detoxify itself and digest the information it has taken in during the day. When the process is complete, eyes pop open. We also agreed that darkness creates another level of quiet that is conducive for meditation practice. The monk and I looked at each other with an inner smile of satisfaction, being okay with being up at three in the morning.

The monk who registered me couldn't sleep either, so he joined us. His presence brought brightness into the dark area. I looked down and noticed that he had a *mala* (a string of beads used for prayer or mantra practice) in one hand and a flashlight turned off in the other. He did not open his mouth, but I heard him in my head or heart, "Come with me." He turned the flashlight on and began walking, leaving the other monk standing there. I followed him to the foot of the stairs. He looked into my eyes with those moon-like eyes, took his *mala* and motioned me to go up the stairs with a wonderful smile on his face.

The stairs were wide and long. It felt like a lifetime climbing the hill to this building and then climbing those stairs. Where could they lead? Not knowing where I was headed, I began, or should I say continued, my journey walking up stairs. I didn't look back, and I could hear his steps walking away. For some reason I knew that this was the last time I would see this incredibly radiant monk. His presence represented the embodiment of compassion.

The steps looked like they were going into the cosmos. As I looked up toward the top, I could see the stars streaking across the dark sky. I finally reached the top, and noticed that I was outside in a garden. The coolness helped to chill my hot bones and calm the rapture. It took a few minutes for my eyes to adjust to the darkness, and as they did I also could hear chanting, but didn't see anyone. The chanting sounded like hummingbirds, very soothing.

As my eyes adjusted to the area, I began to realize that I was in a very sacred, sacred place. There were individual spots in various places for monks to sit. I noticed that there were nuns practicing as well. I didn't know there were nuns at this monastery. I walked around until I found a spot, sat down, pulled out my *mala*, and dove into this ocean of bliss and love.

After a while people started leaving the area. The light of the sun began to consume the darkness. I pulled out my watch to check the time and realized that two hours had gone by. It felt like five minutes.

Not knowing where I was headed, I decided to go with the flow and began walking with the monks in a gentle, respectful way. We ended up in a room where breakfast was being served. I sat down and crossed my legs at a long and narrow table. I looked around and realized that I was eating with at least fifty monks. I didn't see any nuns; they must have their own room. I was surprised that the food was vegetarian, the first all-vegetarian monastery since I arrived in Myanmar.

Returning down the long staircase (the same one I went up after the sadhu/monk with the colorful bag dropped me off the day before), it felt as if I was descending from another heavenly realm. I could hardly feel my feet as they touched the steps coming down. At the bottom, I went over to the other building; I hoped to meet the abbot named Thamanya.

The Western monk who was there to greet me was a most unusual kind of person. He had lived in many different places besides India, and was very un-monk-like in his behavior. He tended to his fire by journeying here. He was devoted to Thamanya Sayadaw and returned to be with him again and again. After the recent experience of the spitting-red-lightning-spittoon monk, I needed to tend my own fire. We sat down and he asked if I had a good rest. I replied that it was one of the best. He said he had made arrangements for me to meet the abbot.

As we walked into his room, I saw him sitting cross-legged on his bed, and I instantly knew that I was in the presence of an awakened being, a highly-evolved person. I knew that I was in the presence of grace, a saint, and tears started running down my cheeks. The abbot had been sick and was in his bedroom, along with two lay attendants and a doctor who was also a monk. I later found out that this doctor had given up his private medical practice to dedicate his life to taking care of Thamanya.

After bowing to him, I was in a deep sweat again. The doctor was his translator and asked me how long I would like to stay. I said with my hands in prayer position, "One day, if I could." I wanted to go up north and visit another abbot named Pa-Auk Sayadaw; my time was getting to be tight. Thamanya told me "Yes" and invited me to use his meditation room above his bedroom to practice in; one of his attendants showed me how to get up there.

The air in the room was vibrant and thick, and I tasted sweetness in my mouth. At one end of the room was an enclosed glass case containing Buddhist artifacts that looked ancient—elaborate jade, emerald, and diamond-studded Buddhas and *lingams* and *yonis*. I found out from the other Western monk that they were all gifts that had been given to him. One was from the King of Thailand.

I began the practice of loving-kindness, sending loving thoughts to myself, and eventually to others, bathing myself in the divine presence. In my meditation, it had become easy to go into absorption states. The pain in my lower back and leg was still bothering me, but I had a choice to ignore it and go into absorption, which is beyond pain. I did this a few times and got self-confirmation that awareness is not the body. I can be in the body but not of the body. Knowing that my body was not physically okay, I alternated between walking and sitting practice for eight hours. Then I rested in lying posture reflecting on my experience.

Just the first view of Thamanya Sayadaw got me thinking about a sadhu whose name is Neem Karoli Baba. I first heard about him from Vishu Magee; I met him when I was in Taos and didn't have a place to stay the night and so stayed with him. A group of us watched a five-minute video about Neem Karoli Baba—over and over again because they wanted to see the huge diamond in Neem Karoli's eye. I had seen this kind of eye gem with the elders on Pawleys Island so it was not a big issue for me. Vishu invited me to stay in his barn, and that was okay since it was reasonably clean and dry in there. The strange thing was the three-ton marble statue of a monkey that stood in that barn. It was Hanuman, the Hindu Monkey God; the Hanuman Tape Library in Santa Cruz was named for him. That was a surprise—a statue of a monkey god in America!

Vishu told me that Neem Karoli Baba had other names like the "Masked Man," and Maharaji, which means Great Lord. Vishu said that Neem Karoli Baba was a saint, an *arhat*, an enlightened being. I wondered if there was a connection between Maharaji and Hanuman? At first, I had serious doubts about all this, but then something happened to make me change my mind and believe that he really was (or is) a Maharaji.

As the months went by, I began to have dreams about him. Then I had a few incidents of meeting what only looked like a human being; other people began sharing their own stories of being with Maharaji. I said to myself, "What's up with this? They burned this person's body September 11, 1973. How could this be?" So many Western people had such vivid stories about being with him that a book was published about their encounters. There were a lot of people, including me, who became quiet when they realized a publication was coming out. We wondered if the publication was the right thing to do. With a being on that level of maturity, there is no right or wrong, just is.

However, being in Thamanya's presence brought these stories up in my mind and brought tears to my eyes. So here are a few of my own stories about this masked man, Neem Karoli Baba. One evening at home in New Mexico, my friends Bruce Smith, Caroline Wareham, and I were taking an intermission from watching a movie. I was making popcorn in the kitchen, and someone knocked on the door. Caroline went and opened the door, and said, "Ralph, there is a person at the door asking if you have any food." Now where my house was, was off the lighted streets. To get to the front door one needed to walk down a dark alley, and my porch light was not on. There is no window on that side of the building to see into the alley or for any light to shine out to give someone the impression that there is anybody at home.

I told Caroline to let him in. He was an elderly looking man. As I gave Bruce and Caroline a bowl of buttered popcorn, I asked the guest to come into the kitchen and sit down at the table. I looked into the fridge to see what I had, and noticed some black bean soup. I poured it out of the jar into the pot and heated it up. I looked for a nice bowl to put it in and gave it to him. I sat down at the other end of the table. His hands were on the sides of the bowl, and they were so big that you could hardly see the bowl.

Behind him, and above his head, was a huge photograph of Maharaji that my friend Amadea Morningstar had given me as a gift on her return from India a year before. The picture was in a frame that I found in my great-grandfather's house. I looked at the picture and at his hands again, and said to myself, "No way." Besides, he had a baseball cap on. He finished the soup and liked it, so I put the rest in a jar for him.

As we got to the door he said, "Do you have a blanket?"

I thought to myself, "No."

Before I could move my lips he said, "Okay, that's all right." We walked up the alley to the street and bid each other goodbye. I got half way back to my front door and was thinking about those stories, and out loud I said, "Holy Shit." I ran back up to the street, which was about ten steps, but he was gone. I was depressed and upset for several days over having lost him.

Later on, I shared the story with a friend Krishna Das who had been with Maharaji in India; he stopped me before I could finish and asked, "Did he wear a baseball cap?"

I said, "Yes."

"And you didn't cut your throat?" he said in a joking way, but I think he was serious.

You could see love for his teacher twinkling in his eyes.

Another time, I was driving from the New York State Correctional Facility to a bed and breakfast in Montreal,

Canada. This was the closest city in the area. It was very cold, with lots of snow on the ground. As I was driving early in the morning, someone threw something at my rental car that left a blue-colored spot. When I came to the border crossing, the patrol person said, "Yeah, kids have been doing this to cars in this area." I wiped it off, except for a little that was in the lower corner of the windshield, for I decided to wait until I got to the bed and breakfast to finish the job. I wanted to get away from this dude, even though he was respectful.

As I was driving down the Canadian highway, there was a guy near an off-ramp hitchhiking. I picked him up, and I instantly knew who he was—big and wearing a baseball cap. I put both hands on the wheel and looked in the back seat to make sure everything was neat and clean.

Most importantly, I tried not to think about anything, which was not easy. I knew he was in my head, but I eventually relaxed and was proud to be with him. I felt that he knew that I knew who he was, and I relaxed into just breathing. Then I thought about how nice and clean my car was, and he instantly said, "What's that?" pointing his huge fingers toward the corner of my windshield. I said to myself, "Oh man, busted."

I told him the story about the paintball attack, and he instantly nailed me about kids.

"You should not let kids get away with anything. You should have turned around, found them, and taken them to their parents. Be an example for them, or else they will run wild because of not having any direction and understanding of what is skillful and unskillful; that's being an Elder. This attitude hurts them as they get older."

After having my ass chewed out, I felt I had just stepped out of a hot shower. I reached over and turned the heat to cool, way cool. His voice became quiet again and I tried to keep my composure.

I said, "Yes, sir," in a respectful and gentle way.

We drove into the community of Montreal and I asked him where he would like to go. He said, "Somewhere up there." He never moved any part of his body, but I knew he meant up toward the left. I took the first exit, and stopped at a park that took up a square block. There were just a few people in the park, and you could see in any direction because there were no trees. He got out without saying anything and began to walk across the park. I sat there observing him walk, and about halfway to the other side, he just disappeared. I put my hands together and said, "Thank you." I never doubted the unseen world or longed for the presence of his form again.

The following day, I went again to Thamanya's bedroom. This time I asked for permission to stay another day and was told that arrangements had already been made for me. This process of asking permission went on for several days.

During one of my sessions in his meditation room, I became agitated because of my back pain. So I did standing practice. Most people in the West think that meditation includes only sitting postures, but there are actually four basic postures of the body: sitting, standing, walking, and lying down. Meditation is about what you are doing in there, not the position of the body. I frequently asked myself that question, "What am I doing in here?" It helped me keep an upright mind, and turned mindfulness into an investigative process.

As I was doing my standing meditation, I looked over to my right at three Burmese monks who were lying down. I began to wonder about them. They had been coming up every day to practice, but the only posture they had been working with was lying. I thought, "Look at those lazy rascals." I went back into sitting posture, but after a few minutes the pain was just too intense. I had learned from my Rains Retreat to be kind to myself, so I got up and did walking practice. The intensity of the pain was still there after about forty-five minutes of walking.

I looked over at those monks who were still lying there and went back into sitting posture. After a while, tears began to roll down my face, and that was a sign that I better change something. I had tried all the postures except lying. I looked around and noticed that there was an extra mat in the corner at the top of the stairs, so I got the mat and began lying down practice. Wow! It felt and sounded like an ocean of sweetness had swallowed me up. The sensation of my body on the mat on the floor was gone. Pleasure and pain were gone; self was gone. I heard movement and opened my eyes; some of the monks were getting up. I closed my eyes again and heard them walk down the stairs. I wondered why they were leaving so early and reached for my watch. I had been lying there for three hours! How could that be?

This was the most beautiful experience I had ever had in meditation. For the first time, I realized that it's not about the posture; it's about what you are doing in there. That experience shifted me to a new level. So far my practice had been focused on sitting, standing, and walking meditations for the development of concentration; now I realized that lying meditation could be used for the cultivation of tranquility as well.

The other monks got up, smiled and said, "What took you so long?"

"What do you mean?" I asked.

"Come on, Punnyananda, we saw for the last few days how you have been struggling in your practice, and your face looked like cold steel. We are all very privileged to be with a senior monk. All you have to do is be aware of your breath and relax, that's why we lay the body down. Are all you black Americans this hardheaded?"

"No! Of course not, I just happen to be a special nut case."

We all laughed and walked on to our resting and sleeping areas.

The next morning I had a conversation with three monks about Abbot Thamanya Sayadaw, and they told me this story: An army general and several of his men drove down from Yangon to Thamanya's monastery. After arriving, they went inside the monastery with their weapons. This is highly disrespectful at any monastery. Thamanya Sayadaw was very calm as the general approached him without bowing. The general then proceeded to speak with an unkind voice as his men stood behind him.

Sayadaw stopped the general and said, "You think you are powerful." The general had a slight smile on his face. Sayadaw raised his right arm and pointed behind the general. The general looked behind him and didn't see his men.

He turned back around and Sayadaw said, "Now how powerful do you think you are?" The general was dismayed.

Then Sayadaw said, "Look behind you now."

The general turned again and saw that his men were back! He turned to Sayadaw, dropped to his knees, begged for forgiveness, and bowed three times. His men behind him also bowed three times; then they all respectfully left the monastery.

We knew that Thamanya Sayadaw was an Arhat, an enlightened person, but we didn't understand how he knew so much about current and future events. I had gotten very comfortable with him, so I asked him, "Venerable Thamanya, you don't have a telephone. I've never seen you read the newspaper, and you seem to always be up to date about the news from around the world. How is that?"

He was quiet for a few moments, and then he said to his interpreter, the physician, "Just as most people around the world gossip and talk to each other, I do the same, but my conversation is with the *devas*, and this is how I find out what is happening around the world."

He gave me a discourse on the Triple Gem: the Buddha, the Dharma, and the Sangha. If my memory serves me right, here is what he said about the Buddha: The highest attainment one can achieve is learning how to become awake. The word Buddha means awake. Siddhartha was the twenty-seventh Buddha. Our universe expands and contracts, just like our bodies, and anything that has a beginning has an ending. To awaken to all this, we work at not clinging to anything and not craving anything, but rather understanding that we already have everything that we need. This reminded me of the Zen teaching that there is nowhere to go, we just need to learn to awaken.

Sayadaw reminded me that taking refuge in the Dharma meant commitment to the teachings of the Four Noble Truths as the foundation of my practice. This, he said, would deepen my wisdom and discernment and eventually help me gain insight into the working of the cosmos and everything within it. The word dharma is made of *dhar* meaning cradle and *ma* meaning mother. That's the Sanskrit spelling. The Pali spelling is *dhamma*, and in Thai it is *dham*, which also means nature. The true understanding of this wisdom can come only through experience, but then you feel it; the breath of kindness becomes the embodiment of our nature.

Through observation of the natural causes of things, he said I would develop insight into how things come together and how things associate and disassociate from each other. He reminded me that through my practice I would come to an understanding that everything is perfect, and gain insight into what is skillful and what is unskillful within this precious environment of the Dharma.

Finally, Thamanya explained that in taking refuge in the Sangha, or community, I would learn to develop a sense of respect for all others and myself. I would come to know that all beings, seen and unseen, are part of my sangha (see appendix: Layperson Taking Refuge). This also includes animals. We all share the existence of making community as we live on this planet, floating through space.

"This is all you need to know to reach your attainment," he said.

After that discourse, I felt complete. I asked his permission to teach after I returned to America. And he said "Yes." He also gave his authorization for a picture to be taken of the two of us. His physician told me that this was very unusual and special.

Thamanya also gave me a photo of a woman with him, saying "Keep that photo between the pages" (in other words, do not let anyone in Myanmar see it). I later found out that the woman was Nobel Peace Laureate Aung San Suu Kyi, the opposition leader who was being held under house arrest by the military regime. Thamanya was her teacher.

The people had voted for her to be prime minister; the competition was not even close, but the military withheld the election results, and Aung San Suu Kyi went to live in Europe. When her father was dying she came home to be with him, and after his death she refused to leave. The government wanted her to return to England where she had a family and where her husband was dying from cancer, but she knew if she left, the military would not let her back into Myanmar. So she gave up being with her family for her country. For me, that was like Siddhartha giving up his family to become awakened—the Buddha—for all beings (see appendix: Householder Buddha).

Thamanya had given me a picture of Aung San Suu Kyi and told me to share it with everyone when the time was right. Seven years later, during the uprising with the monks going against the military, I posted that picture on the web. But for now, I simply bowed with utmost respect and declined going for tea with Aung San Suu Kyi.

I bowed three times, and he said as I was departing, "Be careful about eating red meat, and you will not have any more problems in Myanmar." I remember shortly after returning to America, and six months after being with Thamanya, the "mad cow disease" was discovered in the United Kingdom.

Ten years later I would read in the Irrawaddy News (an Internet journal covering Myanmar and Southeast Asia), that Thamanya had died; government forces had broken into the monastery and stolen his body. They felt that possessing his body would erase their bad karma and unjust deeds, and award them merit instead. There could not be a more valuable example of delusional thinking, which is considered to be one of the three root poisons in Buddhism, like the glue that binds consciousness to suffering. The other two poisons are greed and hatred, and their effects can last for years or lifetimes. These poisons are lethal to one's consciousness. Thamanya Sayadaw was a person who had eradicated these poisons from his consciousness. He was his own physician, meaning he was a master of the Four Noble Truths (see appendix: Four Noble Truths).

Foothills of Southern Myanmar: Two weeks before the Rains Retreat, the Western monks were talking about a teacher in the southern part of Myanmar. They were talking about him like people would talk about a rock star or major football player. They talked about him as though if you had not practiced with Pa-Auk Sayadaw, then you did not qualify as a monastic. They also mentioned that the monastery was located in an area heavily infested with the malaria-carrying mosquitoes. When I heard that, they finally got my attention—because that statement eliminated anyone who carried the concept of "fear" without wisdom. I was asking myself, "Who is this person, and what is he teaching?"

A monk with whom I had sat the Rains Retreat was staying at Pa-Auk's monastery, and I wanted to see him again too. He had helped me out during my visit to the hell realms when I meditated and refused to move, severely damaging my lower back. He had given me some yoga lessons which helped to ease the pain.

I will never forget his comments at the end of the Rains Retreat about the Sunlun Meditation Practice that I was going to study. "You are going to a place where you can kick back and practice at your own pace," he said. "And you are jumping out of the frying pan into the fire." What he said to me carried so much wisdom. Sometimes I could be very stubborn. He was not the first person to say something about my temperament. There was a time in my life when I thought I needed to go back to school for further education, just because my financial situation was not where I wanted it to be. My friend Stephen Levine said, "Man, don't you think you have enough education? You are just a glutton for punishment."

I was starting to realize how the mind works. My life was all about training the mind, stepping up to the fact that my genetic system came from, and was conditioned in, an oppressed culture. Living in a country that rates you by your skin color, race, and education motivated me into the category of "Can Do." At one time in my life that was a skillful concept; then it became unskillful. I found that it's important to recognize when a belief system no longer serves us. Hell, I had to go to the other side of the planet and taste the fire of hell to tenderize my heart, before gaining insight into my temperament. I wanted to check this brother out. I left and found a taxicab to take me to Pa-Auk's monastery.

After arriving at the monastery, I soon found Edward Wood, a friend from the Rains Retreat. We had tea and had a wonderful reunion as I described my journey to him, most importantly the intensity of the Sunlun Advanced Breath Meditation Monastery. He said, "No way would I do that." We all have our path of practice, and it is important that we follow it. Sometimes there is doubt and not knowing which path to take. That's the mystery of life and the adventure it holds. Eventually I came to the understanding that any path has a profound teaching.

Edward said that he was happy, doing very well, and had a wonderful space to practice in. We parted with delight and made arrangements to get together and have tea upon our return to America. That is, if we did return.

I walked around the grounds and found another Western monk. We talked about the mosquito culture, and he told me it did not get any more deadly serious than here. This area was extremely infested with malaria mosquitoes; therefore one's mindfulness needed to be impeccable or one would get seriously sick and die. I had a mosquito net designed to fit over my head; this was one of the eighteen items I had brought from America and never used and so I gave it to him.

I had tea with two other monks. One of them noticed my back pain and said I should take the retreat from Goenka to learn how to work with the breath. He had done a ten-day retreat with Goenka, one of the first teachers who brought this body-sweeping breath technique to the West. It became one of the many meditation skills used in Vipassana when working with the breath and became known as the Goenka method. He didn't know where I had just come from, that I was already staying with another master of the breath, and that I was getting ready to do an intensive practice; I was not going to get into a story about this.

I found that the entire pain syndrome was such an interesting cycle. For example, my inner body had learned how to let go and move the breath energy more smoothly throughout the body. But my physical body had developed a different behavior with regard to the perceived pain. It carried itself more guardedly, more carefully—this is what this monk had noticed.

After having tea, some of the monks took me back to the main part of the monastery where I finally got to meet Pa-Auk. After paying my respects, I asked, "What do you teach?" He told me he mainly taught the practice of loving-kindness. I knew this practice was important to learn, so that when in various stages of *jhana* (absorption), we can call on the retraining of the mind and body, and rough waters won't pull us out of that state. Rough waters are the countless traumas that most humans have experienced.

Trauma, he said, can occur when your mother or father or someone dear to you in childhood yells at you and doesn't quickly support that energy with some quality of loving kindness. Without that support your mind gets a negative coding without being balanced with a positive coding.

I explained that I had only a few hours, and needed to get on the road to the northern part of Myanmar. After my visit with Venerable Pa-Auk Sayadaw, I was ready to head north. But it was not so easy to get permission to leave. I had to be interviewed by one of Pa-Auk's senior monks, along with a few other monks, in order to check out my behavior and to see how I was trained as a monk.

At first, in my exit interview I was focused on (and attached to) my pain to the point that I could not really feel the joy, love, and happiness that this senior monk was initiating. Then, gradually I picked up on his wonderful energy and a dance of laughter came over us. Another monk came over to join in.

"You are an American?"

"Yes," I replied.

"How do you like being with us?" the senior monk inquired.

"Very special. I feel at home," I said.

"How was your Rains Retreat?"

"I experienced grace and hell," I replied.

"So you had a good time," he said.

"Yes, I went beyond pain."

We all laughed. The monks asked if I would stay and practice with them. However, it was getting late and I needed to get going. Arrangements were made for a layperson to take me to the bus and about a dozen monks observed me leaving. The driver introduced himself and reached out to shake my hand, but I didn't take it. That gave me points; I overheard them saying to each other, "Very good."

The sun was setting, which cast a golden color across the blue sky. As we drove away from the foothills of the mountains in southern Myanmar, it was the time of day when nature changes. I knew the mosquitoes would be coming out soon to get their supper. My driver drove off the dirt road that led to the monastery and onto a paved road that took us to the bus station.

It was about six in the evening when the bus left, and I took this opportunity to relax by moving the breath through my body. This practice includes moving the awareness between the eyebrows as the breath comes in and letting the head fill with the breath energy, then moving the awareness down the spinal system as the breath moves out of the nostrils or mouth. This was one of the primary techniques that had helped ease my back pain during the Rains Retreat. Breathing the awareness of breath energy down my spine generated a letting-go process throughout my body, producing an effect of tranquility.

There are many qualities of the breath, endless qualities of breath sensations, and endless ways to breathe—endless because each of us has a different temperament, so our expressions and responses to our bodies are different. Some abbots at the monasteries taught single breath meditation methods and some didn't. Jacqueline Schwartz-Mandell, one of the four pioneers who brought Vipassana meditation to the West, told me that there was an abbot named Taungpulu Sayadaw who taught many methods. His applications were based on one's temperament. He died several years before I came to Myanmar.

There are, however, some basic guidelines. The body is usually breathing in one of the four cycles: long-in-and-out breath; long-in-short-out breath; short-in-long-out breath; short-in-and-out breath. I have noticed that when I tune in to these cycles, it's one of the many ways of communicating with this vessel, my body. And if I pay attention, my body lets me know how it would like the next cycle of breath to be. All I have to do is gently help it along. Then comes the next cycle, and how would you like to dance with the breath this time? This skill became very helpful to me, especially when I had become bored or frustrated with various moods or mental states.

13. THE ROAD TO MANDALAY
(November 1999)

At the end of my time with the Sayadaws in southern Myanmar, I made the journey north to Mandalay. I was the only monk on the bus, and I felt the appreciation coming from everyone. About two hours into the journey to Yangon, we made a refreshment stop, and I got off with everyone else to use the bathroom. Then I sat down at an outside table of a café, next to the restaurant where everyone was dining. A man came up and offered to serve me some drinks, and I drank several different kinds of sodas. Then I did some walking practice until it was time to leave.

It was about nine in the evening when we left the rest area, and it was dark as the bus traveled across the countryside. About an hour later the bus stopped on the highway and a person on the bus walked up to me and waved me off the bus. That person had received instruction when I initially got on the bus. However, I did not know that the bus would stop in the middle of a countryside road, as opposed to a town or bus stop with lights. I was surprised, but I got off, and he noticed that I was surprised, so he pointed the direction for me to go.

Can you imagine being in so much darkness that all you can see is the person in front of you, and a hand appears with its finger pointing? So I just had to wrap my mind around that non-verbal instruction.

The bus took off into the dark of the night. Within minutes it was completely silent except for the sound of my breath, which I purposely kept going on a level course until my awareness had adjusted to the depth of this darkness and silence. There was no other traffic. It was so dark that I couldn't see the road. I knew that there was either a crossroad or a road intersecting the road that I was on because of the finger pointing. I felt with my foot to find the edge of the road on the right, and then went over to the left in search of some indication of the intersection. I put my hand in front of my face, but I could barely see it.

Then I looked up into the sky, and the galaxies and stars began to talk to me; there were so many stars. That was the only comfort besides my breath. My awareness adjusted itself to the starlight, and I began to see the road and started walking. *Yahman*, this was most definitely being born again. My mind and body were awakened to a more joyful, refreshing, and lighter level of awareness. My body was also soaked with sweat from going through the transition of getting off the bus and getting accustomed to this new environment. Fear wanted to come.

It took a diligent effort to be attentive to my breath and mindful of the surroundings, which were black. It reminded of me of Vipassana meditation retreats in America where the sitting periods were forty-five minutes. Sometimes when I would just sit down, or a few minutes into the meditation period, pain would come into my body. If I had a watch, the entire period would be spent opening and closing my eyes to check on the time. Sixty seconds felt like an hour. Why? Also, I would be moving my body, constantly readjusting my position. Why? If "awareness" doesn't have a stable foundation that it can trust, the natural tendency is to look for something stable. Usually it just tumbles through various mental states. How fast it goes depends on the quality of the mental states.

For example, thoughts of finding a comfortable position can escalate to "I am going to hurt myself," to "I am going to die," to "I want the bell to ring," to "Get me the hell out of here." As awareness is tumbling through these mental states, the muscular system is doing gymnastics in the body, thus increasing tension, which increases the perceived pain. When the bell finally rings, the feeling is like being hit by a truck, because unraveling from sitting cross-legged releases the mental tapes of guilt and shame at not doing it right.

I remembered my early days of practice, when I did not understand the importance of applying effort to seek refuge, which is the breath, and I wondered how I had missed it. It was only after becoming a teacher that I realized the mind learns through repetition. It is difficult to be aware of the content of a Dharma talk if awareness is tumbling through

156

mental states. Yes, I remembered hearing words like "pay attention to the breath or object of choice," but I did it so I could get through the forty-five-minute meditation periods. After many years of practice and investigation, I was learning that the purpose of attentiveness is to cultivate a secure foundation for awareness.

Back on the road, I couldn't tell if any other road intersected the one that I was walking on, but I found comfort in the breath, and just continued to walk. I heard some music, but of course couldn't see anything. In one of his songs, the Godfather of Soul, James Brown, has a lyric about being *in a cold sweat*, and that's how I felt. I knew that the temperature at night dropped into the high eighties, but with the humidity, I was in a cold sweat after getting off the bus.

Well, I slowly walked my bones toward the sound of the music. In about three hundred steps, I began to hear voices, then saw light coming through the cracks of what I would call a "sugar shack." That's a building, with walls so flimsy that a gentle wind could blow it down, that houses a bar or restaurant, a place for conversation in the community. On the inside it feels like being in your bed at home, very peaceful and safe.

I just walked toward the sound. It turned out to be voices, instead of music. It looked like a huge tent. My sense door of smell kicked in; I smelled the smoke of cigars, alcohol, and musk. Yes, this was definitely the neighborhood bar. I walked in and the voices stopped. I approached one person and said that I needed a ride to Kyaiktiyo Pagoda, where I could get another bus to Mandalay. He finished his drink and walked me over to a spot where a few vehicles were parked and people were seated in various places on the ground.

They saw that I was a monk, but they asked me which country I was from. I made a mistake and said America.

When they said they wanted money, I said "No" and they said, "Okay then you will have to go on your own."

I began to walk away, and another driver approached me and said, "You are an American and I know you have some money." I did have a little but it was against the rules to even carry or touch money. As my elders said, "Trust in God but keep your mule tied up." I was most defiantly breaking the precepts, and I could hear in my mind my senior monks saying "Rookie." I quietly took out my pouch and gave it to him. He was shocked that I gave it to him. I noticed that he took very little.

He talked to someone who I assumed was one of the drivers, and afterward he walked up to me, gave his respect by putting his hands together in prayer position, and departed. The driver ignored me, so I put my sitting cloth down, and noticed that everyone was watching. I decided to squat down like everyone else, and conversation continued. I said to myself: "Well, you did the right thing, and there's nothing like doing the right thing."

In about one hour the driver came up to me and said, "Are you American?"

I said, "Yes!"

He turned around and went back to his friends and spoke in Burmese, but the word "American" doesn't change.

I said to myself, "There's also nothing like doing the wrong thing."

He began to ask me for more money, and I realized that he wanted to charge me not double, but triple the price. I kept my composure and didn't get into a conversation about money. My realization came from observing how much money other people gave him. Americans, even American monks, are seen as people who are wealthy in Myanmar. In the end, he took a small amount of what I had in my money pouch.

The truck was a 1987 Datsun pickup with benches in the back, a roof, and open sides. I am six foot three inches, so only four people of my size could fit in the back. There were ten people in the back, and I sat up front with three people including the driver. It was almost one in the morning when we left.

About thirty minutes down the road, smoke started coming out of the dashboard. I told the driver to stop. He didn't want to, but because I said so, he did. We all got out of the truck. After walking toward the front, I heard a hissing sound and told them to lift the hood to look at the engine. We found out that we had a broken water hose.

I looked around in the darkness, noticed that there were lights, and realized that there were two homes nearby. Some people came out and helped him because they saw me. I squatted along with everyone else. After about one hour they had fixed the hose and we were able to continue up the road. We eventually came to our destination that was the base of the mountain. It was about three o'clock in the morning.

As I got out of the truck, I noticed that among the people in the back there was a nun. She had a male taking care of her. Keeping my physical distance, I decided to keep my eyes on her, because she was a monastic. The three of us ended up walking into an area the size of one-half of a football field that was a marketplace in the daytime. I could tell because of the wooden platforms and tables made for venders to place their fruits and vegetables upon. Now it was empty. Everything was made of wood; the floors were earthen. The perimeter was made up of shops waiting for occupancy. Beyond the perimeter were tall green trees. We walked toward the center where the wooden platforms (the only structures with floors and no walls) were built-in tables, a perfect place to lie down.

I also noticed that this was the mosquitoes' sanctuary. I do mean sanctuary; it reminded me of being in Vietnam or in the swamps on Pawleys Island. After going through the Rains Retreat, this place was also like a refresher course in graduate school mosquito training. The mosquitoes were all sizes; the larger ones made the loudest sound. Just hearing them activated my nervous system. One of my friends in Myanmar said, "Just let them take a drink, and they will go away." I had brought two kinds of repellant with me. One had more than 75 percent of deet in it, which I never used because of my fear of the chemical. The other had less than 25 percent of Deet. Both containers were the size of my thumb, and during my year in Asia, I did not empty either of them. In fact, later I gave the higher-percentage Deet away. Only later I realized that this was not too skillful because the higher percentage needs to be used with caution.

All three of us got on one of the platforms that had four elongated tables on it. I was not breaking, hopefully, any of the 227 monastic precepts because there was another male, no roof, and no walls. So I felt okay with the nun present. I made sure that the man was between the woman and me, and a table was between the man and me. I lay down and pulled my robe over my head and feet. It was in that moment I realized how versatile my robe was. I was inside a cocoon. I could hear swarms of mosquitoes outside of my outer robe. With gentleness and compassion I turned my body on its right side, understanding that the heart pump was in its most relaxed position, and began formal lying meditation practice.

I never knew that this would become a comfortable posture to practice meditation in. The sound of those mosquitoes became music, along with the sound of nature in the night. It was difficult to distinguish the sound within from the sound outside of my vessel.

After a few hours, I stood up, got my water bottle out of my bag and started to brush my teeth; at the same time I walked about twenty steps. When I turned around, I noticed that the other male was up as well. I hadn't heard him get up because of the sound of me brushing my teeth.

I walked back to my bag and put my water bottle back. Immediately I noticed that my money pouch was missing. I knew he had it, but I didn't know where, and didn't know how to ask since I didn't speak his language. I walked up to him and just listened from within, then my arm reached out and my hand went into his jacket pocket as he stood in front of me.

Inside his jacket I felt my pouch and pulled it out. He was stunned; his face looked as if he had seen death. Perhaps that would have been the outcome in a non-monastic situation, but this was a monastic situation: taking without permission is a high offense in a Buddhist country, especially taking from a monk. He knew he had committed a major act and got caught, which made it even worse.

I questioned him, making gestures with my hands— pointing to him, the bag, and me, so that he could understand. How could you do this? He just held his head down and didn't give a response. I forgave him, by putting my hands in prayer position in front of him, though I knew this couldn't stop his karmic action. When we act upon intention, we are the owners of our action and inherit its results. Our future is born from our actions, and this will be our home. Of all actions with intention, be they good or harmful, we will be the recipients. This teaching from the Buddha continues to be a wake-up call for me. He needed to ask for forgiveness for himself, and that was his personal choice.

As if not wanting to be seen by the "light of day," the man walked away and disappeared as the daylight came. The nun was still lying down, and he left without saying a word to her. I thought it was a classic movie-type exit. The nun stood up and noticed that her guide was gone. She looked at me in dismay. I pointed and made a gesture indicating that I didn't know where he went. In the meantime, a comfortable or respectful distance was maintained between us as we developed a friendship.

As the morning daylight became brighter, burning off the mist, a few other people came to the area. It was too early for the minibus to take us halfway up the mountain, about one or two miles up a winding road. The two of us began to walk, and just as we began, three men came up to me and said, "Good morning." That was good, because they spoke English.

They were policemen off duty and were going up to the top of the mountain to enjoy the day and receive blessings. I explained to them what happened to the nun and why she was by herself. One of the precepts is that a nun is not supposed to travel alone. They instantly volunteered to help her, knowing that they were helping me. They carried our baggage up, and two of them were on each side of her providing support. It is so interesting when one decides to take a leap of faith, like getting up this mountain with a nun's baggage that I was not supposed to touch. The walk ended up being joyful and full of laughter. We stopped several times along the way, and people provided drinks for us. After getting to the top with the police, we all took photographs of one another and bid farewell.

I went to my room and realized that some of the lay practitioners from the advanced breath, rapid breathing, Sunlun Monastery were there. I had a conversation with one of the senior laypeople about the breath practice. The conversation was mostly about pain and how to work with it. He said to be diligent and balance it with kindness. Basically he said that to manage pain is to make it the object of meditation. When the pain becomes too hot, then you should use your muscular system to hold on to that particular pain. While holding on to that pain, you should take a breath, breathing in and out short, with various qualities of lightness or softness.

The essence of his conversation was that pain is unavoidable. There are a variety of ways for working with pain because of our temperament. There isn't a one-size-fits-all except the breath, breath being the various qualities of breathing the wind element into our precious vessel.

It is all about training the mind; therefore this process cultivates more of our uniqueness. The culture of Myanmar is "no pain, no gain." I realized that working with pain, one needs to cultivate an awareness of gentleness to firmness in one's perception of perceived pain. Since I was returning from practicing with an Arhat, Thamanya Sayadaw, I was working on trying to be gentler with myself. I knew that it was working because my back pain had decreased to a minimum.

A woman came to get the man I had been talking to for a meditation session. I knew he was special because they wouldn't start without him, and at one point I could feel their frustration because I had his attention. I thanked him and gave him permission to leave; he departed.

I went and packed my belongings and made arrangements to get down to the bottom of the mountain. I needed to begin to prepare for my journey to Mandalay up north. I only had a few days now before we would all meet again at the country monastery for the yearly ten-day intensive Sunlun Breath Retreat.

Before leaving, I took the time just to walk around. I came across a group of nuns who were dressed very colorfully, like nothing I had ever seen before. They were wearing a bright colorful cloth wrapped up around the top of their heads. They walked with a gentle rhythm. I knew something was very special about this because of the way they carried themselves. They were all walking in a double line toward the sacred rock as if they knew where they were going and what they were up to. They assembled themselves on a covered platform without walls. A crowd of people had gathered to watch them.

They began to chant, and the entire mountain felt even more still. I could feel the *Shakti*, or juice, coming up and down my spine. My body was overflowing, and they were only about sixty seconds into the chant. At least five thousand years ago, the ancient Vedic scriptures from the second century BCE said that chanting or singing about the divine is one of the ways of feeling the presence of energy or *prana*.

This reminded me of my mother, my aunt, and our church choir back home on the island. They would have road trips scheduled to perform at various churches, mostly on Saturday or Sunday afternoons. The majority of the time the driver would get the directions wrong, and we would add thirty minutes to our lateness. We were never on time based on the clock, but always on time based on the right moment.

When we did arrive, the parking lot would be full of cars and trucks. If we were two hours late, no one would have left. They didn't leave because they knew how excellent the choir was, and it was an embarrassment to the individual and their community if someone left. People would be hearing about it for weeks, even though most people didn't have a telephone.

This choir would put their robes on while still on the bus. As they got dressed, the typical conversation in Gullah would be "tis bodee es-ahrade tu raz tha daad?"; "Shoow nuff, uall cum un nuw en las waah en hse ame" ("Are our bodies ready to awaken the spirit?"; "Yes, let's go and walk in the name of our Lord Jesus Christ.") The choir would quickly line up outside of the church and I would open the door. They would walk in singing and the place would light up with energy. Everything came alive.

These nuns were doing the very same thing, except with reverence to the Buddha. After they got through chanting, they went into a silent meditation and we joined them. In about another thirty minutes they got up and left. The air was sparkling like the mist of rain but it was not raining.

I continued my walk around this mountain and noticed so many different kinds of shops and people from all walks of life. People were here from around the world to be at this sacred place; this was definitely an international tourist location. I thought it was interesting that a place like this could function so well without television, telephone, radio, and computers. There was one phone, and that was at the police station. I felt satisfied with my stay on top of this mountain, but it was time to continue on to Mandalay. *Yahman.*

The bus that took me on the next leg of my journey was the size of an American school bus, but with my long legs, it was still like going into a torture chamber. Of course, my seat was up front, which made things worse, because my knees were pressing against the metal panel in front of me. As I said before, all monks are put in the front seat, so if there is a driving accident we get to go through the front windows first. It is also said that monks carry protection because of their merit, and if one's merit is really good, the bus and the passengers will be protected.

Because of the small space, restlessness and fear had a conference with me about how to be calm. Maybe a better word is tranquil. In order to be calm from the inside out, I needed to apply techniques that had a tranquilizing effect on my nervous system. I had many exercises to choose from. One was visualization of different kinds of wonderful images. Another exercise was singing and chanting, with categories like Gospel, Motown, Blues, Sanskrit, Pali, and Country Western. Another calming exercise was working with one of the five sense doors, such as trying not to blink, making a mental note of the various sounds, smelling the qualities of the air, noticing how the taste in my mouth changed with the tension in my body, and feeling the hot, thick, wet air on my skin.

I decided on the breath as a tool for my practice while seated on this bus. I chose the breath because of the pleasant night air moving across the countryside, with its mixture of musty smells from the fields and from people on the bus. Also, it was a way to oxygenate and get the fluids moving in my stationary legs. Using the breath helped my thoughts to settle down, as the Wind Element became my primary point of focus.

As the movement of the bus created a bouncing effect for my body on the seat and I took note of other people's movements, it eventually all became a dance with the breath. I remembered the Hindu god Shiva, who is depicted dancing on one leg with the other in the air, his feet stepping on other bodies with fire all around him. This was the dance I was feeling. It has been called "the only dance there is."

I thought about how life offers a balance of joy and stress, and how being mindful of both requires a skillful dance. In my meditation practice, I was acquiring the skill to cultivate this balance, so that I could eventually transcend it and move on to the next level of refinement.

It would take about twelve hours to get to Mandalay, driving through the night. The driver was supposed to make two kinds of stops: one for dinner and the other for kindness, meaning to use the toilet since there wasn't one on the bus. I had been warned that most drivers would try to get away with just the dinner stop, and this presented two major problems for me. The first was that my legs would start talking to me in an unpleasant way after three to four hours. The other problem was that from my experience of being on a bus without a bathroom, the fifty to sixty other passengers would become restless. Bodies are composed of the six elements, including space and consciousness, and water is the leading tiger of those six, especially when it wants to get out of us and there's no toilet on the bus.

Luckily, I knew that there was a third kind of stop that the bus driver would make, and that was by request from a monastic. It was good for me to know that. The thought itself reduced the restlessness.

How do you know what is skillful and not skillful, especially when you think you are doing the right thing? The Buddha gave emphasis to a view that cultivates a path (see appendix: The Eightfold Path). I thought of them as my Eight Elders because in my childhood years I had the training of elders—grandparents, uncles, aunts, and cousins who were always giving me some form of instruction about how to behave with the utmost politeness and humbleness in their presence. When I was studying psychology and religion in Santa Cruz, I had learned that the translation of Theravada is "The Way of the Elders." I saw the Elders of The Eightfold Path as family. It was more personal that way.

Though there are many cultures in our modern times that continue to give the highest respect to their elders, the family system has changed, especially in America, where "Elder" now means senior citizen—a title meaning you have reached a certain age and you are eligible for benefits and price reductions on various things.

To me, becoming an elder meant earning a title given by one's community, in the recognition that you are someone to go to for advice, a role model. This is very important culturally because, without elders, a disruption in the culture begins to happen.

In the years before I left for Myanmar, youth gang violence had been strong throughout the U.S., and Michael Mead (with shamans Orland Bishop and Malidoma Some, along with poet Luis Rodriguez and Jack Kornfield) had produced the conference called *The Absence of Elders and the Violence of Youth.* This was during the mid-'90s, a time when gang violence was all over the major cities. When Michael had decided to shift his focus to working with these troubled youths, many of his European American supporters stopped funding him. He had to scrape together the money to rent a facility and provide transportation, room and board for a few gang members from various cities; the staff people were basically volunteers, including myself. The youth ranged from age fourteen to twenty-five, and totaled about fifty. There were also men ranging in age from the late twenties to the early fifties from the working class and corporate America; the elders in their sixties and seventies completed the circle.

When the time came for the serious healing rituals designed by Malidoma, we went twenty-four hours without sleep. In one part of the ritual, there was a hole in the ground filled with fine sand from which all the pebbles had been removed. Several buckets of hot water were poured into this hole, turning it into a mud pit; I was chosen to be the Maestro in the pit. It would be during the dark of the night with a full moon, drums beating, and chanting. Jack would open with an invocation, and depending on the location, there would either be a dog or a coyote howling that would acknowledge that it was time to get it on.

One at a time, the participants in their bathing suits or shorts would come down into the pit. The mud was warm and electrifying. I would put that mud on their chests and wherever they would instruct me to. Some of these bodies had two or more beings inside; I could see the faces change from moment to moment; it was like changing a channel on a television. As I held that body, it became lighter and lighter; you could see the uninvited juice jumping out of them. Upon looking into their eyes, I could see the moon in them. It was like someone went into a room and turned the light on. I would stand them up to where they would be looking at the full moon in the sky and I would say, "That moon you see is also in you." In that moment, I could feel the heat jumping off that body.

Helpers would help each young man walk out of the pit to a nearby lake or pond. I would turn my head around, and here would come another body walking on down. I would say, "Come on in here, brother. I got something that you've been waiting for." Those words would help calm them down because, when those entities in that body got restless, the body would start misbehaving and I would have to duck to avoid getting smacked.

Through my teacher Jack Kornfield, I had the privilege to be a part of that conference; as a result we were invited to be on the Dalai Lama's team at another conference, *Peace-*

making: the Power of Nonviolence, which was held at the San Francisco Civic Center in 1997.

To me, being an Elder is equivalent to being an *ajahn*, oracle, *rinpoche*, kahuna, medicine man, *roshi*, shaman or some other monastic who has worked to obtain the best inner qualities and then uses that experience to teach and give advice without regard for color, class, or economic boundaries. It is a title designed, not by a system or organization, but by the human race. The nectar of peace-keeping dwells within our elders, and they of course reside all over our planet so our overall fire can be tended. Now this is where it would be appropriate to say, "Thank God!" *Yahman*, as my grandmother, Sister Mary, would often say.

My favorite way of practicing with my Eight Elders was to work with one of them at a time. For example, when I was working with speech, I would take the whole day, reviewing my words and phrases at the end of each conversation and asking myself, "What could I have done more skillfully?"

My training from my Eight Elders continued at the dinner stop, where I enjoyed the indulgence of a few drinks of sugar sodas that were offered to me. Then I did walking meditation until it was time to get back on the bus and continue the journey.

Another two hours passed and I needed to go to the bathroom, so I decided to have the driver stop the bus. This was easy because there were always people in or outside the monastery who could speak English. We were in the country, and it was midnight-black out there. Deep woods and huge ditches were on both sides of the road. The only place the driver could stop was in the middle of the road. Everyone was glad I had stopped the bus.

The only privacy we had was that black oil of darkness. If a person took several steps in any direction, you could only see a silhouette. The bus driver had turned off the engine and the lights. The sound of the night was talking. The moon was not bright, for it was a few days after the new moon. Adaptable as people usually are, they began to do their thing, and I did mine.

I walked up the road until the voices were low, and mostly everyone appeared to be in groups of silhouettes.

Then I squatted and relieved my body of the excess water. I squatted for three reasons. First, my robes came down to my ankles, so it would be more skillful to bring my bones down instead of pulling the robes up. The second reason was that by squatting one becomes a smaller object. The final and most important reason was that squatting was one of the precept rules.

Since sound moves much more clearly at night, I overheard one woman say, "You better take a good look, you always wanted to know how we do this." I assumed that some of the curious young men were interested in how women urinate. The Burmese culture is very conservative, so neither men nor women walk around showing their skin, except for face and hands. It was a long-awaited break for everyone to pay their water bill to the Earth Element, which they enjoyed. We all experienced a little joy; even the driver paid his bill and smoked a cigar.

We arrived in Mandalay early in the morning around six. I got off the bus and pulled out the address of my supporter, Daw Aye. When a person leaves the mundane world, it is required to give up dancing, listening to and playing music, and at least 227 other precepts that change your life. My son, Clarence, would say it's like going to prison, perhaps for the rest of your life; and in a way this is true, except that this is a voluntary renunciation. People do not have a choice about going to prison, but they do have a choice about how they act inside; you can turn things around within yourself in a positive way or you can deepen your negative process. People living an everyday life also have that choice—to cultivate a positive or negative path.

Monastics leave the life of having wonderful playthings, and even having the necessities, like food. In the Theravada tradition, monks must depend on the community for nourishment, and everything must be given freely, because there is no money. This is why monastics can only stay in the forest or away from non-monastics for a short period of time—we have to eat. Monastics depend on the community for the nourishment of food, and the community depends on the monastics for the nourishment of blessings, consultations, and spiritual services.

For travel expenses, hospitalization, and other expenses, every monk has a supporter, and mine was Daw Aye, who owned two fish markets, one in Yangon and the other here in Mandalay. I took a taxi from the bus station to the marketplace to find her store. It was somewhere in the fish market, I knew, and eventually I found it; and one of Daw Aye's workers took me to her home. As we walked into her neighborhood, I had a flashback of my childhood years on Pawleys Island: the homes here were similar—not expensive looking, but clean and kept up. The yards were dirt, swept with a broom or rake, with a nice landscape of flowers and shrubs.

I remembered sweeping our yard on Pawleys Island every Saturday with a fan rake. It was a wonderful way to settle the mind, a mechanical exercise, like walking meditation, with those movements of the arms back and forth. Working with the various qualities of the breath during that process had been so enjoyable. As a child, engaging the sense doors of the eyes and nose was what I liked most. I liked how the fresh underearth came to the top and the smell of the freshly overturned soil. With each swing of the rake, the smell was so different and unique.

Of course, there were times I had not wanted to do this chore, and approached it with anger, but afterwards I would have an extraordinary peace of mind. And there were times when I looked forward to this process, and afterward the joy was inexpressible. In most monastic traditions, sweeping or raking is a daily morning practice. In Myanmar, we would do it after our meals.

It was so interesting how the cultivation of peace permeated throughout this neighborhood. I am sure that tending the yards was just one of the practices that supported this sweet feeling that made my walk so enjoyable.

Daw Aye was waiting for me. I walked upstairs and sat down on her floor. This was the first time I had ever been inside a Burmese home. I was not sure if I could be with a female alone; however, it was daylight, and she was supported by many monks from my monastery and was held in high regard. Besides, she was my supporter and deep in her own spiritual practice. The natural lighting in the room twinkled visibly in the air, so much that I thought to myself that my blood sugar was low. The building stood off the ground on poles. The roof was made of bamboo and straw, and the walls were of thin, four-inch-wide strips of bamboo. You could see between the strips of bamboo to the outside. The floor was made of wood. A very heavy wind could destroy not just this home, but also all the homes in the area.

It is so important to learn to notice the conditioning process of one's mind. For example, I wrote just now that a heavy wind could blow this building down because my childhood years were spent on Pawleys Island, which is also called "hurricane alley." Therefore, I know that when my mind thinks of homes being destroyed, it initially goes to the experience that trained it. Of course, I think of high winds; it had nothing to do with Myanmar, which hadn't experienced high winds in over fifty years.

Daw Aye's home was warm and comfortable, but it was already about ten and I hadn't eaten yet. I couldn't say anything because it is against regulations to ask for food. So I made a plan. "If nothing happens soon, I'll unpack my begging bowl and walk around the market." What a practice it is to want something and work at being calm about it without suppressing it. I remembered many situations in which I had either directly acted out and made those around me feel uncomfortable or else suppressed what I wanted. Either way the body takes a beating, so I was very careful.

I took my bag and went outside, and soon a small group of people came up with food. It took them a few minutes to lay everything out, which gave me time to unpack my begging bowl. There were at least fifteen different kinds of food laid out on this round table about a foot high. It was a feast. The most interesting part was that they all sat around in front of me to watch me eat. I heard comments being made with regard to which hand I used to reach for the bowl, the motion in taking the food out of the serving bowls, the chewing of my food, where my eyeballs moved to as I was eating. I had learned during the Rains Retreat that it is important to eat slowly.

After I completed my meal, they began to talk. Daw Aye introduced me to her nieces and cousins, including a brother and a sister whose father had died of cancer. Speaking through one of her relatives, Daw Aye advised me that the brother would be my tour guide for the Mandalay area. The sister said that she would like to invite me over to her house for dinner, and I accepted her offer. So they all left with excitement because most of them would see me again.

Daw Aye and I were alone now. She could not speak English and I could not speak Burmese, but we understood each other. She was getting ready to take me over to the monastery where I would be staying, so she stood up and began to change her top. My mind flipped out, saying, "No, please don't do this, I will never recover." Then I noticed that she already had a different top on. How did that happen? All I remembered was her undoing the top button, then doing it up again, but it was a different color top. How could that be? Was that no-self in a zone, a serious dissociation, or what? There was no other room. She was about six feet in front of me.

As she buttoned the last button, her eyes raised up so I could see the light in her eyes and a smile that could melt butter. The energy in the room shimmered around me. My body had a sudden coolness that was comfortable. Then Sister Daw Aye picked up her bag, which was a cue that we were leaving.

I figured that she was taking me to where I would be sleeping. She got a driver and we got into the traffic. Like any city, Mandalay has its own unique feeling of traffic flow. Mandalay is known as the City of Gems and Magic. One of the Sunlun students I had met at an intensive retreat lived here, and I had heard from several people that he could make things move around the room. Yes! That breath energy is potent stuff. But I didn't have a desire to visit with him, nor did I have the time to see his show.

Daw Aye took me to a monastery, which I noticed was a place for children, mostly ages fourteen to nineteen. I learned that there were at least a dozen monasteries for children and youth in this four-block area. Having monasteries for youth is a way to ensure that children get a good spiritual education. The funding for this one came from my supporter and the former Chief of Police of Mandalay. He was there to welcome my arrival.

"Good morning," he said. "Forgive me for not getting on my knees. They are not so healthy." He was an elderly man with a walking stick and wearing a knitted hat and a button-up sweater. He appeared to be in his mid-seventies; his voice sounded strong. The chief introduced me to his two daughters who stood a respectful distance away. They both were wearing a colorful wrap and light-colored top; both greeted me with hands in prayer position. It was mid-morning; even though the sun was shining bright in the clear blue sky, there was a chill in the air that was not unusual for December.

The chief asked how long I would be staying in Mandalay. I told him that I had come to attend the December Sunlun meditation intensive; I shared with him my love for the practice and that it had been the only meditation that had helped me to make sense of my relationship with life. He agreed and shared with me that since childhood the meditation practice had been his support system. He was the first person who was not concerned about my country of origin. We just talked about life.

After a while he got up from the bench he had been sitting on, reached for his walking stick, and bade me farewell. His daughters escorted him to his jeep and I watched them drive away.

I explored this special monastery. How wonderful it was to observe these young people go through the same daily process as the adults—getting up at 3 a.m. and practicing until 5:30 or 6 a.m., then going on alms round. Eating would take place at eight, and after that they would clean the monastery inside and out. From eleven until about two, they would study with the abbot. One day I approached them and asked the abbot what he was teaching them.

"The Abhidhamma," he replied.

"Wow, Buddhist Psychology?" I thought.

He continued, "It takes a year to get through these volumes, and this is our second time going through them. I would invite you to join us but you do not speak Burmese." As he said this, the young people laughed. I bowed and thanked him.

The country of Myanmar is very poor, making it difficult for many families to raise a child with a healthy mind and heart. Therefore, many families send at least one child to the monastery to become a monk. These monasteries reinvent the family system by being a family for the youth. It was wonderful to watch these kids practice at such an early age. Getting up early in the morning and going out to get their food was a powerful endurance test for them, but I could see that their intention to become a monk was so strong that almost nothing got in their way.

Mandalay is a town of carpenters and masons, and my supporter took me to a carpenter to have my Buddha Rupa image carved. I had been advised to do this by my head monk. A Buddha Rupa is a statue or model of the Buddha; the word means "Form of the Awakened One." After the image is carved, it is coated with black lacquer, which is from the sap of a tree. Then it is placed underground for seven days so that the process of drying slows down. As Mother Earth works on this form, other interesting things begin to happen; it begins to look like a newborn. This process is repeated three times, and afterwards it goes through a ceremony.

After the carpenter completes a Buddha Rupa, a *deva* is requested to come and live in it, to bring life to it. As I've mentioned before, *devas* are spirits who can go into different worlds and dimensions. Their idea of time is very different from ours on this plane of existence. For example, the expanding and collapsing of the universe takes thousands of lifetimes from our perspective, but from theirs, it would be like how we perceive one year. Just as we come into a body to bring energetic life to it, so a *deva* comes to a Buddha Rupa.

Stepping into the master carpenter's room where his images were on display was like stepping into an energy field. It was like being hit by lasers from all directions. The sensations of those laser beams didn't just hit the surface of my body, but went in one point and began filling me up. It was quite an amazing experience.

The carpenter asked me what kind of Buddha Rupa I wanted. Having lived in Myanmar for almost six months, I was feeling knowledgeable about the various kinds. For example, there is the Jetted style, which means a heap of gems. This style has straight hair and a swirled wrap on top of the head. Another style is known as Pagan. The hair is matted, knotted, or in mini-dreads with different facial characteristics such as dark skin. One time, I had come across a carved and stone Buddha Rupa in the fields that showed Buddha giving teachings to five students/practicing ascetics who had stayed with him long-term. The artist had done an excellent job of depicting the moment. Their shoulder length hair was matted; their beards were also matted and reached down to their bellies. The artist had carefully depicted them the way they would have naturally looked living deep in the forest, practicing for months on end without any concern for their appearance.

My head monk had suggested the Pagan image with the knotted hair and darkened skin.

"Knotted hair," I said with a slight smile.

He laughed and said, "Do not let your awareness go there," referring to black Americans.

My response was, "I liked that Siddhartha's skin was of a dark complexion, and from practicing in the forest, his hair ended up matted with knots."

The carpenter told me that it would not be completed before my set date to depart the country, so I entrusted one of my many newly established friends to get it to me. Eventually, that special Buddha image arrived in Santa Fe, where it sits in my home and in my heart.

Family and Supporters

Age 3
Dad's funeral 1953, he was 27

House of my birth – me looking at
brother and grandfather

Agent Orange Victim at 2006
Conference, Hanoi, Vietnam

At 1,000 feet
Being dramatic with the bullets

Sabine in Thailand

My supporter Daw Aye

Beginning and Ending

Founder Ralph Steele, Director Sharon Quintanilla, and guest Stephen Levine, Elisabeth Kubler-Ross, Ondrea Levine at the 1986 Inauguration of the Elisabeth Kubler-Ross Hospice Program, New Mexico

Eight-year gathering since Luang Por Chah's passing (for monks known as transitioning) 2000

Taking Robes
U'Janaka Sayadaw 1999

Disrobing Ceremony

Authorization to Teach

Ajahn Jumnien 2000

Ajahn Jayasaro 2000

Thamanya Sayadaw 1999

Blessing received: "Stay healthy Punnyananda"
Venerable Shwe U'Min Taw Ya, 100 years of age
(Elder to Mahasi Sayadaw and Mingun Sayadaw) 1999

Teachers

Kalu Rinpoche

Maha Boowa 1913-2011

Sister Mary 1904-1999

Chanmyay U'Janaka Sayadaw

Maha Thamanya 1910-2003

Sayadaw U'Vinaya Sayadaw
(Sunlun Sayadaw Student) 1914-2012

Variations of Practice

Venerable Bhante Suhita Dharma,
a.k.a. Venerable Thich An Duc
First African-American monk from
the Asian Buddhist Lineage
Transitioned in 2013

The Venerable Monk whom I
reference as a sadhu because of
carrying a colorful handbag
from India 1999

Lobsang P. Lhalungpa 1926-2008
Studied with for 10 years

Ajahn who disrobed, had a
family, and later returned
to become a monk again

Sunlun Meditation, two hours

At Sunlun Annual Intensive

14. PRACTICE, PRACTICE, AND MORE PRACTICE (1970s)

Previous to becoming a monk, I moved to the land of enchantment in 1982 to be with Stephen Levine and Ram Dass, who had opened a Dying Center in Santa Fe. New Mexico is cold in winter, hot in summer, and dry most of the year. After two years in the Northwest, the warm days felt good to my bones. The lower part of the state was once the floor of the ocean, and you can see this in the surrounding geology. The upper part is high desert, bordering on forested mountains. As Spokane, Washington, is based in the Northern Rocky Mountains, Santa Fe is based at the end of the Southern mountains known as the Sangre de Cristo. This is where I went, seven thousand feet above sea level, to Santa Fe—the city of the holy faith of Saint Francis of Assisi.

The Center was a welcoming place to be. We would accept people who thought they would die within six months, but it was so nice there that people would take longer to die. In fact, no one actually died during my time there, but I did learn a lot about the dying process. Dale Borglum, the director, eventually moved the center to the San Francisco Bay Area to begin a death and dying training without walls. This was timely because it was just before the HIV epidemic exploded on the West coast.

I stayed, got my license in Marriage and Family Therapy from the New Mexico Counseling and Therapy Board, and opened a practice in town as a therapist and meditation teacher. My business was named Life Transition Therapy, a trauma-healing center. I also formed a non-profit called Life Transition Meditation Center. I established myself in a charming adobe building in the historical part of town on Delgado Street. By the beginning of 1986 Sabine would join me as partner, business partner, and wife. The center would become an organization without walls, reaching out to people everywhere. I had a special interest in exploring the fear, ignorance, and conditioning that fuel racism—in individuals, families, communities, and in the world at large.

I wanted to illuminate and heal the root beliefs that lead to racist behavior and social injustice, using various meditation techniques to cultivate awareness and compassion. There seemed to be three phases in my work: first, the way in, through meditation; second, the way through, by accepting and loving ourselves; and third, the way out, through accepting and loving others.

Hospices were just getting started around the country at the time, thanks mainly to the pioneering work of Dr. Elisabeth Kubler-Ross and Stephen Levine, and supported by Sogyal Rinpoche and Ram Dass. I had many moments of assisting people through the process of dying at Life Transition Therapy. I came to see it as a special meditation practice for learning about my body-mind, and I realized why it is considered one of the most advanced and insightful experiences in many meditation lineages. It brings up many feelings, both pleasant and unpleasant.

One of the people I assisted was Leroy Brown, who came to my office one very hot summer day. I was sitting at my desk, finishing up some paper work, and appreciating the thick adobe walls because they kept the building nice and cool. Suddenly, the front door opened and in stepped Leroy. I first noticed his white-satin cowboy boots with silver studs, then the blue jeans above the boots, then a shirt with pearl buttons, a white rawhide vest, and at the top a white cowboy hat! The room already was juicing up. Then I saw the face— it was black. Black people were more rare than a monarch butterfly in this town, so a lot of mental states and sensations were being activated in my mind and body. To myself, I said, "Okay, Ralph, one breath at a time."

He walked up to the desk, and I stood up to acknowledge his presence. I was just a little in awe of him. He said with a deep voice: "My name is Leroy Brown." And I said to myself, "Yeah, and *you are the bad-est man in town,*" which was the lyric to a song by Jim Croce called *Bad, Bad, Leroy Brown.*

Well, I quickly snapped out of that state and was about to say my name, when he continued, "I have heard about you. You help people die with grace and dignity."

I thanked him for the complement and asked, "What can I do for you, sir?"

He said, "I have stomach cancer and will be dying soon. The tumor is large and the cancer has spread to various parts of the body."

I asked him where he lived, and he replied Phoenix. I said he would have to move here if he wanted to spend his final days in Santa Fe, but there was no need for that because there were many good hospices in the Phoenix area. I gave him a list, and he said okay and thank you. Then he left.

Two weeks passed, then Leroy called and said, "I am here. Are you ready to work?"

"What do you mean you are here?"

"I have a flat on Canyon Road," he said. It was about three blocks from my office.

I quickly put a team together that included a nurse, three aides, and a medical doctor to sign the death certificate. I also had an incredible team of compassionate supporters, including Richard and Carolyn Canon, who had been together since high school and now in their golden years were devoting themselves to hospice work. We brought in a hospital bed, organized ourselves, and welcomed Leroy.

Leroy would not stop smoking his cigarettes and the medical doctor didn't like that, nor did the nurse. They wanted me to step in and take care of the situation. Now, in Buddhist psychology The Eightfold Path talks about right action, which involves having some awareness about causes and effects before establishing any action. My job was to see that Leroy had as little stress as possible and to eliminate any exterior stress. Since the doctor and nurse were uncomfortable with the status quo, I relieved them both of their duties, and immediately the level of stress went down. We found another doctor and nurse.

Leroy shared his story with me. In his younger years, sometime between twenty-five and forty-five, he had played the streets of Malibu and Long Beach. He would have confrontations with men and knock them out with one or sometimes two punches. He said a recording artist had named a song after him.

Right after an instructional breathing exercise, during one of our bedside conversations, Leroy told me about his childhood and teen years in Philadelphia during the '40s and '50s. He used to skip classes with his sister Zelma. One day the truant officer came to the school and took them both away to a boarding school. At the school, they had to drink a special medicine every day; they were told it would make them strong, and after a few weeks of this drink, Zelma could pick up a bundle of steel rebar weighing three hundred pounds! The other students, all black, thought Zelma was a man, because of her strength. The medication really had enhanced her physical strength. They stayed in that school until their late teens, then left and went back to their family. But the family treated them like strangers, so they left and went their separate ways, and they never saw each other again.

Richard and Carolyn Canon and the rest of us did some research and, yes, we found Zelma in Alabama. We contacted her and she was blown away that we had found her and knew her brother Leroy. She was excited about coming to Santa Fe as a surprise. Traveling was a little issue since Zelma would not get on anybody's airplane. So we put her on a train to Lamy, New Mexico, which is twenty miles south of Santa Fe.

We were there to cherish that blessed moment of brother and sister coming together after forty years. Zelma walked down the hall to her brother's room as if she owned the place; and when she saw Leroy, she yelled out with a sweet tone of voice, bent over his bed, and they embraced each other. Juice was flowing all over the house; we all were in tears. What a moment to experience!

Zelma stayed on and shared stories from their youth. That boarding school turned out to be a place where the government had conducted chemical research projects on black kids in the '40s and '50s.

The days went by, and I could feel that the time was getting close. Conversations were not happening, and I would just sit and hold his hand in an unobtrusive way. I could feel the death pulse now—deep, with a long silence in between. Like Houston Space Center, all systems were ready. One afternoon, as I was about to step out the door to leave for the day, Leroy turned his head toward me as I stood in the doorway.

"Ralph, will you be here tomorrow morning?"

I was not planning on coming until the afternoon, but I said, "Sure, Leroy, I'll be here."

Leroy's room was on the second floor of a two-story villa on Canyon Road, which is Santa Fe's street of art galleries, and his room had an exit door to some metal steps that went down to the courtyard. The next morning, something told me not to use the front door; I could hear people in the kitchen carrying on so I walked around to the courtyard and up the steps to his room. The moment I opened the door, I saw that he was gasping for breath. I pushed the bed away from the wall so that I could be at his head in a comfortable way. I settled down and put my hand under his head.

Then I said, "Leroy, you been waiting for this, let's go."

It is known that if a person exits their body from the waist up, their journey will be much more comfortable; and if they leave from the top of the head, it is guaranteed that they will have an excellent journey. It is like getting a first class ticket. Leroy took two more deep breaths; then, boom, he let go. His body gave out a serious bright hot glow; I could see a younger face for a moment. Without any sign of stress, the energy came out his head, up my arms and upper body to the top of my head, and—gone! Zelma was coming down the hall and knew Leroy was leaving.

"Leroy," she yelled out, "I love you so much! I always will."

Everyone wanted to be at this funeral, of course. I took the primary and support team, all of us in deep sadness, to a flower shop. As we put a flower arrangement together, I could see the sadness dropping and joy arising. We had been saying prayers since his exit.

Leroy wanted to be buried on Native American soil, so after we had cremated his body, we car-pooled up to a reservation. We found a fruit tree and were about to start the ceremony when a car drove up and stopped.

"What are you doing here?"

I told the men, "This is Leroy Brown's ashes, and he requested to be on Native American land."

They said, "Right on. All my relations."

It was a wonderful still, sunny day, but as I delivered the eulogy, a gust of wind came up and shook the tree that we were under, just that tree. Of course—that was the man named Leroy Brown, *the baddest man in the whole damn town*. Thank you, Leroy.

Being with the dying is an opportunity. You come close to the mystery of life; you get to dance with the Divine, God, Ram, Shiva, or Supreme Consciousness. It was wonderful and rewarding work for me. When the Northern New Mexico College, now an undergraduate college, asked me to do a "needs assessment" for a hospice training program, my colleague and dear friend Caroline Wareham stepped forward to help me. She is very skilled in the art of writing, and the assessment resulted in the college putting together, in 1986, the first degree program in the country in this particular field. Stephen Levine and Dr. Elisabeth Kubler Ross were a part of the inauguration; it was a special moment to have them there.

I was involved in all kinds of meditation practices in Santa Fe. With regard to meditation lineages, there were so many available it was like Santa Cruz, California. Some of the best came from the Zen tradition. Three extraordinary practitioners were Roshi Richard Baker, Philip Whalen, and Issan Dorsey; they all had one thing in common—their dedication to practice, practice, practice—which, as I've said before, is the most important skill in meditation.

During that time, Michael Wenger, an old friend and a mature Zen practitioner, came to bless my office with Suzuki Roshi's son Hoitsu Suzuki and his wife. He was visiting from Japan to celebrate what would have been his father's hundredth year; Suzuki Roshi had formed the first Zen Center in North America in San Francisco. This elder and his wife were a bundle of joy and laughter. Their wisdom had great depth. He advised me not to forget my roots, meaning my grandparents and childhood years.

"You are much older and wiser now," he said. "Bring the good and especially the bad together and assimilate your life experiences."

Roshi Baker eventually started another monastery in Crestone, Colorado, to extend Suzuki Roshi's lineage in North America. I loved to go and practice with him up there. The retreats were mostly unannounced, and veteran practitioners from around the world came to practice for three months. This was the traditional Zen practice period where you do sitting meditation about six to nine hours per day and have various group and individual activities, (cleaning the *Zendo*, prepping food, serving food, etc.), between the sitting periods. Towards the end of the three months, the sitting periods increased to about eighteen hours per day, including eating while sitting, so there was little time for group walking, and no time for showering, just some very basic hygiene.

I never did an entire three-month practice period; but I would show up a few days before the ten-day *sesshins* (which means gathering one's mind), and during one of those sitting meditation periods, I received a wonderful gift. Philip Whalen, one of the senior monks, came up and hit this person next to me with a four-foot stick! My inner voice said, "What the . . ?" And then I put my hands together in prayer position to indicate my thought, "No, that's not going to hap---" Before I could complete the thought, the stick was on-and-off *my* shoulders! Whoa, my nervous system immediately felt more awake and in a pool of bliss. I later found out that if you do not want to be hit, you don't move.

I experienced the same blissful feeling when doing Sufi practices with Pir Vilayat Khan and his wife Taj, though the Sufis had greater lightness about them. They danced; they were joyful. Pir Vilayat would give talks that made you feel happy. That was very good for me. Having experienced so much death during the Dr. Martin Luther King riots and in the Vietnam War, I needed to cultivate some happiness.

I met Sabine in the winter of 1986; it was at the Santa Fe psychiatric hospital. Around midnight, I was charting my case notes at the nurses' station. She walked up to the desk and asked me something. What captured my eyes was the long red hair that came down to her waist. Her hair had a glow, and when she walked it shimmered as it swung from side to side. It looked as if the sun was shining on it, even inside the building. Her voice was crisp and straightforward, with a sweet sound. Her eyes were like emeralds. Who *was* this person?

I said, "What man would let you work so late at night?" which brought a smile to her face. Then we went on about our business.

Some days later we found ourselves sitting next to each other at one of Pir Vilayat's public talks. It was during the month of January when it gets rocky mountain cold in New Mexico, which to me is seriously cold—these kinds of temperatures should be against the law. After the talk, Sabine and I ended up in a restaurant drinking hot apple cider with a cinnamon stick, telling stories and challenging each other. Within a week, we moved in together. The little house on Delgado became home and work space. We had found each other.

There are many things I could say about Sabine, who had left Germany for the U.S. in 1980. Originally, she came to study hands-on healing arts in Santa Fe and Boulder, Colorado. She had quickly fallen in love with the light and colors of Northern New Mexico and recognized Santa Fe as her spiritual home. She was born in 1953 in Berlin to refugee parents and had felt burdened by Germany's Nazi past, the silence and denial of the war generation.

In 1991 Sabine received a stage-two breast cancer diagnosis after a routine mammogram. We found that no one had anything hopeful to say. Women were dying like leaves falling off the trees. The death toll was very high. Many women received a single or double mastectomy and later found out that it was not needed.

We were in shock, but quickly rolled up our sleeves and began researching medical approaches and alternative therapies, though data about complimentary medicine was only slowly building at that time. If I had not had my meditation practice, I am sure I would have relapsed back into drugs to keep from losing control. There were certain physicians we decided not to work with. It was difficult to say no to any one of the doctors, and it felt as if we were walking around in a fog. Finally we assembled a team of kind and knowledgeable caregivers.

In the end, we decided to take both routes. We found a superior doctor of oriental medicine in California who had a large caseload of women with breast cancer; then we located Daniel Bruce, a doctor of oriental medicine of the same quality in Santa Fe, who was supervised by the California D.O.M. About the same time, we found a medical doctor of oncology Timothy Lopez who was open-minded and on top of his game. This was the person we brought the kitchen sink to for decisions about what to do, and when.

At that time Sabine received a lumpectomy, chemotherapy, and radiation treatments. Both of us kept our composure. She had the hair of a model; when the moment came for me to shave it off, we both wept. The good thing is that Sabine survived, and her hair grew back as good as it was before.

Sabine is also an artist, and later she collaborated with other breast cancer survivor artists who worked to draw attention to breast cancer and lobbied for research. They created a breast cancer art show that opened at the State Capitol in Santa Fe. She also connected with "Art.Rage.US," sponsored in part by the Susan G. Komen Breast Cancer Foundation. This organization set up exhibitions all over the world, of artwork created by women touched by breast cancer. Two of Sabine's pieces went as far as Hong Kong.

During the time of her cancer treatment, in the summer of 1991, Sabine was introduced to the Tibetan teacher Lobsang Lhalungpa, a fellow cancer survivor; his friendship and guidance as a meditation teacher was medicine to her. Lobsang became a beloved teacher and friend to both of us.

15. PEOPLE OF COLOR
(1990-2000)

I had not done a Vipassana retreat for some years, and in the late eighties I was invited to take part in a ten-day loving- kindness retreat in Yucca Valley, California, the first or second of its kind in America. The primary teachers were Sharon Salzburg, Michelle McDonald, Steve Smith, and Joseph Goldstein.

About two hundred people showed up, and for the first time I wasn't the only person of color. There was one other— a Vietnamese monk. "Wow," I said to myself, "This is incredible." The Vietnamese monk and I were in the same group with Joseph.

Joseph told us, "You two are the old students."

We turned our heads toward each other with a puzzled look, as if to say, "What is he talking about?"

That's when I heard myself say, "Joseph, something has to change."

Joseph looked at me in a quizzical way and said, "What do you mean, Ralph?"

"Just look around," I said. "This is not right. We are the only people of color, just two of us. Something has to change."

He paused for a moment, then said, "Yeah, you're right. But you're here now, so let's do the practice."

And I said, "Okay. I can do that."

I learned something very important from this exchange. I realized that *I could* take this practice and not look at the issue of cultural diversity; but the truth was I needed to look at it, and I wanted to. This was supposed to be a conscious community, yet the teachers were missing something important—the real suffering that exists in American culture and how that suffering affects us all. Our country began with separation and violence between people of European descent and people of color, and between men and women, and we were still working at healing that separation.

191

Despite my long personal history within Buddhism, I suddenly felt like a person from another planet, as if I didn't even belong in the room. Luckily, there was the Vietnamese monk, and he said that, like me, he felt very alone. After all, this was the oldest group of Vipassana practitioners in the country, and as we looked around, we saw who we had and who we didn't have, meaning people of color.

It was a good retreat for me. We spent all day saying kind phrases to ourselves, as part of the loving-kindness practice, and this resulted in extraordinary levels of concentration. I was beginning to understand that kindness is the foundation to all aspects of meditation practices. We need to be looking at our inner environment with the same kind of awareness which we have when holding an infant. From that understanding we build our various meditation skills.

In the fall I was teaching at the Lama Foundation near Taos, New Mexico, with Jack Kornfield, and I brought this concern about people of color to him. I said it as clearly as I could, "Jack, something's got to change. None of the leading teachers are doing anything about the imbalance. If I continue, I'll have to be some kind of closet practitioner. Sitting here feeling isolated at a big retreat is just too weird."

We talked about it. Women had been feeling this way for years. During the late seventies and early eighties, Ruth Denison had been offering Vipassana retreats specifically for women with great success. It gave women a place of safety with regard to gender, especially those with traumatic experiences. I would hear conversations among women saying, "If you want to be somebody, then you need to sit with Ruth." The teachers would frequently mention Ruth's women's retreats as rites of passage. They were different; she even had a dog that practiced with everyone else.

Then, in the eighties, there were gay men's retreats. Like the women's retreats, they were also full with waiting lists. I had the privilege of being on a teaching team with Robert Hall and Jack in one of those retreats, and again you could feel and see how comfortable and relaxed everyone was. It was a retreat of pure brotherly love and joy. The gay, lesbian, and women's retreats continued. There was a wonderful feeling about all of them. The Vipassana teachers supported those retreats in many ways, but in particular by addressing the issues in their Dharma talks. I felt that because they were teacher-supported, it helped to decrease negative attitudes like, "Why do we need to have a separate retreat? Doesn't this further segregation?" I believe that the healing of a community is most effective when it happens within that community, and before going into any other community.

English colonists living in what is now the eastern United States first used the phrase "People of Color"; the colonists were collecting people from around the world to help them build America. Because of the variety of skin colors, this name had seemed appropriate at the time, but then it slipped out of the language until the '80s.

Wasn't it time for people of color to have their own retreats? I had a conversation with Jack Kornfield, Julie Wester, and Mary Grace Orr and we agreed: "We need to do something about our sangha. It's much too European-American." We wanted to bring people of color into the American Buddhist community. We wanted to "mix" the practice, working like the Equal Opportunity Commission that helped people of color get into college during the '70s. So, Marlena Jones, Linda Velarde, Jack Kornfield, Julie Wester, Mary Grace Orr, and I created the Inter-Racial Buddhist Council.

We talked about getting People of Color Retreats started at Spirit Rock Meditation Center in Woodacre, California and at the Insight Meditation Society in Barre, Massachusetts. A meeting was arranged for the administration and teachers at the California center; I was invited to attend. At that meeting, the majority of the administrators were present, but fewer than four of the twenty-plus teachers came. Here we were having a major discussion led by a facilitator from the prestigious Institute, it was an important event costing a few thousand dollars, and the teachers who are the spinal system of this meditation center made their statement by not showing up. *Yahman,* that was a new awakening. I thought, "The heat is on; let's dance."

193

A few meditation practitioners from the community went around and around about the pros and cons of this new idea, and I was mostly quiet. Then one person stood up and said, "I am a practitioner in this community, and I've been coming here for a long time. If people of color start coming here, I don't think that I will be able to continue practicing here." This practitioner was so real and I felt that. For the first time in the meeting, I stood up and acknowledged my respect to him. It took a lot of courage for him to say that.

We could see it was going to be a tough struggle. Just looking around at all the established teachers, even those who might be interested in involving people of color, I thought, "Why bother?" I didn't see much reason for them to take the extra step to bring people of color to their retreats. Vipassana retreats were already full; there was no reason to go out and hustle new members, especially unfamiliar ones. Most teachers simply want to teach. However, Jack vowed that from then on in his Dharma talks he would bring up the subject of racism in this country. For many years he would be the only teacher to respond, as others only gradually got involved. No one expected anyone to come to People of Color Retreats (P.O.C.R.) because, as the myth goes, *these people do not meditate.*

The first day-long meditation retreat for people of color was a non-residential event held in 1992 at Spirit Rock Meditation Center, California. About fifty people were present—Hispanics, Afro-Americans, Japanese, and Koreans. Jack Kornfield, Michele Benzamin-Miki, and I were the teachers.

As we were about to begin, something quite amazing happened. The three of us were seated so we could see outside through the open main doors and, as if in a dream, we saw a Theravadin monk walking toward us. He was wearing the robes worn by the monks and nuns that sat in the presence of the Buddha twenty-five hundred years ago.

"Jack, do you see what I see?"

"Yes."

The Monk had dark skin, and he glided into the building as if he belonged. We shifted our bones around to make space for him. The room was still; I was stunned. He offered the invocation, and we chanted along. Afterward, he greeted us and then walked out into the abyss from which he had come.

The first People of Color Retreat was being authorized by a monastic. Wow! But who was he and where did he come from? I later found out that his name was Venerable Bhante Suhita Dharma, a.k.a. Venerable Thich An Duc.

A brief story about the first African-American Buddhist Monk, from the Asian Buddhist lineage. During his childhood years he witnessed several deaths by hanging and other violence by the KKK. He became a Trappist monk at the age of fourteen, just before the ordination age was changed. After Vatican II, he was sent to study Buddhism in Thailand, Vietnam, India, Bhutan, Taiwan, and Hong Kong. Bhante Suhita took refuge in the Triple Gem and was fully ordained by the Most Venerable Thich Thien An, with the Dharma names of Suhita Dharma and Thich An Duc. Bhante was ordained in the Theravada, Mahayana, and Vajrayana lineages of Buddhism and rose to the rank of Maha Thera in Sri Lanka. He spent fifty-eight years of monkhood serving others and inspiring others to help homeless persons, former prisoners, people with AIDS, and many more. In the last few years of his life, he founded the Semillas de Compasion (Seeds of Compassion) Sangha in Juarez and the Hermita de Guadalupe. Bhante died in 2013. I, along with so many others, offer a Deep Bow, *Anjali.*

Everyone was so glad to be there, sitting in a place that had seemed to us for so long to be "Whites Only." For the first time, we people of color were able to feel that perhaps it was *our* home, too. Jack and I were pretty much in tears the whole day. We noticed, of course, how being around people of color was different; the whole retreat had a different flavor.

The Inter-Racial Buddhist Council lasted until the mid-'90s, and its presence stimulated a few non-residential retreats. Some of the teachers were Jack Kornfield, Julie Wester, Michele Benzamin-Miki, and me. There were no People of Color Retreats for several years. During the late-90s the Diversity Council was formed. It engaged in different projects and activities at Spirit Rock to include people of color again.

Our way of doing things in the meditation community was still segregated; but that was okay if, and only if, diversity eventually followed. People of color were being invited to regular retreats, and scholarships were even provided, but the meditation community still had this segregated point of view. It was very white, also very middle-class, with this idea that people of color were lower class. There seemed to be no awareness that there are different classes in all cultures.

There was a lot of resistance from the teachers and the staff to the idea of a People of Color Retreat. "Why do you want to do this?" they asked. "Why can't you just come in with everybody else?" But we were patient, and explained how Ruth Denison had instigated many retreats just for women, and how the gay and lesbian community had been such a strong force in initiating its own retreats as far back as the '70s. We had to explain that the first step in working with a traumatized individual or community is safety.

Vallecitos Mountain Refuge in New Mexico, a small organization for activists, hosted the first P.O.C. residential retreat in 1994 with Jack Kornfield as the pioneering teacher. Those retreats continued yearly throughout the '90s. Some of the teachers were Joseph Goldstein, George Mumford, Linda Velarde, and myself.

Gradually they began to understand that people of color needed to have their own retreats. It took ten years and a lot of patient teaching and explaining, but finally it happened. Perhaps the administration respected Jack who was the most senior teacher on the faculty. The administration gave me permission to rent their facility.

Pond Foundation, who initially supported me in starting People of Color Retreats, wrote a check; this led the way to support P.O.C.R. A year before leaving to Asia, in 1998, I funded the first residential Native American Vipassana Meditation Retreat at Sunrise Springs in Santa Fe, New Mexico. The teachers included Sharon Salzberg and Joseph Goldstein, with seventy participants. The retreat managers, Herb Lewis, Karen Waconda-Lewis, and Bonnie Duran followed it up with two more retreats due to its popularity. This included Linda Velarde and Bonnie Duran, along with Joseph Goldstein as teachers.

In 1999 the first residential P.O.C.R. opened to all economic groups took place. I also encouraged Pond Foundation to create a scholarship fund at Spirit Rock Meditation Center (S.R.M.C.) and Insight Meditation Society (I.M.S.) for people of color who would like to become teachers. The teachers at the retreat included Marlene Jones, Margarita Loinaz, George Mumford, and Jack Kornfield. During the time of this retreat, I was a monastic in Asia receiving and experiencing the nectar of Buddhism.

After returning from Asia, I had the privilege to attend an African-American meditation retreat at S.R.M.R. around the year 2000. There were about a dozen African-American teachers from various traditions. Jan Willis, Gaylon Ferguson, Angel Kyodo Williams, and Joseph Jarman all gave sweet talks. The retreat was very rich and effective.

Then one of the teachers named Rachel Bagby brought some empty plastic five-gallon buckets from the kitchen with wooden spoons. We used them as drums. For some reason, at this particular retreat, 90 percent of the people were styling their dreads. I was among the 10 percent with short hair. Those drums started making a harmonious sound; as I looked out across the sangha, it appeared that everyone had checked out of their bodies while their ancestors had checked in. Hair was flying, bodies and feet were moving every which way. That went on for about fifteen minutes, and at the end the ancestors gave everyone their bodies back. "What was that?" people said as we wiped that sweat off our foreheads. The room was luminous. You could feel and taste the magic in the air. It was like being in church on Pawleys Island during my childhood and in the Burmese and Thai monasteries with their communities. Yes, the Dharma has many forms of prayer.

After her talk and as she was leaving, "Sister" Alice Walker said, "Well, you just can't take that music out of us; we do need that." In that depth of her wisdom, I knew that she was saying that if the teaching and practice of the Dharma are going to take root with all people of color in

America (not just African-Americans), it has to change its form of presentation and encompass all cultural forms of presentation. After all, this is a culturally diversified country, and eventually our planet will be that way. *Yahman.*

After that Joseph Goldstein of Insight Meditation Society in Barre, Massachusetts, agreed to host a People of Color Retreat; they received a letter of threat from a member from the community, stating that it is illegal to hold this retreat. I.M.S. pushed on to make this retreat happen, even though their calendar was full. So, the initial retreat on the East coast happened instead at the Garrison Institute in Garrison, New York, with Joseph, Gina Sharpe, and myself as the teachers. We had one hundred people, "including white people" and a waiting list almost the same size. As at Spirit Rock, the experience was extraordinary. It was so very special to come together like this. It took a while for the I.M.S. to come around, but eventually they, too, started annual P.O.C.R. and offered scholarships to people of color, to attend the annual three-month retreat.

In 2008, eleven years after the first People of Color Meditation Retreat, Spirit Rock Meditation Center in California invited me to their twentieth anniversary. Marlene Jones, a special person on their staff, and I were acknowledged for bringing cultural diversity to the community, and we were asked to say a few words. I shared a moment of reflection that it may be possible for American people to practice the Dharma as a multicultural community. We were sitting on the lawn outside the community meditation hall, in the shade of a large tree. Sunlight was shimmering through the branches, and as I came to the end of my address, I felt the sensation of the sun rising in my heart, and at the same moment a large bird took off from the tree where we were sitting. It was a moment of generosity shining on our community—as a result of the practice.

Marlene Jones died during the month of January 2013. She was the embodiment of sunshine. Her pioneering work in having Spirit Rock Meditation Center acknowledge cultural diversity will leave an imprint forever.

Diversity was coming like molasses, but at least it was coming. For example, presently at Spirit Rock and Insight Meditation centers, a People of Color Retreat has been held annually for the past decade. Heartfelt thanks to all the teachers mentioned, including Gina Sharpe, Larry Yang, and Mushim Patricia Ikeda. Finally a deep bow to Venerable Bhante Gunaratana and Thich Nhat Hanh for supporting the People of Color Retreats.

16. WALKING IN THE NIGHT
(1999)

My time in Asia was passing fast, and I needed to get back to Thailand for the next part of my journey—a retreat in the forest monastery of Wat Pah Nanachat. However, I was already having strong feelings about being a monastic for the duration of my life. Like during my drug-addiction years, I told myself, "Oh man, this stuff is good." I now understood why so many Westerners who took robes never returned.

Upon boarding the plane, I was invited to go with the first-class ticket holders. This reminded me of when I was a soldier during the Vietnam War. In the early days, soldiers boarded international flights at the same time as first-class passengers, but as the war proceeded and the soldiers were more looked down upon we boarded like everyone else. In fact, people said that if you were doing air travel it would be wise to travel in civilian clothing, which was against military regulations, but it was safer. I remember hearing comments like, "What's that soldier wearing that uniform for? Doesn't he know that the war is a joke?" I was nineteen, serving my country, and not yet able to question the justifications made for that war.

As I took my seat on the plane, I reflected on how special it is to be a monk especially in a Buddhist country. You are looked upon as someone who is a healer of the mind, and the community comes to see you before consulting with their physicians about illnesses on the mental or physical plane. They know that you would sacrifice your life for the sake of the Dharma in a heartbeat. Monastics know that Yama, the Lord of Death, is like our shadow, and all monastics are supposed to embrace Yama permanently. Since the beginning of time, death has been our biggest teacher. What a change it would be in America if everyone were trained to consciously embrace death.

During the onset of the HIV crisis in America when so many were dying, people came together in such a warm and respectful way. Those who didn't even have the infection

201

exemplified compassion. People were more respectful in public. After the attack in New York City on September 11, 2001, people were respectful of the presence of death, but also fearful.

Among the other people getting on the plane was a missionary carrying a four-foot statue of Mother Mary. I saw him as a fellow spiritual soldier in robes. Being from New Mexico, I thought, "Could this be Mother Mary Guadalupe, known locally as 'Our Lady of Guadalupe'?" The artist had done some impressive work. It is such a good feeling when people take pride in what they do. When that happens, the creation usually becomes bigger than the person. This was definitely the case with this beautiful Mother. They sat her across the aisle from me and were bold enough to put a seat belt around her.

There was a group of people with this missionary. They all sat behind me and seemed to speak English. Trying to be an excellent monk, I did not turn my head around, but I picked up on their conversation about my interest in or opinion of the Mother. They knew they had something special, and I suspect that it wasn't an accident for her to be sitting across from me. In fact, if one understands the relationship of cause and effect, there is no such thing as an accident. Our entire cosmos is in perfect harmony. As our intelligence moves further from non-understanding to understanding, there is a respect for this harmony that arises in us, resulting in a motivation to cultivate integrity with loving kindness for what is comprehensible, while humbly experiencing what is incomprehensible.

The stewardess brought me a tray of assorted drinks. It was afternoon, and I had already had my meal for the day so this was all I could consume. The topic of the missionaries' conversation was Buddhism and Christianity, and being a former Religious Studies major, my ears perked right up. It is interesting what kind of desire makes the mind more attentive, whether it is skillful or unskillful. For me, it was like listening to National Public Radio in America, or hearing a group of people carrying on with ageless gossip.

"What does he think about her?" one of them asked, speaking of Guadalupe and me.

"He's a Buddhist," said another, "and they don't have respect for other religions, or maybe they do. I wonder—does he feel uncomfortable sitting next to her? I would."

Then another, "We should go and talk to him about Jesus."

The plane landed in Bangkok, and we began to get up and move forward. When it was my turn to stand up and move my bones I heard, "What is he going to do?"

I stood up, looked toward the back, and made contact with a bunch of stone faces with eyeballs in them. Then I looked across the aisle at the Mother and reconfirmed to myself that she was indeed a beauty, a beautiful carving, and I smiled so they could see it. My smile melted those stone faces and released the tension. "That was a potent smile," I thought as I began to walk toward the door. "How can I package that?"

I stood in line with everyone else to go through customs, and saw that I was close to the back, with forty to sixty people ahead of me. Because of my height, I could also see that there were only two customs agents working. Okay, standing meditation. After being mindful for a few breaths, I noticed that one of the customs officers got up from his desk and walked to the area where no one was standing in front of him. He just stood there and I saw his face lighting up. I finally got it—this brother was waiting for me to come toward him. I began to move my bones toward him and saw heads turning. I was tempted to turn back but just took a deeper breath and appreciated even more the experience of being in this monastic tradition. When I approached him, he bowed and said, "How long would you like to visit us?"

"For about eight months," I said.

"Welcome to Thailand." He stamped my visa and I moved on with grace.

My destination was Wat Pah Nanachat, an international western monastery that was started by a great teacher named Luang Por Chah. People had been talking to me about this man for years, long before I came to Asia. The primary practice at this monastery is the Vinaya, which is the monastic Code of Conduct, and Jack Kornfield had told me that my shit would hit the fan here because the primary spoken language is English.

I had written a letter from Myanmar to the abbot, *Ajahn* Jayasaro, asking if I could practice there. I also knew that practitioners from this monastery go into the jungle along the border of Myanmar and Thailand to do intensive practice. This was a major interest of mine.

I needed to find a place to stay, and as a monk that's never an issue, and I mean *never*, because if you can't stay inside there is always outside. I looked up the name of a monk that someone had given me, and his driver picked me up and took me to where he teaches at a Buddhist university in the city. The traffic in Bangkok is equal to downtown Manhattan at rush hour. We eventually arrived at the campus; classes were over for the day. I walked into the monk's office and saw him sitting on the floor going through some papers. I bowed three times and shared my story. Then he gave me his driver and his room at a *wat* in town to spend the night, as he was staying at the Buddhist university. He wished me well. Now I had some wheels to take care of some business.

One of the 227 rules of conduct is not touching money. I had about $800 left out of my original $2000. Several times I had been denied a safe deposit box at the banks because that required more money than I had, but after researching the Lonely Planet Guide, I had found a safe deposit box in a hotel off the beaten path in a wonderful residential section.

So here I was standing at that hotel desk trying to get my money put away in a bag. My driver was waiting outside, and I called him in and told him to take as much money as he needed to get me to the airport. I did not dare touch that money. He took what he needed, put the rest into a pouch, and put the pouch back into the safe. Both the driver and the desk clerk saw that I was working hard at honoring the precept, and they were putting their best foot forward to support me.

Then we got back into his car and headed toward the airport. I was relaxed and at ease because the most important work was completed. I already had my ticket, which was purchased when I arrived from Myanmar. Then I noticed that the driver was looking confused. He couldn't speak English, but I realized that he was lost. Oh man. We finally did arrive at the airport, and I smiled at him, which was a way of saying thank you. Then I stepped out of the vehicle and walked briskly into the airport. At the ticket counter they told me that my flight had left an hour ago!

My driver was gone, and for several minutes I totally flipped out inside myself. I couldn't even make a phone call, no phone card. Nor could I ask someone for money to make a call. I turned back to the person at the counter and asked if I could use her phone to make an outside call. She said that the phone system was designed so that outside calls cannot be made. Great! So then I asked her the time of the next flight to Northeast Thailand or Ubon Ratchathani. "Eight in the morning," she said. I took a slow deep breath, then another, and another. Okay.

I saw that there was an area of the airport that was just for monks and I went over there and sat down. I scanned my mental faculties to investigate what to do for the next seventeen hours, and I came up with four things: sitting and walking, no eating or sleeping.

Walking meditation practice had become my favorite practice during my Rains Retreat in Myanmar. Of the four postures—sitting, lying, standing, and walking—it is the most mechanical. Therefore, it is a wonderful break for one's mental faculties. Walking meditation is an excellent ingredient in working with restlessness, agitation, frustration, and anger. There are also many other benefits to walking in the cultivation of tranquility and wisdom (see appendix: Walking Instruction).

Practice and more practice, the opportunity is always available to tend one's fire. I walked through the night in Bangkok Airport. Nothing else was going on in my mind except walking and sitting meditation in the chairs. Though at one point, I remembered the island during my childhood years and how most of the African-Americans didn't have cars. Transportation was by horse and wagon or most of the time by walking. In summer, when that sun was peaking, the sand could be like a hot iron on the bottoms of our feet; we didn't have any shoes except for church and school. We had to be careful not to wear them out so we were not allowed to go out and play until after the sun had peaked. But then, when the time was right, around mid-afternoon, the sand was perfect—not too warm and not too cool.

I remembered a game we used play. We would see this spot about half a mile down the road, and my younger brother Jimmy would say, "Here comes someone." Then we would see who was able to identify him first. We would take turns in winning. That spot might turn into Uncle Sam who had come to sit on the porch and visit with Sister Mary. Looking so peaceful with a halo around his head, he would take a handkerchief out of his back pocket, wipe the sweat off his face and say, "How you boys doing? Who's winning?"

We knew from past experience if we said who was winning, he would have the winner give the other person some marbles, so we had this answer: "We're even, sir."

"Yeah, you boys take care of each other." The dogs would come up to him and help to walk him to the front porch. Even dogs have their form of practice.

The airport terminal was cold from air-conditioning, and around four in the morning I took my practice outside. At about six I went to the washroom and cleaned up, then back outside to continue walking until the counter for my flight opened.

The population began to increase. I could feel the energy movement in the air slowly shifting from still to semi-stillness, and the coldness shifted to coolness. The same woman who had closed the counter the day before came to open it up again. "Were you here all night?" she asked.

"Yes" I said. She bowed and gave me my boarding pass, and then she bowed once more. I eventually boarded the plane and, surprisingly, I got fed—which took care of my alms round. Upon arriving at the airport at Ubon Ratchathani, I was directed to the information booth and a soldier proudly gave me a ride to Wat Pah Nanachat.

17. BOOT CAMP
(January 2000)

*Just know what is happening in your mind—
not happy or sad about it, not attached. If you
suffer, see it, know it, and be empty. It's like a
letter—you have to open it before you can know
what's in it.*

– Ajahn Chah

The ride from Ubon Ratchathani airport took me out across the Thai countryside. I remembered this flat landscape of rice fields and irrigation systems; it reminded me of the war. As a helicopter door gunner, this was the majority of my visual experience every day. I remembered once when we had to go in and fetch a Marine who had stepped on a mine. Several soldiers were down because of that misstep. The entire area was rice paddies; so water, mud, and blood were all over the floor of the chopper. Most importantly, I remembered that we got everyone out of there, and that was a wonderful feeling.

As we drove along the rice paddies toward Wat Pah Nanachat, I noticed water buffalos hanging out on the high ground. Anyone who was ever really "in country" in Vietnam has a water buffalo story. It's a magical animal.

Then I saw a most unusual forest up ahead. Unusual because it took up less than a square mile in this flat open area. Could this be where we were heading? The vehicle was going toward it, and my curiosity level was at "awe." I needed to breathe to keep it under control. Sure enough, according to the sign at the entrance of the forest, it was Wat Pah Nanachat.

There was a circular concrete drive, and in the center of it were two concrete pillars, each about six feet high and ten feet long. There were three feet between them. What were those things? Outside of the circular drive was a tree that had grown horizontally and created a loop that was at least four feet in diameter. I thought, "Okay, here's Grandmother Nature dancing the dance." I stepped out of the vehicle, retrieved my small backpack from the driver, and said thank you. He frowned at the pack, and I knew that as a monk I was carrying a little too much stuff.

This place was a tropical garden with lush-looking plants, and in the center was the meditation hall with a moat about twelve inches wide. I had never seen anything like this before, and my curiosity was up. Getting closer to the entrance of the hall, I saw a pool of water sitting in stone. "What's up with that?"

Being aware of my breath, I slipped out of my shoes and mindfully placed my right foot onto the composite stone floor of the meditation hall, tracked the left foot forward, and continued on until I was up front with the Buddha Rupa. There I prostrated three times, then moved my head in an unobtrusive way so I could see around the hall. On one of the longer sides of this rectangular building was a platform for monks to sit on, with a door next to it that went into another room. Across from that door was the Buddha Rupa. I knew that was the abbot's seat.

The Buddha Rupa was so huge it made me feel like a grain of sand on a beach. Baba James would say, "Don't forget that we are nothing but a grain of sand with regard to the ocean, so be careful, pay attention, and have respect when you go swimming in the ocean."

The abbot came in to give me instructions. His voice sounded British, and it had this unbelievable kindness and sweetness to it. This was an international monastery, and English was the spoken language.

"My name is *Ajahn* Jayasaro. Thank you for your letter. Was your traveling rewarding and growthful?"

I said, "Yes" out loud, and then to myself, "If only you knew."

He said, "I do."

I said to myself, "Shit!" and he just looked at me and smiled. I took another breath and quickly worked at becoming stone quiet.

He gave me instructions.

Alms round begins at 5 a.m., we eat at 7 a.m., and do cleaning from 7:30 a.m. to 11 a.m. Then we return to my *kuti*, my living quarters, and clean, sweeping inside and outside. Practice until 4 p.m., tea with the community from 4 to 6 p.m., and practice at my *kuti* from 6 to 10 p.m. At 10 p.m. there is a choice to lie down until 2 a.m. unless there is a full moon, new moon, or quarter moon, when it is 3 a.m. Then there is a community meditation, until 5 a.m.

I bowed three times, and a monk took me to my *kuti*.

This *kuti* was at least ten feet off the ground with stilts holding it up because of snakes, especially cobras. Underneath the *kuti* was a slab of concrete. There was a water pipe coming up out of the ground at one end of the slab, with a waterspout on it. I noticed that this would be an excellent area to string a line and hang my robe after washing it. The water faucet and bucket next to it were my washing machine and my shower.

Next to my *kuti* was my track for walking meditation. It looked more comfortable than the airport with that cold air-conditioning. However, I had never seen a walking meditation track. The track was approximately twenty-seven steps long and about two to three steps wide. Around the *kuti* was a four-foot empty space, and beyond that was the forest. It was amazing to me that in this flat open area of Thailand, which is almost entirely rice fields, there was this forty-acre jungle.

My *kuti* was square and made of dark wood with a pitched tin roof. On the same side as my walking path there were stairs, with eleven steps from the small porch down to the slab of concrete. The windows were open spaces with shutters.

The mosquitoes at Wat Pah Nanachat were small and gentle. They felt like warm fuzzies around you, and their wings looked almost luminous. Perhaps that's one of the consequences of cultivating concentration–one perceives things as they truly are. After all, there is a quality of light that's generated from anything that has a beating heart. My mind was far removed from the thought of killing. It is so surprising what training the mind can do. Even to this day, my attitude toward mosquitoes and all insects is the same. I know that I have some level of a relationship with anything with a heartbeat.

Looking out of the window, I could see another *kuti* about fifty yards away through the vegetation. I later met the monk who lived and practiced there, a wonderful man in his late sixties. He had been a monk for ten years, which gave him the title of *Ajahn* and the right to give teachings to others. Then he disrobed, got married, and raised several kids to their adult lives, and now he was back in the monastery. He had always said to his older kids, grandkids, and wife that one day he would become a monk again. They had never believed him and just laughed (it became part of a family joke), but one day he didn't come home. At first, no one except his wife thought anything of it, but after a week they reported it to the police.

Months went by and there was no word from anyone about him. They checked the monasteries in the area, but he had gone to a monastery far away so that they couldn't find him. After a year of practicing he was granted permission to take robes again, and at that time he contacted his family and invited them to the ceremony. Of course they were all in a state of shock, but eventually were honored that he would do such a thing.

He had already completed five Rains Retreats when I met him. He would begin his walking meditation just after tea, which would be about 6 p.m. I could sit in my *kuti* and observe him walking. At the end of his walking track, he had huge candles that were the size of a baseball bat, the kind that are used in cathedrals. He had them at both ends of the track, and I could see the light of the candles easier than I could see him. Somewhere around 10 p.m. he would go inside and continue *bhavana*, or meditation practice.

I recall a conversation this monk and I had during tea.

He asked, "Did you hear me chanting last night?"

"Yes," I replied. The sound of our voices was mixed in with the wind, making the leaves talk with a crisp raspy sound, along with the various sounds of insects and monkeys.

He said, "Excellent. All chants are sacred. This is a prayer to the intelligence of our universe." He went on and said that when we connect by chanting it's like joining in an ancient chorus across time.

"I am so joyful that you were able to hear me," he said. I understood that he was offering a blessing and that nature was acknowledging it. Whoever heard him was blessed. He inquired if I had a good rest.

"Yes," I said. "I was able to lie down for three hours and was refreshed at 3 a.m."

"Very good," he concluded.

I was one of eighteen monks, and three of us were from America. All the monks at Wat Pah Nanachat were younger than I, and taking orders from a monk in his twenties was difficult for me especially when there were issues. Jack, my primary teacher, had told me to prepare for a storm at this *wat*.

The primary practice was *Sila*, the practice of right conduct. The body movements and how people responded reminded me of being in a Zen *sesshin*, gathering one's mind.

I later came to realize that the Thai Forest Monastery tradition contains in its cup all the various meditation practices, including the Vedic traditions. In some of the monasteries, they follow the practices of Rinzai Zen. In some, they have a skeleton, an infant in a glass jar, or other objects associated with death, which is also a Tibetan Bon Po practice. Some of the monasteries have gargoyles and other statues that were excellent candidates for causing nightmares.

I eventually found out that the concrete object in the center of the circle drive in front of the monastery was a place where the bodies of the dead were burned. The family brings the deceased to the monastery and the monks put them up in smoke. A family can make a donation of any amount. It is a very inexpensive way for them to have a funeral, and doing it at a monastery creates merit for the deceased and the family.

The forest monastic practice works with nature with regard to the phases of the moon and the three phases of the twelve-hour night—from 6 p.m. to 10 p.m., 10 p.m. to 2 a.m., and from 2 a.m. to 6 a.m. Every twice-a-month quarter moon, we did standing, walking, and sitting meditation from 10 p.m. to 2 a.m. with no lying down. We did this individually in our own *kutis*. Every new and full moon we practiced as a group instead of individually. It was like dancing with the elements of nature, as I wrote earlier.

The full moon practice brought several special activities. We had to shave our heads and all of our facial hair except the eyelashes. This was good because I didn't have to worry about hosting conventions and parties for the mosquitoes as I did in Myanmar. Another activity was washing our robes, which was the best because we got to be social and exercise wise speech as opposed to idle chatter in what was almost an all-day process. A few monks would get a fire going in the morning. They used a huge wok about three feet across, filled with water and chips from a jackfruit tree. After a few hours, when the water had a deep dark color, we would take that liquor and put it in a wooden trough to wash our robes. The jackfruit took the soil out and gave the robes a sweet smell and a color like chocolate. The joke we had was that we looked like a herd of cows going on alms round.

We wouldn't have tea at 4 p.m. that day because of the busyness. At 6 p.m. the meditation hall would be full of people from the community who would join us in practicing throughout the night. For monks, there's a senior order in how we sit, according to how many Rains Retreats you have done. I had only accomplished one, so I was almost at the end; but, yes, there was a new monk next to me. I must say it felt good to move up the pecking order, even if it was just by a breath. It must be a great feeling to be further down the row, I thought, but I knew that they had earned it.

There were two monks who had been in robes for only six months, and they had not completed a Rains Retreat. They were in their early twenties, from Malaysia, and they seemed surprised that there was an African-American Buddhist. One said, "This is the first time I have ever met an African-American Buddhist." He was sitting next to me in a full lotus posture, which means both of his legs were crossed. I was impressed because I thought if he could do that, then his practice must have some depth; but I did not appreciate his shooting off his mouth. I was a little more than twice his age, and I thought I was a better monk than he was. I was a little beside myself with him sitting next to me, and my mental qualities were in the neighborhood of such words as "piss off!"

Through thinking that I could practice better than him, I had created a competition in my mind. Every few hours I had to get up and do walking practice, while this young blood did not move. I used walking practice because that's the utmost effective way to work with a restless mind, but my mind got into a sluggish state. Then I turned around a pillar inside the hall and made eye contact with an elderly woman who was doing yoga. She lit up with a smile that just lit me right up too. I got back up on the platform and continued with my sitting practice.

After a period of time I felt a cold draft and closed the shutters behind me. No one else had the shutters closed. Less than five minutes later, mosquitoes started hovering around me and, of course, tanking up with my blood. I quickly understood why the shutters were open so I reopened them.

I began to settle back down in *bhavana* when someone started snoring. "What's up with that?" I thought, and opened my eyes and realized that the young monk I had developed an attitude about was sleeping. This was a wake-up call for me. It's not about posture, it's about what you are doing in there. I was playing games with myself and, of course, lost most of the night to unskillful practice. However, through mindfulness and discernment, I was able to change my unskillfulness into tremendous insight and skillfulness during the final two hours, until 5 a.m., when I got up and prepared for alms round.

Later I had another experience of getting schooled when a monk and I were cleaning one of the outhouses. These were uptown outhouses compared to what we had on Pawleys Island, where my grandfather once sat down and got tagged by a black widow spider. These had flush toilets and tile floors, but still they were outhouses. I had left my timepiece in my *kuti*, and it felt to be around teatime, which was 4 p.m., so I wanted to go back to the *kuti* and wash up first. This was usually the time of day when all monks wash up.

"When will we be having tea?" I asked the monk.

"Pay attention," he said.

I flipped out. I went off with my inner voice, "Who in the @#@# does he think he is? Just because he's done more Rains Retreats than I have doesn't mean he has control of me. I've been working my #@#@# off cleaning this john, and all I wanted to know is what time is tea."

I grimly continued with my work and afterwards we began to put the supplies away. In the process, I noticed some monks walking in the direction of *Ajahn* Pasanno's *kuti*, which is where we had tea. *Ajahn* Pasanno was once the abbot, and the old abbot's *kuti* was referred to with his name. Knowing this, it made the knitted cap (that he had given me back at Abhayagiri) even more special.

That same skin-headed monk said, "See, pay attention. Look, there are monks going over there. It must be getting around to tea time."

This senior monk was only trying to get me to pay attention to my mind—which is everything in the inner and the outer world. I had been so full of myself, going off on myself, and cultivating suffering instead of tending to my fire.

The precepts reminded me of being in basic training in the military. These precepts would yell and scream at you, but once you got used to it, by letting awareness relax in the present, the quality of mindfulness became even more alive. This made it easier to deal with the evil forces of *Mara*, the demon that tempted the Buddha.

Once I heard the abbot giving a tongue-lashing to a nun from Malaysia. It was so intense that I decided to drop in. *Ajahn* looked at me, and it was as if he gained more juice to continue with her. He told her that she had broken a major precept by traveling alone when coming here to practice, and he had a major point, because she was exceptionally beautiful. He said she was allowed to practice, but she couldn't leave until she had someone with her.

When he had excused her, *Ajahn* turned and said to me, "I have never seen anyone so selfless." It was a compliment to her, for not being attached. Interestingly, it took me two days of skillful practice in my mind to detach myself from her.

18. SWEET NECTAR
(January 2000)

Abbot *Ajahn* Jayasaro took several other monks and me over to Luang Por Chah's monastery in the van. This was the eighth anniversary of Luang Por Chah's death. I had heard his name at so many Vipassana retreats. Listening to other monks talk about him, it sounded as if they were talking about the Buddha.

It was late in the afternoon when the van drove into his monastery, a place that was utterly peaceful. The van stopped, we got out, and everyone seemed to have an agenda except me. I watched as they began to walk in different directions, to visit a friend from another monastery or something. *Ajahn* looked at me and I began following him into the ocean of energy; no verbal conversation was happening. I was working my bones to be as mindful as I could because I was tired of his reading my thoughts. We walked toward a building on the famous cobblestone drive that was handlaid while Luang Por was still alive. This path was made to carry his body to the *chedi*, the place where his body was cremated, and that is now a shrine for the world to visit.

Ajahn said that when Luang Por was ill, the monks started to construct this quarter-mile-long drive. It took a few years for them to complete this process, and all the while they knew that this would be the drive that they would take his body down. From the outside, the *chedi* looked like a tall smokestack. Its base was about fifty feet in diameter with entrances from the four directions. A cobblestone street circled it. We went inside. When I arrived at this monastery, I had found the juice very sweet but, wow, this was going to another level of sweetness and intensity of energy.

There was a huge photograph of Luang Por Chah. It had a pedestal above it, and on the pedestal was a glass dome about twelve inches in diameter. I noticed large and small pieces of crystals underneath the dome, and thought, "This is an odd place to have crystals."

So I asked *Ajahn*, "What are these crystals doing here?"
"Those are his remains after cremation," he said.
How could that be?

We knelt down in front of his shrine, and I joined my abbot in bowing three times. Then he began chanting a very special chant that I knew was for me. He was giving me a formal introduction to Luang Por Chah. I felt an invisible movement in the sweet sensation of the room. As it got stronger, my physical body felt like it wanted to explode because my inner body had become enormously huge. The saliva in my mouth tasted like honey, which reminded me of another time I had been in a situation like this.

I remembered meeting a ninety-plus-year-old devotee of Neem Karoli Baba in Taos years before. This devotee's name was Dada, and he had known his teacher since he was a child. When he told us about Neem Karoli Baba, that honey taste came into my mouth, just as if I had put a piece of Taos honeycomb into my mouth. It was then that I realized what my cousins and friends meant when they would say, "Sweet Jesus," after having a religious experience.

After *Ajahn* got through chanting, we got up. I bowed three times and walked around the inside of the building. I ended up spending the night at the *wat*. I was given a *kuti* where the toilet didn't work and had been used. It was amazing. After practicing for a while, I lay down and rested in a sweet in and out breath.

One afternoon Abbot *Ajahn* Jayasaro and I, along with about a hundred monks, gathered outside to wait for *Ajahn* Maha Boowa, the most senior forest monk in Thailand. Luang Por Chah and he had been very close. Both of them were students of *Ajahn* Mun, who was the most influential monk of the twentieth century in Thailand. Being in *Ajahn* Maha Boowa's presence was a way of seeing the Theravadin Lineage, the "Way of the Elders," dance right in front of my eyes. They said his presence created a sense of magic in the air.

We gathered at Luang Por Chah's *kuti*. Like most Thai *kuti*s, it was about ten feet off the ground, but this building was bigger and had more rooms than the standard one-room building. His wheelchair was up there, which we took turns sitting in, you know, soaking up those healing fumes he had created. Serious medical complications had put him into that chair several years before he died.

Ajahn Jayasaro shared with us that when Luang Por Chah was ill the monks took turns taking care of him. *Ajahn* was one of them and he made a vow not to lie down until Luang Por would die. He had been given three to six months to live but, as I remember, he died something like six or seven years later. *Ajahn* told me that this was a good practice to learn how to rest the body.

I asked, "You never laid down during that time?"

"No," he responded. "I would just sit and lean up against the wall; eventually it became a routine or habit. Understand, that's how we learn, through repetition. However, some behavioral patterns or habits cause suffering. You need to investigate with a wise mind and experiment."

Several of us thanked him for his teachings. I later realized that this is how various teachings were given in the forest tradition.

We were taking up time waiting for *Ajahn* Maha Boowa to arrive though, of course, "taking up time" is a timeless event when one is constantly practicing mindfulness of the present moment. I found a spot to sit under the *kuti* because this was where *Ajahn* Maha Boowa would be giving us teachings. A monk brought us news that the motorcade was about fifteen minutes away.

On one side of his *kuti* was a green lawn that extended about forty yards to the edge of the forest. I had heard stories of the deer coming from that forest to eat out of Luang Por Chah's hands. Several monks got up and walked to the edge of the grass and began gazing into the forest as if something was coming out of the woods. Full of curiosity, I left my place under the *kuti* and walked toward this mysterious group of monks. I didn't have a clue what or whom I was looking for, but it felt good getting into this particular zone.

Suddenly, the wind began to create a gentle breeze that came across my face. It felt as if a person with endless compassion was caressing my face. Then it picked up to the point where leaves flew off the trees, and a sound like a roaring tiger came from the forest. "Could this be a tiger? Okay, if it is, then I will go down with my brothers." We all had to hold onto our robes to keep our respectability. Some of the monks hurried back underneath the *kuti*, but I just stood there with a few of the *ajahns*. The roaring sound disappeared as the wind slowed down. I turned around and walked back to the *kuti* to join everyone else. By the time I got back to my spot, and had taken in one cycle of breath to join the tranquility of my sangha, the wind had stopped. In the same moment, *Ajahn* Maha Boowa's motorcade arrived.

These masters of awareness always make an interesting entrance. I remembered seeing His Holiness the Dalai Lama my first time. The energy had been incredible: I could feel him in my bones, and everyone around was making aha sounds.

Ajahn Maha Boowa got out of the vehicle, walked over, and checked the toilet to see how clean it was. Just that says everything about a monastery's hygiene. Then he took a few steps toward the rest of us under the *kuti*. As he walked toward us, what I saw was not a solid human being in any shape or form. It was a liquid-like, luminous body that I could almost see through. I said to myself, "I just went into a delusional state, and it will go away." He then sat down, and we all bowed three times.

He began to give a discourse about his phases of development. This was the first time I had ever heard anyone who was already awakened talk about his awakening. I had read about it but this was different. It was coming straight from the heart. He told about how his last phase toward awakening was the most difficult because it involved sensuality, and this was something not to take lightly. It doesn't matter if you're living in the forest and never have contact with another human being. Sensuality is deep-rooted in everyone, and gender has nothing to do with it either.

He reached into his bag and pulled out a betel nut, which he put into his mouth and began to chew, chewing and talking at the same time about his path to awakening. He explained that sensuality is a sweet nectar that is deep in all of our systems. It doesn't matter if your intention is on the avoidance side or the attraction side, because sensuality is always associated with desire, and desire can be used skillfully or unskillfully. When used in a healthy, skillful way to decrease stress, desire can be beneficial. However, it is most important to ask oneself this question first: "What is my intent?" One's intent sets the foundation for the right quality of desire to come to maturity. A skillful intention means not causing unnecessary harm to oneself or others.

Ajahn went on to describe the difference between sensuality and death. "Sensuality brings pleasure to the body and mind," he said. "And dissociation happens easily, whereas death brings alertness, which can be fearful because one knows that a permanent dissociation from the physical body is happening. From a physiological perspective, sensuality releases dopamine, which cultivates tranquility— while death releases endorphins, which cultivate alertness. Therefore, sensuality and death are two of the most powerful objects of meditation."

At the end of his discourse, we all bowed three times. Then we stood up, and a strange feeling passed through me like a combination of the Three Stooges, Laurel and Hardy, Fred Simpson, Amos 'n Andy, Redd Foxx, Jackie Gleason, Richard Pryor, Jackie Chan, Chris Tucker, and Chris Rock being channeled into my system. We were all drunk on love. As the Sufis would say, we were drunk on God. I looked over at *Ajahn's* body, and it was luminous and extremely bright. Every cell in my body was exploding; it felt as if I had nowhere to go or hide. I just tried my best to continue seeing things as they were. For me, that meant keeping the breath in mind.

After collecting myself, I walked over to the public meditation hall. Who and what was walking was the question. Everything I looked at had some form of light in and around it. I thought that I was having an acid flashback after thirty-five years. A gentle quietness of the night was all over me.

Up ahead I could see the building that housed the meditation hall. That hall is a room the size of a cathedral, with a huge stage about three feet high. The ceiling was twenty feet high, with huge wooden shutters for windows that went from floor to ceiling. The shutters were open to give an inside-outside effect. This enabled people who couldn't get inside the hall to see and participate in the evening chant.

It was about six o'clock in the evening, and approximately five thousand people were gathered outside the building. I walked inside with the other monks. The main meditation hall had room for about five hundred of us on the stage, and maybe a thousand lay or non-monastic people in the audience, all dressed in white. I came onto the hardwood stage with the other monks and I put down my sitting cloth. Then I knelt down, put my hands together, and bowed three times to the golden Buddha Rupa. Then I got myself into an upright posture and looked out. Every molecule in my body changed. The sensation was as if I had been ejected from my body. I didn't know if I was breathing or if I even had a body because it felt as if all those thousands of people were looking at me. This was an experience beyond words.

The senior monks were in front of us, and in front of them was a huge chair, about five feet high with a back and arm rests. The seat was big enough to easily cross your legs, which was the purpose of the design.

Ajahn Maha Boowa came in and sat up in the chair, and we all began the evening chant. It was my first time chanting with that many people, and that alone took my mind and body beyond the beyond.

After about forty-five minutes of chanting, he gave a Dharma talk. Speakers were set up outside the meditation hall so that the people outside in the grove could hear him. The setting for his talk seemed just like that of the Buddha when he gave his talks in Jeta's Grove in Anathapindika's Park, India. It felt timeless.

He continued chewing on betel nut. One of its attributes is that it makes your saliva red. In the middle of his talk, he stopped and gestured toward a spittoon. One of his attending monks got up and gave him the spittoon, and he reached for it and brought it up to his belly button. He slightly tilted his head and began to spit. You could see a long red line of liquid coming out of his mouth going into the spittoon. Then he cleaned himself up, got a clean spittoon, and continued with his Dharma talk. The whole process took up about five minutes. The monk sitting next to me was from India and spoke English very well. He turned his head toward me and said, "Is he for real?"

It was so interesting observing my own conditioned Western mind. I just couldn't and wouldn't let that experience go. In America, spitting like that would have people walking out of the room saying, "How disgusting, how dare you do something like that? Doesn't he know how to act in public?" Who knows, people might be consulting their attorneys for compensation because of the "trauma" that was caused to them. The culture in Thailand is different. There, people see you as an individual and support you in being yourself.

Then I remembered the famous story about a sadhu, or teacher, who was walking along a path with one of his students after a rain. They came upon a muddy spot as a woman on the other side was approaching in the opposite direction. The sadhu took off his outer shawl and laid it across the muddy path so that the woman could get across. The student looked surprised, but knew he was studying with a wonderful and famous teacher. So, after about one hour of walking, the student asked his teacher why he had taken his shawl off and let it get muddy by having a woman walk on it.

"Oh, I see that you are still carrying her," said the sadhu. "I left her back there after wrapping my shawl around me. How sad that you missed the blackberries, the plums, the flowers along the path."

"What blackberries, what flowers?" asked the student.

Attachment clouds the mind.

After *Ajahn* Maha Boowa's talk, a monk from Yugoslavia asked if I would like to walk back to Wat Pah Nanachat with him.

"Yes, of course." We had left our shoes in the van that brought us over, in order to save time, but the van had already left.

He said, "Don't worry about the shoes. The walk is just a few miles."

"Okay, no problem," I thought.

Now, I did not know that this road was full of rocks, especially small pointed ones that would love to jump up under your feet. Actually, the entire road was covered with these stones nature had designed especially for me to walk on. At first it was okay because of the thick skin on the bottom of my feet, but after about half a mile, my nervous system began talking to my brain in a not-so-friendly way. The muscular system in my body was fighting with me. It wanted to be tense, and I wanted it to be soft. My associate, walking with me, noticed that I was struggling with myself, and occasionally he would say, "Soft Belly." My inner voice could only reply, "Shut the %%## up."

I was breaking some serious rules here with regard to right speech. When people think of the precepts—such as sexual conduct, no killing, not taking what is not yours, no false speech—we assume that this is guidance for how to perform in the world. This is true. But the precepts are also guidelines about how to perform within ourselves, and that is more important than the world outside of our bodies.

It got to a point in the walk that I had to not only work the cycle of the breath but also say to myself, "I can do this."

"We only have just one mile left," he said.

My thoughts were, "Well, we have come too far to turn around, just take one step at a time, and then the next, without putting any pressure down on any of the steps." I never engaged in such a mindful walk. I noticed that when I focused on keeping the belly soft, just as he said, there was a dramatic decrease in the intensity of the perceived pain. So my mantra became "Soft Belly." It was incredible how everything else fell away.

I had always been interested in sound, and I realized that the quality of my tone when saying "Soft Belly" had a tremendous impact on the pain intensity. After I got attuned to the feeling or sensation of that tonal quality, I was able to let the verbal drop and just hold on to the sensation. I realized that this sensation had a different quality from the breath.

I also became aware that this distinctive sensational quality had a sound, a sound that others have referred to as the sound of silence, a hum from the big bang, the distant ocean, *prana*, a swarm of bees, a pitch coming from an electric line, and a waterfall to name a few. Luang Por Sumedho, the most senior Western monk, described his experiences with that sound in his book, *The Sound of Silence: The Selected Teachings of Ajahn Sumedho.*

As I dropped into that "Soft Belly," the breath energy and the sound became one; the feeling of ecstasy was overwhelming. How could there be a greater experience than this? I wasn't happy, but I was joyful. It came to me what was really happening was getting to the monastery and not to the hospital emergency room. When we finally arrived at our *wat*, it felt like coming home from Vietnam—a sensation beyond words.

I slept almost all four hours of that night. The next morning at three o'clock upon arriving at the meditation hall, I felt a little tenderness on the bottoms of my feet, but since the soil around the *wat* was soft, it was not too noticeable. When I went on my alms round, the road was paved, and my tender feet felt like I was walking on nails or broken glass. The other monks noticed a serious limp in my stride. I continued my alms round on down the dirt road to the village and onto the railroad tracks, and you know the kind of rocks that dwell on the tracks. Those rocks immediately brought up the traumatic, and priceless teaching from the previous night, and the lesson of those rocks followed me into the village as I got my food and gave my blessings from a joyful perspective.

One of the Buddha's quintessential teachings for practice was the Seven Factors for Enlightenment or Awakening, and I reflected on them in relation to the previous night. They are: mindfulness, investigation or analysis of qualities, persistence or effort, rapture, serenity or calm, concentration, and equanimity (see appendix: Seven Factors for Enlightenment).

It became a joy to work with these factors once my sense of self was able to settle down. I learned when to pick up the pace or slow it down, when to adjust my stride, how much air to take in, and not to hold my breath. All this was being mindful while in action—putting it into words just does not do justice to the actual experience. Keeping my belly soft, I was opening into a new level of existence, learning how to dance with pain.

It took about ten days for my feet to recover, but they did. The story got around about what had happened, and a monk from Russia came up to me and said, "You should have told me what you were up to. I would have given you my shoes. That monk from Yugoslavia is known for having no feeling in his feet—his feet have no nerves!"

The monks would school me constantly with regard to becoming an excellent monk and cultivating the path to freedom. And every so often we would get a visiting *ajahn*. A senior monk at a monastery had told me you could take a test to speed up the process of getting this title, but I later found out from *Ajahn* Thanissaro—an authority on the sutras—that there is no such test. Getting a credential through examination and instantly calling oneself *ajahn* was false. In this particular tradition, one has to walk the talk. There was a monk who said he was an *ajahn*, but he was bending the rules. I found out he had a beach-type dune buggy automobile that he used when he was on the beach with tourists, and he received payments when he gave advice!

Having a visit from a Forest *ajahn* was a special gift; we didn't know where they were coming from or where they were going. Some would be dropping in from a mountain cave, some were abbots at other monasteries, some were just floating around the countryside, some came out of the deep forest, some were from other countries, and some had started their monastic practice at Wat Pah Nanachat. All of them knew that this was a training monastery for Western wanna-be monks.

What's so special about these Thai Forest *ajahns?* First of all, they are a community of monks and now nuns, including Westerners, who have reached a special level in their practice. Their teaching comes directly from their experience in the practice. They have read and practiced the sutras and various written and unwritten meditation techniques, and now they have settled into their own way of just being. It is like going to chef school or any graduate school—we all come out basically the same, learning the same skills and philosophy—and it's not until many years later that we finally become a unique individual and master at what we do. That's what's special about the traditional term "Thai Forest Master." This particular forest lineage goes back to the time of *Ajahn* Mun in the nineteenth century, and some of the practices go back twenty-five hundred years to the Vedic and other ancient traditions.

It was wonderful to have tea with a guest *ajahn* at four o'clock. One never knew what would happen, but everyone knew that we would be in for some wonderful stories, which is where the depth of the teaching exists. Also, much can be learned from just observing a Thai Forest Master's body movements. After some of those teas, I would be so juiced up, it felt as if my feet were no longer touching the ground as I walked back to my *kuti*. I would just take that sweet bliss and use it as medicine to practice through the night. We often desire that sweet nectar, but it is important to have wise intention about what to do with it. Having that nectar creates a perfect opportunity to deepen our insight about our relationship with life. It's like putting money into your savings account. It strengthens your character and integrity.

There was one *ajahn* who came from England. He stood about six feet five inches, and this brother was so slender that his robes looked like they were hanging off a pole. One good thing about being like that is there is no fat on the body, but the most unusual thing about him was his begging bowl. I noticed this when we had returned from alms round one morning and were preparing to sit down and eat. He was sitting up front in the abbot's seat since he had more Rains Retreats than the abbot. Offering merit by helping attend to this *ajahn's* needs, our abbot pulled out his bowl; it was the tiniest bowl I'd ever seen. Not even the youth in Myanmar had a bowl that small. A newborn infant couldn't even fit inside. It was about five inches in diameter and about the same depth. All of a sudden I saw him as a professional basketball player spinning a begging bowl on one of his fingers.

It is so interesting what perception does to the mind. I could see so clearly how life is an illusionary play on the mind, and how holding on to fixed views perpetuates suffering. Science has confirmed that our mind sees 10 percent of things as they are; the other 90 percent comes from our personal view. The English *ajahn* was, of course, content with the size of his bowl. It was my mind that was flipping out, making judgments, and putting him in a mental box.

After eating, this *ajahn* called me up front and asked where I was from and what I did in America. Our conversation got into a two-way street and ended when he said, "Wow, you are very psychic. Be careful."

"What do you mean?" I asked.

"You were verbalizing almost everything that I was thinking about. This could make people feel uncomfortable; do not worry, you will learn how to manage your mind."

I remembered another Thai forest monk whom I had met in California telling me something similar. "You are going to be an incredible person," he said, "once you get a handle on how psychic you are."

I mentioned to him how my Rains Retreat in Myanmar had been my hell, and he pointed over to the jungle, where all kinds of crawling things dwell, and said, "That was my hell while I was practicing there."

I bowed three times and left.

Our monastery would be leaving to go into the deep forest in a few days, so the days ahead were about getting things ready. I knew that I would not be coming back to this monastery. So I spent some time walking around the property to experience the illusion of being in a deep forest while at the same time knowing that outside of our property everything was flat fields. Modernization had taken over Mother Nature here. At one time, all of Northeastern Thailand was a jungle with tigers. Most of them have either been killed or have escaped across the river into Laos. As I walked along the sandy footpath to my *kuti*, I wished that I had a torch, even though the path was ten feet wide with nothing but white sand. I wanted to make sure that I didn't accidentally step on anything, like a cobra or a viper that had made these woods its home.

The following day we spent most of our time around the sewing *kuti*. We had to put our mosquito nets together for the jungle and a tarp to cover the net. All the materials were there, we just needed to cut it out and sew it up with the foot-pedal Singer sewing machine. After going through a box of needles with my mindless actions, I was reminded how you can take your practice and put it into your daily life. The monks thought that I was used to doing this, but I had never sewn on a machine before and started breaking needles. One of the senior monks smiled with only his eyes: they were like airport runway lights blinking on and off as he got within one step of me. "If you break another needle," he said, "you will have to hand stitch this." That was impossible from my view.

It is so interesting that when our backs are up against the wall in a pass-or-fail situation, we only have the choice to be mindful or mindless. It must be like doing surgery; you are not all there until a serious situation arises and the mind/body gets a boost of adrenalin. It is important to know what to do and how to use that rocket fuel. We can burn ourselves up by self-destruction or manifest an accomplishment and teachings for others. Looking at that needle was like treating the breath as if it was my last, but I listened carefully, with mindfulness and concentration, and was able to get through that process. I had my net and tarp.

I stepped outside and there stood a visiting Forest *ajahn* beside a jackfruit tree about forty feet tall. This *ajahn*, who was from Australia, had come down from the caves in Northern Thailand. He told me that this used to be the edge of the forest. He pointed to an old, abandoned, falling-down building and said, "This was the sauna that Luang Por Chah would come to relax in. We constructed it for him. He would walk over from his monastery, which was in walking distance and take refuge in the sauna with us Westerners."

Ajahn looked at me and knew that my awareness had zipped off somewhere.

"Are you back?" he asked.

I put my hands in Anjali, the praying position, and said "Yes!" *Ajahn* continued with his story.

I felt that the time was slipping away, and after a few more sentences I said that I must get going and finish packing because the bus would be coming to pick us up in the morning. I didn't look at my watch until I was a ways down the path, and sure enough, it was getting close to teatime. So not only did I have to pack, I also had to get cleaned up for tea.

At tea, this *ajahn* told us all a story about being in a cave in meditation when a cobra entered. My mental thoughts started up, "Oh man, why now, just before we get to go into the jungle." He told us that he didn't have his upper robe on when he was meditating (because of the heat), so he was naked when he heard something that made him open his eyes. Moving along the ground, less than six feet in front of him, was this long black snake. He estimated that it was six to ten feet in length.

The *ajahn* said, "I can't remember how I did it, but my body rose up on this ledge behind me. Then there I was on this ledge about four feet high, with nowhere to go." The cobra had risen up to the height of the *ajahn's* belly button who just sat there with his legs crossed, and the cobra touched his belly with its tongue! Then it went back down and slowly disappeared into a sliver of the rock that went outside.

After this story, the room was still. Nobody was breathing until the *ajahn* reached down to pick up his teacup. Then you could hear everyone take in a breath, and we all reached down and picked up our teacups. He ended the story by saying that death is a wonderful teacher, and he hoped that one of us would die so that we could learn from its teaching. Oh, man, why did he have to say that? It wasn't a bad statement, but depending on your point of view it might feel bad. If one sees the death of the body as something bad or the end result, then you would have a meltdown. If one sees death as just a part of our passage through life (including before and after the death of the body), then you might find that statement wise and nourishing. One thing was sure—death was in the room with us.

He reminded me of our administrator in Vietnam who would say to us helicopter gunners as we were leaving for a mission, "Hey y'all, please don't die on me today. I'm too far behind on processing the papers of those who have already died, so let me catch up." No one talked like that since the War, and here it came again. At least I was used to death and dying after my training with Stephen Levine, Dr. Kubler-Ross, Ram Dass, and Sogyal Rinpoche. If I considered my history—racial tensions in America, the war in Vietnam, my conscious dying education, working at a hospice, starting the first higher education degree hospice program—I had a relationship with death. But I was not ready to die. Life was too sweet and mysterious.

19. GRANDMOTHER NATURE
(February 2000)

The forest was magnificent. I had never seen woods like this before. The trees made my childhood woods in the swamps of South Carolina look like a little garden. The average height of the trees was ten to fifteen stories high. The vines on some of those trees could be called trees, and the way they wrapped around the trees was amazing. Some of those trees were twenty stories high. Whoo! Was I really on planet Earth? The monks said they were Banyan trees—the kind of tree the Buddha sat under during the process of his enlightenment.

I had visited a snake pit in Bangkok before becoming a monk. They had many native snakes, including various types of vipers that hang out under green bushes, bamboos, and other objects of nature. They also had cobras and Burmese pythons, which are the largest snakes on this side of the world, just as the anaconda is the largest on the other side of the world. It would have been interesting if nature had put all these snakes on the same side of the planet. For snake lovers, this was paradise. For me, it was a serious wake-up call to another level of mindfulness. I called it, "Be mindful or die." Jon Kabat-Zinn, the founder of the Mindfulness Based Stress Reduction lineage in North America, would have called it "Mindfulness on all levels," meaning the four basic levels of mindfulness presented by the Buddha as the foundation for practice, life, and awakening (see appendix: Levels of Mindfulness).

At the snake pit in Bangkok, the snake doctors had several king cobras crawling around. They are very aggressive snakes. The audience and I noticed how they would fight with one another and attempt to swallow each other headfirst. It was amazing to see more than half of one snake going down inside another snake. "Is this for real?" I thought, "How cool." Then came others voices, "Shut up, this could happen to you," "I never knew that snakes liked each other so much that they would do that," and "This is

233

very educational." Some of the audience had walked out, and I assumed they let their thoughts walk them out of there, which is okay. Thoughts are just a fabrication anyway.

The king cobra likes the mountains of Chiang Mai, in Northern Thailand. I had seen the dried skin of a twenty-foot cobra, with ribs about twelve inches across. I was six feet three inches and realized that a snake like that could easily rise up to the level of my head. Knowing that I was going into that kind of woods made me mindful with my next breath, and the next, and the next.

Later I would see lots of snakes, and about every other day there would be a viper. An agreement that the monks shared about the viper was that if any of us were bitten then out of respect the others would find some shade to lay his body down, so that the sun wouldn't decompose it so fast. There would be no chance of survival. To get to a hospital took four hours in a four-wheel drive to get to the blacktop, then several more hours into town. You would be dead within fifteen minutes. In Vietnam these snakes had a nickname, "the two-stepper." I thought the name was right on, at least it got to the point. I did hear of a soldier who was bitten in the arm and survived, because he was wise enough and wanted to live enough that he amputated his own arm.

There is a practice called the Thirty-Two Parts of the Body (see appendix), in which the primary purpose is for the mind to come to realize that it is not the body. There are, of course, benefits to this practice. I had had a student with a tumor the size of a grapefruit, and this person didn't want chemotherapy or surgery. After one month of working with the body parts, practicing four to six hours per day, the tumor began shrinking according to the MRI report, and eventually it went down to nothing. She completed the practice in four months.

Non-monastics and therapeutic communities have used this method for the management of pain. Instead of cultivating pleasant or unpleasant sensations, you cultivate neutral sensations, and this takes you deep into the sanctuary of concentration. The power of this is extra-ordinary. It supports the mind in cultivating the perception of dispassion, which can be difficult because of the belief systems that surround it. For example, you might fear that if you are dispassionate, you will never be able to love or be good at accepting love. This practice helps you experience things as they are, and your mind/heart develops a new level of passion—the passion to experience true essence. I practiced in the Hindu lineage of Neem Karoli Baba, and one of his statements was, "See God in everything." This was easier and more meaningful for me to work with after the Bangkok snake pit.

As we walked deep into the jungle, I saw many beauties. You could go with your imagination for the color spectrum of butterflies, communities of twenty-five to fifty of them in this direction and that. And the flowers—what an assortment of beauty! There was one flower that looked like a black rose. Wild orchids were in the hundreds, looking like rainbows. At one point, I looked up at the limb of a tree that was at least one-story-building high and it was covered underneath with orchids and fan-fern plants with leaves six feet long. Nature's beauty took my breath away.

We were each assigned a *diang* the size of a queen-size bed. The closest *diang* was at least a hundred yards away, so we felt that we were the only humans in the woods, especially at night. I chose a spot at the end of this area of the jungle where we were staying because I thought that, there, my chances might be better for an encounter with a tiger, or something else seriously wild. Now I wonder, what would I have done if that had happened?

I walked across a bridge over a stream of water that was about ten feet below. The bridge was made of two large bamboo trees to walk on and a railing on one side. The non-monastic laypeople make these footbridges and platforms for the monks. My *diang* had four legs, which put the construction about three feet off the ground. There was a six-foot pole at each end, with another pole connecting them horizontally at the top. This was for me to hang my mosquito net and my rain tarp. The four corners of the rain tarp were tied with string to nearby trees. I was so excited about my area that I took my flip-flops off and walked around to case the area.

235

Following a footpath I came to a hole in the ground with strips of bamboo on each side so that I could place my feet and squat. Walking back to my *diang*, I realized that there were several banyan trees there. I got up on the *diang* and crossed my legs to check out one of those trees. It was huge, and even though it was alive with birds, it emanated a stillness.

I realized that one hour had gone by so I better set my home up. Upon uncrossing my legs, I noticed that on the *diang* where I had stepped there was blood. I wondered, "Where did that blood come from?" I looked around and noticed blood in several places on the top of my *diang*. "Were those my footsteps?" I looked at the bottom of my feet and saw that they were all sliced up. "How could this have happened?"

I realized that I had been walking on strips of bamboo that were used for ground cover. I never felt a thing. I put on my flip-flops and walked down to the stream for some water to wash my feet off.

If you have ever gone camping in the woods or taken a walk in a park or in the countryside at night, then you will have some experience of what nature does during the transition from light to darkness. One time I was doing my walking meditation at dusk (which is when the mosquitoes come out). Instead of taking cover under the mosquito net over my *diang*, I kept walking. This area is heavily infested with the malaria mosquitoes. I had never seen one and, of course, was curious about what they look like. I knew they were the smallest of the mosquito family, so I just kept walking my bones up and down my walking track. It didn't take long before I spotted one and then another. I stuck my arms out and noticed that they were extremely delicate and didn't make any audible sound. It was interesting to experience how tiny these things are and how they can pack such a deadly punch. Those few seconds were enough. I kindly blew them off of my arm and swiftly got my bones under my net to begin sitting practice for the next several hours.

Getting settled, I reached for my torch so that I could get my thermos of hot water. I wouldn't keep my torch on too long, just long enough to make sure everything was in its place, less than sixty seconds. But underneath these huge trees, even the middle of the day it looked like dusk, so you can imagine what it was like at night. Then there was darkness, the kind of darkness that looks like tar; you could put your hand in front of your face and you would not see it. It was as if the darkness was ready to swallow up my torch. Like all of the major cities on our planet, the jungle comes alive at night. Okay, let's party.

The sounds of nature were so loud that you couldn't hear yourself talk. I would do my chanting, and the only indication that I was saying something was the sensation of the vibration of my body. Sometimes trees would decide to come down at night. A tree in the forest does not fall by itself; it brings other trees down with it because of the density of the vegetation. Nightfall would be an indication to me that it was time to ride death through the night.

This darkness reminded me of the time when the bus driver dropped me off in the dark of the night in the countryside of Myanmar and I had to find my way. The thick darkness made me feel like I was blind. I could rely on my instincts and nothing else. The crashing trees reminded me of Vietnam, when I worked the night missions as a door gunner. I would start delivering food and ammunition to the troops in the evening. Having that ammunition on board meant one spark and I would be in another realm. I would work myself up to pay attention to what I was doing, not letting myself get distracted by stray thoughts, what I called my cousins. They would just get me in trouble. We would get a call that a base camp was getting hit, and would quickly fly over there, and nothing would be happening except darkness talking to us.

So we would spend time in the chopper hovering over where the gunfire came from to try and draw fire. Sometimes we succeeded and sometimes we didn't. Usually when we did succeed somebody took a bullet, though I never did. If I had, I would have had to put $10 in the company "party kitty." If you died, everyone in the company would have to put $10 in.

There had been times back in America when flashbacks of the war and dreams of racial riots in the sixties had been a major problem for me; now these night experiences were starting to upset me. They needed some adjusting to. I had to find a way to chill, and began chanting to cultivate concentration, tranquility, and calmness. I would then transition into breath practices.

One night there was a huge sound like a bomb dropping but not going off—a big thud and then what sounded like something walking and breaking branches, the sound getting louder as it came closer. The only practice I knew that could maybe deal with this situation was "death practice." Although I was not in a situation where I knew that I was going to die, it felt like death might be coming up quickly. Then I heard my inner voice: "Oh shit, now what are you going to do? Your bones are far from home, and you can't dial 911."

I had been warned not to turn on the torch, because it would make "them" angry, whatever "they" were. The light would make "them" come right after you. Sweat was pouring down my face. There was no space for physical pain to enter my body. Being present was an understatement. I shifted my intention to loving-kindness practice, toward myself. This is a gentle concentration technique in working with one's self, cultivating the oil of honey into one's nervous system for tranquility. I could hear that whatever was walking in my direction was breathing heavily as the stepping sound got louder and closer.

I knew from my years of meditation that only when my sense of self was satisfied would it leave me alone, so I needed to be mindful of meeting my own needs myself: "What kind of breath do you need now? Sweetness? Long-in and short-out or long-in and long-out? Should we do some body sweeping?" I knew that if I didn't satisfy my sense of self, it would throw a mental state at me—like the fear that I was going to have a heart attack or that I would make a mindless mistake, like getting up and running or turning on my torch. By now I was getting hot. Sweat was coming out of my ears and all my pores. This was not boot camp nor a

Rains Retreat. It was Grandmother Nature taking me to the next level of practice, practice, practice in tending the fire.

At that very point I was able to gain a tremendous insight into the situation. The insight was that if I was on the dinner plate, then so be it—what a way to go, doing what I love doing. Suddenly, a wave of tranquility and calmness passed through me, a cool sensation running over my bones. The unknown creature walked right by me, and the attitude of a forest monk settled deep into my heart.

Another day I was late getting up because I didn't want to move from my six-hour meditation. Being a monk for the duration of my life in the body was all that mattered. It was five o'clock and sunlight was slowly moving into the darkness. If I wanted to eat, I needed to walk—now! I got on the trail and headed down the mountain for our daily meal. The path lay along the ridge of the mountain, through trees ten to twenty-five stories high and huge vegetation. The root systems of these trees ran across the footpath, and there were roots a foot high every few steps. Well, I was ten minutes late for the meal and walking briskly; I thought that I was being very mindful with my steps, until my foot was not raised high enough to go over one root and crashed right into the side of it. I felt a crunch in my toe but needed to keep going, because it was about a thirty-minute walk down.

About two hours later, after eating and washing my bowl, I realized that it was difficult to walk normally. By the end of the day, the *ajahn* had decided that I should have one of the laypeople take me in to see a doctor. That was a day's journey into town and a day back. Another monk from Russia came along. On the way, we talked about what life would be like if we were not monks, and we realized that it just couldn't get any better than this. However, he was due to go back to Russia and serve in the military.

It was dark by the time we arrived at the doctor's office in Kanchanaburi. His tech took an x-ray of my foot, and afterward I sat in the waiting room with my friend. His office secretary was seated in the same room and I noticed her shoes. They made stilettos look like flat shoes. "How can she drive in those things?" I said to the other monk. He chewed me out up and down for disgracing a woman, even if she had not understood what I said. As he chided me, it was clear that she knew what was going on—what a lesson in wrong speech!

I ended up in the orthopedist's office, and he confirmed that I had fractured my toe. He said the best thing was to stay off it for the quickest healing. Then he gave me some pain pills, and I put them in my bag and hobbled out. Our driver took us to a nearby monastery for the night, but it was difficult to rest. I was worrying about going up and down that mountain, wondering if I could heal this in a short amount of time. The monk from Russia said, "Would you stop worrying so I can get some rest?"

I said, "What about your worries upon returning to Russia?"

"Yes, my country is so backward and a dictatorship. It will be difficult to give up my monastic vows, especially leaving Thailand."

"Yes, living a monastic life is so sweet and demanding."

He said, "Demanding—isn't that what learning to be a mature person is about, except with some spice and joy?"

We both laughed and closed our eyes on that note. He was such a kind and gentle person and spoke Thai fluently. He eventually disrobed and made Thailand his home.

After staying the night at a monastery in town, we went back to our monastery Dow Dum in the mountainous jungle. We arrived in time to eat our only meal at 11 p.m. Everyone knows that with any kind of leg injury the quickest way to heal is to stay off it. I was restricted to my *diang*. The sangha made arrangements to bring my food to me, which involved someone making a thirty to forty-five-minute hike down to the kitchen and up to one hour and fifteen minutes back up. The sangha also made arrangements to bring me hot water for tea and wash my begging bowl. The monks also brought me chocolate. Being embraced by my community like this felt like a mother's touch of loving-kindness. Loving-kindness is the first of the Four Immeasurables that we cultivate in Buddhism (see appendix: Four Immeasurables).

The only time I moved my bones from the *diang* was to use the toilet. The rest of the time I did lying meditation practice. I never thought that I could do something like that. My body went from being drowsy to awake and from lying-down pain to pleasant sensation. I got into such a pattern with this method that when I did get up to go to the toilet, I was excited about getting back into that posture. Practicing through the night was beyond words, just unbelievable, with nature dancing and me joining the dance with the breath and breath energies.

This went on for seven days. Afterward I could walk without limping, and this was deeper than a mother's touch, it was Grandmother Nature's touch. Returning to the roots of the word, *dhar-ma* (the first part means cradle and the second part means mother), my sangha had me in the cradle and the cradle was rocking. Also in the Thai language *dhamma is tham-ma,* which means nature (see appendix: Dharma and Dhamma).

20. LUANG POR JUMNIAN
(April 2000)

After coming out of the forest, I moved to Luang Por Jumnian's monastery. Luang Por is one of the few forest meditation masters who had stepped out into the public with regard to actually healing people. I had heard that he was like the ministers at those revival conferences where they touch your head with what is known as the "Holy Spirit." From the 1920s to 1960, Bishop Grace from Cape Verde was one of the pioneers in this area of ministry; his church was in the northeastern part of America. In the southern states he was known as Daddy Grace. Reverend Oral Roberts was another.

People said that in Luang Por's presence, one would forget about the world. The only thing of any importance would be the practice of mindfulness, wisdom, and trying to stay awake. They told me that he would lie down for only one to two hours every twenty-four to seventy-two hours, and that once he had gone eight years without sleep! I noticed that most mature or awakened people have similar behavioral patterns; their rest is zero to four hours every twenty-four hours.

His monastery covered about a hundred acres of land. It included several meditation halls, and one of these called the Tiger Cave can hold several hundred laypeople and monastics. There was also an outside meditation hall for monks only, caves to do solitude practices, a jungle area with Banyan trees for forest practice, living quarters to house seventy-five to a hundred monks, living quarters for fifteen to twenty-five nuns, and 1,008 steps leading up to a mountain top where there is an imprint in marble of the Buddha's footprint. All this is on the tourist map as the Tiger Cave. I came to realize that this was an excellent monastery to continue my monastic practice for years to come. I met monks who have been here for thirty-plus years and were content. I told myself, I can do that.

When *Ajahn* Jumnian was at his monastery, about 97 percent of his time was spent in a room about the size of an average American household's living room. There was a door leading to a smaller room, and in that room were various Buddhist artifacts, some dating back to the time of the Buddha. The only other monk I knew of who had had a situation like this was Thamanya Sayadaw. What both these monks have in common is an unbelievable quality of compassion.

In the larger, rectangular-shaped room was a large seat on which he sat. At any given time, from fifteen to thirty laypeople would always be in that room. They would come for psychological advice, business advice, and healing for various illnesses. We would be in that room all day and all night. My way of spending time with him was to be in that room. Because I was a monastic, I was able to sit right up next to him.

Now the practice of being present for twenty-four hours was much easier said than done for me. During my first week with him, I would begin to get tired around 1 a.m. My eyelids would begin opening and closing, my head bobbing up and down, my torso moving this way and that. Eventually Luang Por would tell me to go back to my quarters and lie down, by just making a hand gesture. That dance with sleep went on for at least seven days.

It was like observing Muhammad Ali in the 1964 Summer Olympics in Tokyo, Japan. This unknown brother was knocking people out in a matter of a few seconds. Before a cycle of one breath . . . Boom! His opponent was down. Everyone was saying, "What happened? How and what did he do?" His opponent would slowly get up (sometimes) and would be given a second chance. You could feel the intensity within the audience because we were given a second chance to watch this brother dance, and I mean dance. Honestly, I didn't know which was faster, his hands or his feet. I watched his footwork because I wanted to pick up some steps for the next time I was on the dance floor. This was during my teen or acting-out years in high school, and all the ladies and gentlemen appreciated someone with new steps. Boom! The opponent was on the floor again and I missed it.

This time the audience and I were cheering, "Please get up! Please get up!" Ali would be cheering with his gloves as he continued dancing. "Yeah, get on up!" The ref would stop him from saying things and jumping up—you know, those Olympic rules. This one brother got up twice, and this time I vowed to not watch his feet but just his hands . . . Boom! The punch appeared to lift the brother up off his feet, then he came down on his back, and no way was he going to get up. Ali's dance was so juiced. The audience was stunned from the knockout and moving with the juice. It felt like he was everyone's "private dancer," as Tina Turner might say.

Well, that's how it was for me, trying to dance with being awake. I couldn't wait to get to my *kuti* and lie down. Sleep was knocking me out again and again and again. This was the most perfect teacher to study with for years to come.

On one of the many days I was dancing with sleep and was determined to knock it out, Luang Por noticed what was happening and abruptly moved himself to a standing position. I got the message to stand my bones up. He took me over to the monks' ceremonial hall. There were twenty to thirty other monks who came with us to this hall for monks only. I thought it would be a public ass-chewing-out going down. After we entered the hall I noticed that the lights were low, and I sensed a feeling that was familiar, another juicy zone where they make that moonshine whiskey that's aged and seasoned with cherries. I said to myself, "Whatever it is, it's going to be special." He wouldn't let me sit below him. I sat next to him with an interpreter below both of us.

He shared with me how to practice and how to see life: breathing in through the third eye, filling up the head with the breath energy, and going down the body with the breath energy. That breath energy is like oil; it lubricates your joints and all the areas where you have been so hard on yourself. He went on: the out-breath would bring the breath energy down the spine and out of the sacrum. At times you may want to bring it out of the bottom of your feet. After the exit of the breath energy, float your awareness through the air in front of you and bring it up and into the third eye again. It is important to note that when your point of awareness is in the air, the breath energy is much more refined, so it will take time to train your perception to this quality of sensation. That was one of several breathing practices. This particular practice calms the nervous system and brings a sense of grounding to one's state of being.

Another practice to develop compassion was to see the Buddha-nature in everyone. I took this to mean: to perceive that everyone has the potential to become awake. Just wish them joy and happiness for their travel. We need to realize that it's human nature to become attached, especially to pleasant things, to get close to what we enjoy. It is like when we have been on a hike in the mountains, and the view is just wonderful—a sunrise, a sunset, a misty day, a foggy day, or a bright day. We want to stay close to that. But eventually, with maturity of practice, we can come back down the mountain and see things from a different perspective and attitude; that helps cultivate dispassion.

Luang Por gave me many other ways to view the world and work with the breath. For example, another instruction was to see through everything. When looking at a sidewalk, let perception go through it and see the earth underneath it. After giving me all these instructions, he advised me to go back to my quarters and practice.

He reminded me of Sister Mary when he said, "Go and practice." During my childhood years on the island, there was a situation when Sister Mary had a conversation with her neighbor Sister Edna and, who knows, maybe a distant relative. What made the situation magical was that Sister Mary was standing in the front yard. During that time period we had the swamps on one side of the house and on another side, fields for planting that eventually went off into the woods. At the backside of the house was the outhouse, a stable for the horse, the shed, and more woods. The front side of the house included the front yard with all kinds of flowers, the dirt road, and more woods on the other side of the road. Sister Edna's house was in those woods about one-quarter of a mile away as the eagle flies—about one or two city blocks. The two of them would have a conversation that would last for at least thirty minutes.

Afterward I would say, "How do you do that?"

Her response in Gullah, my childhood language, was just "Wo un du uro shors, ant kep prakacing," which translates "Would you do your chores and keep practicing," meaning keep listening. In my sixties, I would go back to that spot in the front yard of Sister Mary's house, and I still could not comprehend how they did this.

The next day when I walked up to the healing room, Luang Por had left to do house calls into the surrounding towns. No one at the monastery could ever keep up with him with regard to his whereabouts and what he was up to. Walking into that room reminded me of when I was at a special event at the Neem Karoli Baba Temple in Taos, New Mexico.

The event called offers homage to the god Shiva. It begins at sunset and goes until sunrise. A brother named Mr. Tewari and his wife came from India to conduct this practice. The ceremony was in four sections. I remember between the second and third sections, about 1 a.m., we were outside bumping into each other drinking chai tea and smoking these cigarettes called *beedies* (like smoking two Camels without a filter). After one toke I said, "No thank you." Mr. Tewari was in the yard smoking and then he started to do *pirouettes* that would make a world-class ballet dancer stop and take note. In one of his moves, he placed his *beedie* into Jai Uttal's mouth; then he took it out again. Jai was so stunned that he turned to a crowd nearby and said, "Did you see that?" He told folks what had happened, and their response was "Yeah, right." That was the beginning of a serious energy shift for me.

I went back into the Temple for the third set. It was like stepping into a sauna turned up to the maximum. This sweet brother began to sing and chant to the point that tears were running down his face like a waterfall. My head started spinning as if someone had me in a spinning wheel. I looked around the room to see who was around, but I didn't want to move from my sitting posture because folks would start talking about me. My mind was stirred up with guilt and various other delusional mental qualities. I knew if I

247

didn't do something I would pass out, but the juice just kept coming, sounding like a swarm of bees.

Mostly everyone had ducked out of that third set. I began pushing my body backward on the floor, just needing to put some space between this brother and me. A wall stopped me, so I just glued my back up against the wall and began breathing deeply. My body was soaked in sweat. He finally brought the third set to a close. He was soaked in sweat too. Although it was dark outside, I had never seen so much light in this room. It was lovely but all I wanted to do was get out. I crawled to the door, pushed my bones to a standing posture, and drank in the fresh wet early morning air. When he walked by me, he said, "Un-huh," as electricity shot through my bones. That's how it felt stepping into Luang Por Jumnian's room. He wasn't there, so I went into self-retreat and practice.

When he returned to the monastery, the first thing I did was to visit Luang Por in his room, and the activities were business-as-usual. You could tell from the faces and behavior of the people in his room which group was there and which part of the day it was. The morning group had a zesty, bright, and eager temperament; it was at times over-energetic. The afternoon group was slower, more easy-going, and their energy was a little low and subdued. The evening group's temperament was almost like the morning group with a mellow and exciting feeling in their energy. The late-night group's temperament had an even, relaxed energy. They weren't tired or excited, but they were looking for something to turn them on, like the rapper Jay-Z's song, *Show Me What You Got.* Yeah. Each group had a different behavior.

It was about one in the morning, and I was with the late-night group that had come in about two hours ago. For the first time, I was very alert and I realized that Luang Por was trying to tell me something with his beautiful smile and the movement of his pinkie finger: "You are finally on the dance floor of the energetic ocean."

I was able to be there with him for a few days, and he would interpret what he was doing when he was healing people. He said that the most important practice is no-self, meaning to get his sense of self out of the way and not let his ego get involved. That meant not thinking, "I am doing this healing." One of these people was a woman who had pain in the midsection of her body. Her tone of voice would change from a very deep masculine note to a soft note and back again. I immediately recognized that she had something else going on. From past experience I knew that she was possessed by some other entity.

When I looked at this woman in Luang Por Jumnian's room, I saw several faces. Luang Por jumped up, chanting as he moved, and went into the other room. He came out with some of his potion. I knew this was going to be more than just an ordinary healing. The entities in this woman's body picked up on what was getting ready to go down. Luang Por motioned to me to open the main entrance door, which looks into the Buddha Hall. The Buddha was right there, so huge that you could only see part of his leg from the room. That was not important. What mattered was the sacred juice coming into the room to support Luang Por.

This body started rolling up and down the floor like a barrel. It was so obvious that something more than just this person was in that body. Luang Por gestured to me that he wanted to use part of my robe as an energetic barrier. I took my outer robe and held it up on the other side of her body opposite from the open door of the Buddha. With Luang Por chanting and sprinkling that potion over her as she screamed and rolled and with the juice coming from the Buddha Rupa, that body eventually had a meltdown. Finally she just went limp, soaked in her sweat. Luang Por looked at me and smiled. I smiled back, knowing that those rascals were gone. I also realized that my robe was something more special than I could comprehend.

As the other laywomen and men helped her up, she had a slight smile, big enough to show her teeth. You could see steam-like energy coming out of her. The other women were crying with joy. Luang Por was back up on his bench and the business of addressing healing questions continued. It was about 3:30 a.m. Within half an hour people started leaving. Someone brought Luang Por a plug-in vibrating mattress and he decided to go lie down for about thirty minutes to try it out. I decided to go to my *kuti* and practice.

Luang Por had several bags of metal amulets underneath his robes. That would give him an added weight of fifty to seventy-five pounds. He would walk through the airport metal detector and it would not go off.

One day at his monastery we were in the Tiger Cave, the main meditation hall. It was in the early evening. I asked if I could take his picture. He said sure, and he began to take off those packets of amulets as I took his picture. Many other monks gathered around because they had never seen this before, even his most senior monks. As he advised me to continue taking those pictures, this was indeed a very special moment of being with a Master. Also, in addition to becoming more of an object of curiosity, I gained a little more respect from the monks. It felt like I had found a home.

21. LIFE TRANSITIONS
(1950-2000)

For a Theravadin monk to disrobe is a very serious matter. Taking robes is for life, regardless of the situation; it is not a part-time affair. As the singer/songwriter Curtis Mayfield would say, "There is one way in and no way out." I knew deep down (or at least I thought I knew) that this was the most long-term, peaceful, painful, joyous, and transformative situation I had experienced since my early years on Pawleys Island and as a young man in Japan.

I could feel a storm brewing deep in my bones. On one hand, I wanted to support my son, Clarence, and my partner, Sabine. As I was growing into being an Elder, I also felt strongly pulled to support cultural diversity in the lay community. On the other hand, it was inconceivable to walk away from a community that cultivates higher consciousness 24/7; being in that community felt like being in a healing stream with no end.

I could hear my dear friend Patty McNulty's voice say, "You are almost fifty and just going through another turning-of-age crisis."

I said out loud "Be quiet!" and looked around to see if anyone heard me. I had been carried away with my inner thoughts. I needed to stop these narratives. Nothing made sense anymore, and I felt a headache rising up. I took my bones for a walk.

Disrobing is an insult to the community and oneself so it was important for me to work on cultivating thoughtful and well-considered reasons for going through the process. What is a person to do in this situation? I had the privilege to study with esteemed meditation masters and lay practitioners in Myanmar and Thailand. To walk away from this priceless relationship was incomprehensible.

I saw staying at the monastery as a way of not accepting my responsibilities in the world. Siddhartha came from a family of wealth, I did not. First, there was Sabine. I don't know any other woman who would have given me a year's time off to go and fulfill my dream, without knowing if I would return.

I also had to consider my son, Clarence, who was not even halfway through his twenty years in prison. I remember going to Harlem to visit with him and his legal guardian parents, Reverend and Mrs. Pendarvis. He was the pastor at one of the churches in Harlem, and he took us to church where I was the topic of his sermon. He said, "Lord, this is the happiest day of my life. I don't need to be around here anymore, but if you think I do, I will stay." Within twelve months, Rev. Pendarvis died at the age of eighty-six. Mrs. Pendarvis followed shortly after in her early eighties, leaving me as Clarence's only family. Grace was giving me the opportunity to parent and support him through his transition after his twenty years of being locked up.

Lastly, there was my work on diversity—introducing people of color into the applications of meditation to support their maturity. I had worked hard at that, and I hoped that something was achieved at the first retreats at Spirit Rock in 1992 and Insight Meditation Society in early 2000.

My father died in 1953 at the young age of twenty-seven in a car crash. His death was connected to the Ku Klux Klan, a white organization in America that doesn't like anyone other than a particular type of white Anglo-Saxons. My mom was very angry because there was no way she could directly deal with them. She had an early death at age sixty-four resulting from alcoholism, and so did her second husband at the age of sixty-three. It was in an era of American history when many blacks were killed by the Ku Klux Klan, and I mean many. Thank God for cause and effect—every good deed you do returns to you; the same is true for unkind deeds. In the late 1990s and early in 2000, a few, just a few, of the old guards were brought to trial. I personally feel that there are still many more out there, living their lives with blood on their hands and in their hearts.

The Ku Klux Klan trauma haunted my mother for a long time. Forty years later I visited my dear friends and her in Spokane, Washington. She gave me a business card that was placed on the windshield of her car as she was grocery shopping in the city. The card read, "Ku Klux Klan—we are watching you."

So cultural diversity was a big deal for me. Diversity is natural; when a society is culturally diverse, people accept the uniqueness in everyone. In Western Buddhism, the Vipassana lineage had introduced more people into meditation than all the others combined, but it was still predominately white. Even though it is a small percentage, there is now more cultural diversity in the other lineages as well. Any Buddhist lineage is for all people. Eventually they would have to become diversified and embrace people of color. I knew that maturity needed to develop within the community and the teachers, including myself, and I knew I had a small part to play in that dance.

I reflected on the man who was a monk for ten years. He had the desire to have kids and ended up disrobing. I, too, had strong worldly desires and unfinished business; I knew it would take the duration of being in this vessel to take care of it. Remembering the awakened laypeople I met over the years gave me some assurance on my path of reentering the world.

The first step in my disrobing process was to contact the most senior monk at the monastery so that he could select the day. He reached into his bag and pulled out his astrological calendar to select the appropriate day so that the entire situation could be in utmost harmony, and the inter-connectedness of everything would be taken into considera-tion. After thoroughly looking through the days of the month, he decided on a day and time.

The night before the ceremony, one of the senior monks I had selected to be present at the disrobing ceremony took me around to the quarters of the monks. One of them graciously agreed to witness the ceremony, but he wouldn't let me walk away before I had coughed up some chocolate for him. Chocolate is an inside monastic addiction that goes way back, but how did he know that I had some? Before I gave it to him, he looked at me as if to say, "Well, what's taking you so long?" I gave him a big piece.

Even though I was fifteen to twenty years older, this monk had done at least 100,000 hours of just sitting practice. To put that in perspective, when I was not in retreat, my hours of practice of just sitting would be 6 hours per day or 180 hours per month. During retreats, this would jump to at least 12 hours per day or 360 hours per month, and during my Rains Retreat, which lasted four months, just my sitting practice came to 1,440 hours. My total for the year was about 3,000 hours of practice. This monk had thirty times more than that.

I am emphasizing this because I had heard so many times, from various teachers in America, "Be patient and keep practicing." It takes time and consistency in one's practice to train the mind. All professionals can relate to this. It takes a training and practice to be an effective professional and the same applies to meditation.

I was instructed to get a white top and bottom as my first clothing to be worn after the disrobing ceremony. That was to represent coming down from the monastic realm to the ghost realm. In becoming a monk, one leaves the world of worldly things and desires and enters into the ghost world to progress on into the monastic realm. Now I was coming down from the monastic realm to the world of possessions. Have you ever been in a situation where you do not know what you are doing? Sometimes these are the best situations and sometimes the worst.

I continued walking toward the entrance of the monastery, thinking, "How in the world am I going to go into town and buy some clothing? No way," I thought. "Monks don't buy things, at least they're not supposed to." Money was looked upon as poison in the forest lineage that I practiced in.

As I got closer to the monastery entrance, wondering how I was going to solve this problem, I noticed a familiar woman sitting on a bench. "Is it really you? Sabine—it's you!" I knew that she was coming; however, I didn't know when.

What do you say when you are a monastic and have not seen your partner in twelve months? How could she be my partner? I have let go of all worldly passions, I thought. I stopped and so did she. It was like a silent comedy routine—Amos 'n Andy, and Laurel and Hardy.

"You can stay in robes if you want," Sabine said. "I just came to check, to see what you want to do." She activated all of my emotions. However, the skills of meditation include excellent ways to transcend emotions. It was interesting that not a drop of sensuality was running through my veins.

There was a Thai chaperone monk sitting with us at the table; we all sat down. As we continued talking, I told Sabine what I needed and the time of the ceremony the next day. It was not a problem. She would take care of getting the clothes. I walked away thinking, "You take care of the Dharma, and it will take care of you." That classic phrase has been said in so many ways, in every culture and every part of the planet. The fact is, our family is bigger than the cosmos. *Yahman.*

The ceremony began in the latter part of the next morning. Everyone was present, including Sabine. It was nothing joyful like they told me. It was more like going to a wake or a funeral back home.

I was about to leave something that I had worked hard for and had a loving relationship with.

So often we don't let ourselves grieve, and we can always come up with an excellent reason. But what happens when that energy of loss isn't allowed to release in a skillful way? Most people know this part of the story, so I will just name a few examples. The person looks for more work to do and avoids the pain of that loss, and this becomes a habitual pattern. It can get buried so deep inside of us that whenever a situation or conversation touches upon it, we become emotional in either a gentle or violent way. The same was true for me as a veteran of the Vietnam War, dancing with post-traumatic stress disorder. Suppressed grief can manifest itself as various kinds of illness; it can motivate a person to use intoxicants for the purpose of temporarily forgetting about the loss.

From a monastic perceptive, disrobing is like the death of a close family member. I felt I might as well be dead. Perhaps being dead would be a healthier environment. I went to each of the five monks to ask for forgiveness, and bowed three times. Then I knelt in front of the Master of Ceremonies.

This was the moment. He reached for my sanghati, my monk's outer robe, which is as formal as a tuxedo and carries the authorization of being a monk. Without that, you are not a monk. His hands got a few inches from grabbing it when I leaned back. "What's going on?" he said. "If you want to change your decision, now is the time."

He said to take a walk and have a conversation with the Buddha, because it was between Him and me. So I got up from the floor and took a walk over to the Buddha. I listened and listened. Was this the right thing to do? I got to the point where I didn't know if I was standing or kneeling, front or back, up or down; but I did know that at the right moment, desire would bring me out of this state.

I needed to complete this ceremony and prove to myself that one can be an excellent practitioner in a non-monastic setting. Most importantly, I wanted to prove that I could become a mature person as a partner, father, teacher, and therapist.

I didn't know that I was in a meditation posture in front of the huge Buddha statue until I opened my eyes and realized that my knees were screaming from kneeling on the marble floor. I bowed three times, walked with two stiff knees back over to the others, and completed the ceremony. The *ajahn* reached for my outer robe that was folded and hung across my shoulder. This process felt like I had given someone permission to take off all of my clothes. It required a certain quality of effort—including guarding, abandoning, cultivating, and maintaining balance.

I remembered teaching a retreat at Insight Meditation Society, along with several other teachers, and toward the end we were addressing questions about how to maintain and integrate one's practice in everyday life. One of the practitioners said, "I have been coming to this particular retreat for the past ten years. I have been a meditation practitioner for at least twenty years, and I am a college professor. After leaving this retreat and returning to work, in a few weeks I will be back to my usual self and feel that whatever I have learned in this retreat is all gone. What can I do to work at maintaining and cultivating my practice?" The answer is guarding, abandoning, cultivating, and maintaining balance, which are the Four Right Exertions (see appendix: Four Right Exertions). It was a must for me to apply these skills. Luang Por Jumnian, U'Vinaya Sayadaw, Thamanya Sayadaw, the sadhu/monk with the colorful bag, Maha Boowa, and *Ajahn* Jayasaro were excellent role models.

Without my robes, I realized what a "bean-pole" I had become. It was a phrase used back home when someone has been deprived of food. If I had stood in front of a full mirror, you would hardly know I was there. I reflected on the starving people around the world, especially in Africa. How could we continue to let people starve when there is so much food in the world? The white top and bottom that Sabine had bought looked extremely white. I had worn only my robes for a year. At the same time, my skin looked extremely dark. For the first time, I could say that my skin was black or at least *very* dark brown!

I had agreed to meet Sabine in a few hours, so I went back to my *kuti* to pack my stuff, which all fit into one small bag. Several monks crossed my path on my way out, and they held their heads down because of the loss. One stopped in front of my *kuti* for a few minutes, with his head down, then continued walking. Letting go and holding on both take effort, and both have an element of grief and loss as well as something to gain.

Sabine and I had made plans to travel to Koh Phi Phi for a few days, then spend my fiftieth birthday at Ayutthaya, the ancient capital of Thailand. Well, we hung out on this island, and all I could do was let the process be. I got up, read the newspaper, lay back down, and got up and ate what is called lunch. I had forgotten that meals had names depending on the time of day; I needed to adjust and go through the process of grief. It felt like jetlag magnified by a hundred. After lunch I lay on the beach and let my grief run its course by practicing letting go and gently embracing myself with love. Eventually Sabine came to get me in the late afternoon. Then I attempted to eat dinner, but it felt like an overload. I tried to be present, but it took me many weeks to delete chronic depression.

22. TENDING THE FIRE
(2014)

Tending the fire is about being mindful and responsible for my own fire, taking responsibility for all of my actions, and increasing the practice. Tending the fire is mindfully stepping up to the plate with pride and dignity, and this is what gives us confidence in utilizing the Noble Eightfold Path, mindfulness being one of those paths.

The definition of mindfulness can be as simple and as complex as our cosmos. Tending the fire is as simple as being aware of the words coming out of our mouths and as complex as having the intention, physical awareness, movements, and sensation of picking up a glass of water and tasting it while having a conversation about global peace. It is about increasing the goodness in myself so that deep peace awakens somewhere along that journey. This is a personal decision in working toward generating my fullest potential.

You can say that tending the fire means work on two levels: one is deepening practice, maintaining compassion, and working for benefit of the global community; another level is applying practice and right action to my personal situation and my personal practice. Together, these two generate a powerful fire!

I can't have one without the other: a growing awareness of my own right actions, applying wisdom to my health, my personal relationships, and my care for myself. And then building practice around me: nurturing the wisdom and teachings in my community, increasing inclusion and mindfulness of all peoples in how we treat each other and in how we envision our world.

I am now sixty-four years old, and my life experiences have led me to see that tending the fire has no beginning and no ending. If we take responsibility for what we know and how we act, we will continue to work on ourselves and also to apply our knowledge to the world in which we find ourselves. We will offer help and we will seek out help—for our health and spiritual care (for spirit, mind, and body). If we do this, there is no reason we cannot become awakened to the truth of our lives.

After my return from Asia, tending the fire meant fulfilling the responsibility I felt to bring change to the Buddhist community. It was time to move forward with the People of Color Retreats. I had a lot of energy, and within weeks of my return, the Pond Foundation gave me funds to create a series of meditation retreats for people of color—not just day-long retreats as we had done before, but residential retreats for a week or longer. Those retreats were and continue to be good medicine for our community. They demonstrated that healing is possible if there is support from the community.

We can have a separation of people of color from the European-American culture or an integration of the two. We can have a diverse community. I am sure it will happen, but the soup needs to have the proper ingredients. Well, it is pretty clear that we are dancing in that direction—slowly, and that includes the one percent.

Gradually, more people of color are being drawn to meditation, and we are beginning to train teachers. Hopefully, if we have teachers of color, this will encourage people of color to go neck deep into practice. It would help if we teachers—all of us—encouraged our sanghas through Dharma talks to create more diversity and address the issue of the integration of people of color into our groups.

As a war veteran, tending my fire means finding a place for vets in the world of American meditation. Our Buddhist community has held a deep silence with regard to this topic, and it was never easy for me to feel comfortable with this. The precepts describe the way we are to conduct ourselves, and all meditation centers adhere to the precept that we should not cause harm. Just to hear that, or read those words, is difficult for a vet. In our minds and hearts, we understand that we are not accepted, and a certain amount of guilt is already there.

During my tour in Vietnam, I supported in spraying the deadly defoliant chemical Agent Orange. Sometimes, meditation practitioners ask me, "How could you do that? How can you call yourself a Buddhist or meditation practitioner if you fought in the war?" And it touches on a tender and important point. This is why so few vets go to meditation retreats. It makes me really sad, because *we* are the ones who were traumatized through war and gave our lives.

The military falsely convinced our youthful minds to believe that it was a fight to keep America safe. After coming home, being shamed, and coming to the realization that the war was about greed, my fellow soldiers (including myself) were traumatized at a catastrophic level; the healing work has been going on for years. Therefore, I can either learn to tend the fire or let it burn me up.

In Myanmar, the military are not excluded from the temple. I remember several meditation centers where the military would come in groups, wearing their uniforms, to practice for several days, as an assignment! When I shared this story with a senior American teacher, she was upset and said, "How could those soldiers call themselves Buddhists if they are in the military?" I would say that anyone can benefit from practicing Buddha's teachings. We all have issues and we all need to pay attention and tend our fires.

Pushing other people away is oppression. The more modern day phrase is to be "traumatized," but the Buddha called it oppression. War veterans have experienced this, and all people of color have experienced it. We all have some degree of post-traumatic stress disorder. Well, meditation, chanting, healthy eating, and an Ayurvedic lifestyle all helped with my PTSD, without needing to take truckloads of medication (see appendix: Ayurvedic Medicine, Elements Ayurvedic).

Taking responsibility means exercising discernment, especially in looking after the body. Before I went to Mayanmar, I took an Ayurvedic cleanse from my doctor, Sunil Joshi, M.D., and it prepared me very well. During the year, we lived in harsh conditions, especially outside. At least two monks had to leave the country because of illness, and around half a dozen went to the hospital because of malaria. I did not even catch a cold. However, I had herniated a disk and broken a toe. Through all of this, and most importantly, these practices have helped me face my shame and grief.

The most heartfelt part of tending the fire is learning to love without any dirty water, meaning to love without any prerequisites or conditions placed on oneself or someone else. Love happens. It is a natural ingredient in our mind/body system; part of the practice is to love yourself. It is said that Love is God, or God is Love, and that's our own true nature. If that is true, then love is more potent than any drug, and I need to practice holding that level of awakening. The challenge is to take that loving intention we give to our children, our partners, our pets, and others whom we deeply love—and applying it to ourselves! However, our eyes need to be open, meaning wisdom has to be a part of applying that intention; we have to see ourselves not as "me" or "self," but as what our makeup actually is. Then, be gentle.

I disrobed out of love and a deep caring for two people in my life. I needed to make sure that my partner, Sabine, had personal support in her life transition with cancer. After returning from my year as a monk and after twenty years of living together, Sabine and I married; that was shortly before her second cancer diagnosis. We have been joyfully tending that fire. I also am taking responsibility as a father to my son, Clarence, who is serving a twenty-year prison sentence. In addition to regular communications, I visit him several times a year on the East Coast. I also want to be there to support him when he is released, as he transitions into his new life.

The Buddha was clever in pointing out the Four Noble Truths as a way of teaching us to become our own physician. The healing process is about full awakening to freedom from the diseases of greed, aversion, and delusion. To awaken is to realize whom we really are *not*. By going deeper into the forest of grace, we can eliminate our unskillful qualities and unhealthy behavior patterns. A very important point is coming to the realization that we are *in* this physical body but not *of* this body. Through practice I came to the understanding of the preciousness of being in a body: I became more respectful. Living in the body gives us the rare opportunity to listen to the Dharma—and practice.

For me, the road was and still is the practice, practice, and more practice of meditation and everything that goes into the preparation for meditation. This includes eating healthy food, yoga and exercise, singing and chanting love songs to all those (Sister Mary, Thamanya Sayadaw, Kalu Rinpoche and so many others I had the pleasure of spending time with) who were such excellent examples of how to work with love in difficult times. It includes nurturing those I love and following through with my relationships. It includes being gentle with myself and continuing to build awareness of my actions. Continuing the practice.

This is the heart of my tending the fire. Meditation is where I started this book, and meditation is where I would like to end. So, with a humble heart . . .

We begin by setting our intention to express good will in our own way, toward ourselves, our Elders, and others (see appendix: Meditation Application).

Consciousness does not have a self until it is recognized. I still have much work to do on myself. Becoming a mature person takes practice, practice, and more practice. The same is true as we become a diverse community—with respect and kindness being a priority, along with an openness to learn from other communities globally. Finally, we need to be joyful about our uniqueness. This also takes practice—community and individual practice—and more practice.

Peace be with you.

Appendix

Agent Orange and Forgiveness p. 62

This is what I wrote in 2011 and presented in August at the 50th Anniversary Conference of the spraying of Agent Orange held in Hanoi, Vietnam.

The time is now! War has a beginning, middle, and an end. Another way of saying this is: There is a disagreement, violent interaction, and reconciliation.

Right now, we are at the point of reconciliation. It is a time for acknowledgement, taking care of one another, person to person, country to country, and healing the damage done to our planet. This requires much integrity from all involved. Today marks the 50th, or one-half century, anniversary of the spraying of Agent Orange.

I am a disabled vet now; I was a nineteen-year-old door-gunner then, when I participated in spraying the deadly chemicals from a helicopter. I didn't know how devastating their impact on all living things would be. We were not informed about the details. It was almost like any other mission until we actually got to the site. From that moment on, the four of us—two pilots and two gunners—went silent. It felt as if we were witnessing a mass funeral; everything was dead, especially nature. At that young age it was just a feeling I experienced, without intellectual understanding of the future impact of this mass destruction on the people and the land. We were soldiers. I recall a vet's comment at one of our meetings in America after I shared about this mission; he said, "If I knew what you were doing, I would have shot you down myself."

After the First Agent Orange Conference in 2006 we toured the country, visited victims (many of whom are dead by now), and are being replaced by a never-ending stream of new victims. The chemicals have affected the genetics, and have caused mutations that are expressed in a myriad of diseases. Today a part of this country is uninhabitable because of the contamination Agent Orange left behind.

Our original five-member team (Marine, Air Force, and Army) has lost two, Joan Duffy and David Cline. All five of us had shared intimate social meetings with fellow soldiers, who at one time had fought against us. In one of those conversations, one of my new friends and I realized that we were in the same firefight. A comment that stood out was, "If we could only get an acknowledgement from the American government," healing could begin.

Many years later, after fully understanding the devastating power of this chemical, it has been impossible to fathom how we as humans could authorize such an act.

Personally, I became addicted to heroin and other drugs as a way to cope with my traumatic experiences. Later I had the insight and support to seek professional help for my problems. Finally, my conscious healing process began in 1999 and recently came full circle at an international Buddhist teacher's conference. It takes time to heal, like taking care of a fruit tree that has been damaged. The most important thing that I have learned is to never stop giving wise attention to the task, especially when it involves oneself; just continue to make adjustments.

Standing here now at the age of 64 and getting a little closer to the end of my life cycle, I ask myself, "What do I have to give that would promote some kind of justice, retribution, or healing?" I am not a lawyer so I can't create a good argument; I am not a medical doctor so I can't administer medicine; I am not a construction worker, plumber, or electrician. However, I am a Meditation Teacher, and once was a Forest Buddhist Monk in the monasteries of Thailand and Myanmar. I had the privilege of studying with esteemed Meditation Masters from Asia: Thamanya Sayadaw from Myanmar, Maha Boowa and Luang Por Sumedho from Thailand, and Venerable Thich Nhat Hanh from Vietnam. I can share my practice.

I attended high school in Japan, was a soldier in Vietnam, and finally came back to Asia to begin my healing process. I can and will offer my personal apology for the contamination of this beautiful country, which I have supported.

There is hope. We live in a different world compared to fifty years ago. I will name a few points that are relevant to the change that we are witnessing. One is the concept of Green Living, which promotes creative solutions to the environmental problems that plague us. Because of ignorance, we as custodians of our planet have committed so many unskillful acts, greedy consumption of fossil fuels, and soil contamination, to name a few . . . These and many other harmful actions have caused a shift in our climate and weather patterns. Hopefully, these dramatic results will bring us to our senses and put an end to our indifference.

Secondly, we are learning to embrace the concepts of diversity, interconnectedness of all living beings, and gender equality, all of which are aiding in our evolution as human beings.

Thirdly, we are a global group of wonderful people, supported by technology and the worldwide web. We can come to the table and have a conversation; we can all be heard.

We continue to learn from wars; hopefully, today's acknowledgments will accelerate our emotional and intellectual growth. This is not about what happened fifty years ago, it is much more important—this is about what we can do right now.

I am asking all those who are listening, near and far, to share this acknowledgment in your own words, with the proper authorities who can contribute to the change we seek.

I ask you and our earth to forgive me for the endless devastation that I have caused. Please, forgive me for this senseless act . . . please, forgive me for the destruction of our environment . . . please, forgive me for spraying Agent Orange that has affected our soldiers, innocent people, and our planet . . . please, forgive me for causing the catastrophic illnesses that are seeded in our children and children to come . . . please forgive me.

Since the beginning of time, whenever we encounter some-thing that's bigger than we are, we need to counter the situation by giving appropriate attention to something that is bigger than our sense of self, in order to restore balance.

From the goodness that has arisen from my talk, may the guides of great virtue, our mothers, our fathers, and our relatives, and especially all the virtual leaders of the world— be called into the circle. Those who are friendly, indifferent, or hostile—may all take heed of the injustice that has been done. Through this action may all become alerted to supporting the process of acknowledgement, so that we can cultivate a greener planet and healthier people.

I ask those people in positions of authority and the guiding spirit of our earth to give attention to this matter. Through this act of sharing, may the healing sun shine on all who have been effected directly or indirectly by this deadly chemical.

Ayurvedic Medicine p. 261

Ayurvedic medicine, the science of life, is an ancient system from India. It reminds me of Sister Mary's way of healing on Pawleys Island. She had no knowledge of medical doctors; her way of medical care came from the ancient African system called *Voodoo*. On the island it was called *Root*. Herbal medicine and prayer was the heart of my childhood life. However, unlike Ayurveda or Ayurvedic medicine, very little of my childhood medical system was kept intact.

Ayurvedic cleansing, called *Punchakarma*, is about cleaning your system of various toxicants. For example, can you imagine getting a warm oil massage with four hands on your body? Then someone puts you in a steam box, after which you get a delicious vegetarian meal plus various other kinds of treatments—every day for nine to thirty days.

Briefly, in Ayurvedic medicine, each of us is made up of three kinds of subtle energies. These subtle energies are viewed as three combinations of elemental forms–they are the Doshas. The fire-water dosha is Pitta, the air-space dosha is Vata, and the water-earth dosha is Kapha. Doshas are how the physiology of the body is organized, and a balance of the Doshas is required for good health. Pitta dosha works with our metabolism; this includes our digestion, liver, skin, eyes, thoughts, and even our awareness. Vata works with movement, separation, deconstruction, including our colon, lower back and pelvis, bones, ears, skin, mind, and senses. Kapha works with cohesion, endurance, reconstruction; this includes our stomach, heart, lungs, joints, tongue, and nervous system. "Tending the Fire" is a sign of respect for all three *Doshas*, as we strive to become a *mature* person. I use the word "mature" carefully, rather than "awakened" or "enlightened."

Breath Meditation Methods p. 109

Breath meditation methods include awareness of the breath only at the nostrils, awareness of breath and rising and falling of the chest, and awareness of the abdomen swelling and collapsing. Other methods involve following the journey of the breath and feeling the breath energy moving from the core of the torso to the surface of the body. These are some of the different applications and methods to begin your meditation practice.

Desire pp. 56, 121

Desire is one of the three primary forces of destruction investigated by the Buddha during his quest to understand the nature of suffering. The other two are hatred and greed. Let's explore desire; it can become a healthy tool. When you are in a destructive state or your behavior is out of control because of desire, you might as well jump into a hornet's nest. Who knows how many times you'll get stung? But it's going to happen. Getting stung generates suffering for yourself and others. Our prison system is filled with those who have been unable to control desire.

Earlier in my life I did not have access to the teachings of Buddhist psychology to work with the raw energy of desire in a healthy way. Later I learned that one could practice restraint of one's body, speech, and mind; this provides the opportunity to be discerning in a situation that involves desire. This discernment enhances the practice of mindfulness; when faced with desire it is helpful to be mindful of one's behavior, feelings, and mental states. As a quality of concentration begins to deepen through persistent focus, the resulting tranquility can bring balance that helps to support healthy decisions.

However, until a certain level of concentration has been achieved, there can still be distraction that may come in through any of the sense doors including our internal senses. The skill of discrimination needs continuous cultivation. Discrimination is one of the qualities that most helped me in facing desire in my own life. Desire can therefore be a powerful tool in training one's mind—it can lead to suffering, but in working with it skillfully with concentration, persistence, and discrimination it can be part of an active practice that frees us from suffering.

Desire is how we were all born, and it's how families, cities, and communities are created; but it has been looked upon in some meditation arenas as an unskillful process because of its association with suffering. However, there are ways to utilize desire as a skillful tool toward awakening— for example, the desire to maintain a level of good concentration to get through one's daily activities, or the desire to attend ninety Alcohol Anonymous meetings in ninety days, or the desire to become more skillful in one's practice, or the desire to experience the body as constantly full with breath energies. Desire used with intention and wisdom is a wonderful asset in furthering one's practice and growth.

Dharma/Dhamma p. 241

These two words basically have the same meaning—to cultivate respect toward natural, sacred, and spiritual embodiment of the cosmic flow of the universes and all that they contain. We can also learn how to cultivate that natural path. This is why, in Thailand, the language sound of nature (Tham-ma) and Dharma are the same. As we learn how nature flows within our bodies and all things, a compassionate and respectful awareness arises.

The Eightfold Path p. 166

The Eightfold Path, which is the fourth of the Four Noble Truths, includes: right view, right thought, right speech, right action, right livelihood, right effort, right mindfulness, and right concentration. The Pali word for "right" is *samma*, which means thoroughly, to the point where awareness sees and understands the cause and the effect.

This made sense to me; it was something that I could work with through my activities. Years ago when I first began to work with these eight skills, my attitude began to change. For example, I would say, "Today or this week I will work with right speech." During lunchtime, I would take a few minutes and evaluate the different communications I was engaged in during the morning hours. I would look to see how I could make my communications more skillful, especially the ones that I thought were good. Then I would do the same exercise in the evening.

I understood that meditation is actually about training one's mind. Just like when I was a kid, my mother and grandmother would ask, "Did you wash your hands? Did you brush your teeth?" and sometimes I would forget. But after many repetitions of doing it, my mind was trained with that skill. I worked the other factors of The Eightfold Path but have yet to come to the point where I can say that the skills have been mastered.

I still need to work on what I call buttons. Buttons are issues, situations, items, people, concepts, point of view, and other things that I am attached to. There is nothing that can push your buttons more than those people who are close to you. I didn't think I had any more buttons to push. What a joke on me! If you want to skillfully cultivate the human spirit, work on what pushes your buttons. I eventually realized that this Buddhist concept is a lifetime practice. If one is skillful and persistent enough, the path is endless.

The Eight Elders are responsible for three areas of training one's mind. The Eight Elders are the eight perspectives that the Buddha noted as The Eightfold Path. The three areas are conduct, concentration, and wisdom.

These three areas have many levels. They range from the farthest part of our cosmos to writing our names. I will just speak of a few simple areas, because of my love for simplicity.

Conduct includes the cultivation of respect for one's body. The body is made of all the elements of nature; therefore, conduct also means having respect for the environment. If we abuse the body, the awareness that resides has repercussions. The size of those repercussions depends on the level of abuse. For example, if I drink too much alcohol, it is taxing on my liver and my decision-making. I experience the suffering first, and then it affects others who are close to me and even not so close to me.

Similarly, if I abuse the environment that I live in, it will affect everyone else who lives in that environment. For example, our planet is in a crisis situation because of abuse by us as individuals, families, groups, cities, towns, provinces, states, and countries. Al Gore, the former Vice President, has toured the planet giving lectures informing us of the crisis situation that we are in as a planet. Not skillfully learning about how to train my mind regarding conduct can destroy both me and my environment.

Conduct is not a law that man made; it is the law of nature. I said earlier that our bodies are from nature. It didn't take long for me to understand that there is a natural rule, and I have a choice to either respect it or suffer the consequences. I am sure that we all remember the times that nature and our bodies just did their own thing. Because of having consciousness, I was able to bring some reasoning to these unexpected circumstances. However, to come to the absolute understanding of a situation is mind boggling, because of the law of cause and effect. The absolute cause and effect of anything is endless. My teacher instructed me to just work with what is, and try my best to be skillful with that. After getting into a situation and realizing that it is causing harm to me or someone else, then I stop what I am doing.

Concentration is the second group of Elders. I continue to realize the importance of the application of cultivating concentration. I will never forget some of my first experiences with the result of the cultivation of this technique. The feeling of tranquility was overwhelming. It was difficult to separate myself from any other object. The sensations of bliss and being in a zone reminded me of my days riding the "white horse" of heroin. Hafiz, an eighteenth century poet and master at training the mind relates the result of being concentrated as being "drunk on God."

At one of my first Vipassana meditation retreats with Jacqueline Schwartz-Mandell and Jack Kornfield, I recall considering if the experience of being concentrated was better than marijuana, acid, and heroin. I wonder if it is better than sex—"no way." If it isn't, then it sure is up there in the world of addiction, or is it just a natural thing? I said to myself, "I wonder if I could package this stuff." This was my delusional self speaking. Hell, all the other drugs have a price tag with regard to money. Then I realized that it is packaged, and it does have a price tag—this is America—and I paid for it by coming to this retreat.

It took a while for me to understand the process of concentration. I remember a chanting and silent sitting period at the Hanuman Tape Library in Santa Cruz, California. I looked over at a female friend and I could see through her body. After one of the sitting periods, I moved my arm to begin getting up, and noticed from the arm movement that I had many, many, many arms. That experience felt like I had dropped several hits of purple microdot acid.

When Sabine, my life partner, and I went home to Pawleys Island, South Carolina, we went to visit my uncle who lives in another town. He is my dad's brother. After he got through giving me forty-five minutes of tongue-lashing for not being around, he went upstairs and came back down with a gallon-sized glass apple-cider bottle with red liquid in it. He set it on the table and invited me to partake of his home-made "moonshine" that had been seasoned with cherry. He said that he had had it for several years, and only pulled it out on special occasions. Sabine wouldn't touch it. It was as smooth as silk going down to my stomach. After three cups, everything appeared to be double, triple, etc. The feeling of tranquility was all over me. But clarity of seeing things as they are was not there because my mind was dull from the alcohol. It took a while for me to become comfortable with and get used to this level of sensation.

I am sure that we all have some stories with regard to this sensational effect of concentration. Knowing that it could be induced without any outside agent was the surprise for me. In the late '90s various news magazines carried articles stating that the brain has two potent chemicals. One is dopamine, which makes you feel extremely relaxed. The other is endorphins, which make you feel very excited. Some of the agents that can activate these chemicals are heroin, happiness, coffee, meditation, cocaine, exercise, shopping, sex and sensuality, yoga, music, and grief, just to name a few.

Concentration alone can cause one to get out of balance. During one whole week of the Rains Retreat the only thing I practiced was concentration. This resulted in a very painful situation wherever my awareness would go across my body. It felt like I was being sliced by a knife or stung by red ants. I could not stop this process and didn't know what was causing it. During my interview with a more senior monk, he explained what had happened. He said, "Just work on spaciousness for a few days and balance the concentration practice with insight practice." That took care of the pain. I was practicing concentration but wasn't balancing it with mindfulness and insight. When concentration isn't balanced, it is like driving a vehicle while intoxicated. One is susceptible to dangerous encounters.

Wisdom is the final group of Elders. Getting to know these Elders requires more practice, as opposed to simply reading about them. Wisdom in particular only comes from the experience I gain from my practice. For example, a very wise person may give me some advice or teachings. What is coming out of another's mouth is his or her wisdom. However, what is coming into my mind is words. My mind and body need to assimilate those words through my own process, and that may result in some insight. If so, that becomes my wisdom.

The same is true whenever I am doing my own formal practice. At the close of my sitting, walking, lying, and standing practice, I always do an evaluation that takes only a few seconds. I ask myself, "What did I learn? Did I get any insight about this particular practice? If and when I do it again, what could I do to be even more skillful?" This has always been an effective tool for me because mediation practice is about training the mind.

Another very helpful skill in the cultivation of wisdom is working with discrimination. This word can be a little more user-friendly than the word wisdom, which can seem too overpowering or intimidating. I have found that this process helps me to understand the nature of my suffering. Sometimes I couldn't cultivate my path alone and needed to seek advice from others.

Working with conduct, concentration, and wisdom have been healing. They all dance together after you get to know them. I feel that it's like a show and we all are on stage doing this cosmic dance with one another. Conduct has the components of speech, action, and livelihood. How I dress and move my body, my expression, and the tone of my words all make a statement. Concentration has the components of the application of effort or persistence, the many levels of mindfulness, and the abundance of concentration skills. Wisdom has the components of having a healthy view and being able to resolve internal conflicts.

Working with an exercise on a daily basis continues to be rewarding.

Elements Ayurvedic p. 261

Understand that most cultures have a different view of the elements. Here is a twenty-four-hour view from Ayurvedic that's out of the Hindu culture and Vedic system. (The active elements dominate particular times of day.)

The earth element does not change; it represents structure.

- The active elements (water, fire, and air) influence nature.
- Each element dominates during a four-hour period of two twelve-hour cycles of a day.

- From six to ten when the air is heavy, cold, and damp with dew—the water element dominates.
- From ten to two the sun burns through the heavy atmosphere and the stars begin a steadiness that makes it look brighter—the fire element dominates.
- From two to six the wind produces its cool and dry influence—the air element dominates.

The Four Immeasurables p. 240

Loving-Kindness
Loving-Kindness is the first Immeasurable skill; it is wanting all beings to be happy. This love is unconditional and it requires courage and self-acceptance. It is the wish that all beings, without exception, be happy.

The meditation on loving-kindness: one extends loving kindness to those whom one feels close to, to others whom one may know only slightly or not know at all, then to all beings in all the realms of existence. The practice of loving-kindness entails unconditional acceptance for oneself and others, and the cultivation of boundless tranquility and confidence. In the early years of my practice, I used to distract myself by always being helpful toward someone else, but giving very little help to myself. Traumatic experiences can play a part in avoiding or not wanting to give that tender loving kindness to oneself. Even during my Rains Retreat in Myanmar, I had just sat with the pain and wouldn't move, which caused permanent damage to my spinal system.

Compassion
Compassion wants all beings to be free from suffering. Compassion refers to an unselfish emotion that gives one a strong desire in wanting to help others. It is the wish to free all beings from the sufferings of cyclic existence and to become fully mature.

The meditation on compassion has to reach beyond the beings that one loves or cares for. Compassion has to be extended to all beings in all the realms of existence. The second Immeasurable, compassion, is sweet and juicy due to its close connection with sensuality, and it takes a serious mindfulness practice to make sure the right intention is there. I had to constantly remind myself, "It's compassion, not passion, Bro . . ." In the old days, I used to turn a friendly compassionate relationship into a steamy passionate encounter, regardless of the conditions. Ethics, what's that? The end result was always, "Whoa, what happened there?"

This practice was difficult for me, I think, because of my temperament: I always wanted so much passion. Sensuality was a part of my childhood within the extended family system in a wonderful way. However, being born in a community where one's mind is conditioned for passion can cultivate trouble. Also, dealing with sensuality can be difficult, especially for those who have been sexually traumatized. It's possible for a person to be sexually traumatized even when he/she is not physically touched. As you can see, the practice of loving-kindness may involve serious work on oneself.

When the intent is clear, compassion cultivates a sweet juice . . . *Yahman!*

Sympathetic Joy

The third of the Four Immeasurable skills is gladness or joy. Sympathetic joy is being happy for all being's good fortune or happiness. It is the potential of bliss and happiness of all beings, as they can all become mature people.

The meditation on sympathetic joy is good medicine for depression for oneself but, more importantly, it is rejoicing in others' progress. This application is the opposite of jealousy and resentment; it's about cultivating a healthy attitude that is beneficial for oneself and others.

The energy has lightness and one becomes elated. This is not the superficial selfish joy of a salesman nor simply bringing gladness and joy upon oneself, but also bringing joy to others, sometimes without words even being spoken.

This energy can make anger melt like butter. I experienced this genuine gladness when it was time to get out of high school and college, and also on my first day of school each year. That feeling of the first day of school was off the charts. I had already set my intent on that wonderful sensation of seeing old friends and meeting new ones. Part of the skill of gladness is remaining mindful, because gladness can become superficial.

Equanimity

Equanimity, the fourth Immeasurable skill, means to have a balanced and tranquil mind. It is an unselfish, detached state of mind that helps to discriminate what is a negative and what is a positive action.

Equanimity is the basis for loving-kindness, compassion, and sympathetic joy for another's happiness as well as one's own happiness.

The meditation on equanimity is looking at or visualizing someone until you see yourself in that person; there is no inequality, just a pure state of wholesome oneness. The light within me is the light within you. The final skill of boundlessness is equanimity. Equanimity is sort of invisible, but the practices of loving-kindness, compassion, and gladness all support me toward mastery of equanimity. As you work with the others, you are actually being trained in working with equanimity. An example is watching someone keep their composure even when they are arguing. Doing this practice includes making sure that the body is not too tense and not too soft.

Equanimity is noticing how to move from the gross energetic qualities to the more subtle qualities, like a New Mexico raven taking off. That raven stands at least two feet high with a wingspan the size of a swan and a body three times its size. It just sits there, then with intent it spreads its wings and flaps to get that enormous body into the air. The wings keep flapping as the bird gets higher and higher and then the flapping is less and less until it finally stops altogether. Then that bird just works with the subtle air currents to move along. This is how one moves toward the mastery of equanimity in practice.

Four Noble Truths p. 149

1. There is suffering, stress, or disease.
2. What is its cause?
3. Curing it.
4. The Eightfold Path, a prescription to work on living a healthier life.

Four Right Exertions p. 257

"Right effort" is one of the skills on The Eightfold Path. The traditional language translated by Thanissaro Bhikkhu is guarding, abandoning, cultivating, and maintaining. I will make it more personal.

The process of "guarding" requires one to be mindful of the many good skills and qualities that one has accumulated. So often in the past, during my non-monastic life, I had completed a meditation retreat and done very little reflection on the insight that I gained from that retreat. I had not integrated my practice into my daily life. By not doing this, the old patterns I was accustomed to had slowly taken precedence again.

"Guarding" is guarding against unskillful qualities coming in and destroying the skillful ones you're trying to cultivate and maintain. "Abandoning" refers to abandoning the states of mind that come up and say, "Was this the right thing to do?" It has already been done and can't be retracted. So many times, I have done something and gone for days putting myself down, wondering if I did the right thing. I have learned that before every decision, one needs to ask, "Am I working toward healing myself and others, or creating more suffering?" After the decision has been made, if I notice that it is causing more harm than good, I will stop it if I can.

When I am exercising mindfulness, not only am I abandoning old qualities, but I am also cultivating new qualities within myself. It is like in Alcoholics Anonymous when one makes a commitment to do ninety meetings in ninety days; there are days that you don't want to go because of whatever, but you find a way to attend. That's "cultivating."

The fourth and final part of this effort is maintaining "balance of mind." This is where I bring the process of mindfulness up front. I understand what needs to be done with regard to guarding, abandoning, and cultivating. To exercise these functions, I need to maintain consistency with being mindful. Understanding the importance of applying this view can't be stressed enough.

When I studied with Tibetan master Sogyal Rinpoche in Santa Cruz, at one of his retreats he started talking about the importance of "understanding." Every sentence contained the word "understanding." If you do not understand, how do you know wrong view? If you do not understand, how do you know if you have faith, energy, attachment, or right view? I realized that mindfulness gives birth to understanding. This went on for about thirty minutes. Rinpoche concluded with, "Do you understand?" We were frozen and needed to take a break, and no one asked or talked about understanding, because it had thoroughly washed into our bones.

Householder Buddha p. 149

According to the Theravada lineage, a Buddha is a single person who becomes awakened or mature; he/she is completely free of attraction, aversion, or any sense of "I am," and is not involved in a sexual relationship. According to Zen, Tibetan, and other lineages views, a person does not have to leave his/her family nor live a life of celibacy in order to awaken. This would be a Householder Buddha.

Layperson Taking Refuge p.148

A layperson is a person who is non-monastic and has decided to practice the principles of taking refuge in the Buddha, Dharma, and Sangha. Taking refuge in the Buddha means that I will practice toward becoming a fully mature person in this lifetime. Taking refuge in the Dharma means that I will compassionately, respectfully, and with joy take care of my body, speech, and mind. This will reflect into the world I live in. I will cradle the natural teachings like a mother taking care of her newborn child. Taking refuge in the Sangha means that I will maintain my practice in a community of other committed practitioners and that I will give support to my friends, relatives, and all those in need. The Sangha provides endless support for our growth in the practice; we support each other to succeed in awakening. At the end of each ceremony, Kalu Rinpoche always tells us: "Look around you and see your brothers and sisters for this life."

I remember first moving to the "hood," usually a lower socio-economic neighborhood, where it is customary to meet the people up or down the road from you, or across the street, next door, above, or below you. My move was from Pawleys Island to Myrtle Beach, South Carolina. People lived in apartments, and you could hear conversations and other things going on in the next apartment. This was my first time living in such a close proximity with people.

My mother wanted my younger brother and me to stay with her and go to elementary school. It was the usual story for so many single-parent families. When we left for school, which was within walking distance, she would leave for work. The neighbors would take care of us, if and when we got home before she did. Several of the neighbors were single-parent women themselves. I learned that this hood was a community that took care of each other, which was the same on the island except there was distance between families.

Back home on Pawleys Island, on special holidays we would go visiting throughout the community. During my childhood years, when someone's house was on fire it would usually burn all the way down. Afterward, the community would come together and help that person rebuild their house. I am sure that there are a lot of people who know about community, and yet there are those who don't.

These days, sangha specifically means a Buddhist community that one has been practicing with for a period of time. Most sanghas try to cultivate an environment that exemplifies right livelihood, right speech, and right action. Of course conflicts do come up in these sanghas; these conflicts may promote health or they can destroy or make the community toxic. If nothing ever happens, how could a community grow?

With that said, it is very important that we as individuals try our best to be proficient about wise action and livelihood. Cultural change takes lifetimes, even if a particular culture would want a change to happen. It is up to each individual to make a change within, which then reflects outward. An awakened person has never changed a culture in a day, a week, a month, or a year. Putting sugar in a glass of water takes time before the water is sweetened; and effort decreases the time, but it still takes an immeasurable amount of time. A layperson is someone who walks with "grace."

Levels of Mindfulness p. 233

The first level is mindfulness of the body: taking into account one's nervous energies, the energies that produce tension in the muscular system, and the energies that produce holding of the breath, resulting in various body sensations. Working with the breath can support the relaxation and calming of all these energies. I needed to be particularly mindful of these various systems of the body in order to stay calm.

The second level of mindfulness is noticing one's feelings. In the past, when I heard a snake make that maddening hissing sound, I would feel a shift from dancing with the Thailand heat and humidity that had finally begun to feel pleasant, to an extremely unpleasant sensation that made me want to be instantly back home, anywhere but where I was.

To feel neither pleasant nor unpleasant feelings in the body is a wonderful skill to cultivate, because it puts one's perception into a neutral zone. With unpleasant sensations, mental qualities like fear, dislike, anger, and restlessness tend to present themselves. With pleasant sensations, mental qualities of liking and wanting more tend to present themselves. Most of us have conditioned our minds to liking or disliking. With a neutral sensation we have an opportunity to cultivate a middle ground. In the sitting posture, the skill used in cultivating neither pleasant or unpleasant sensations is focusing on whatever the body is in contact with—the clothing on the body, the air moving across the skin, or the hair of the body.

The third of the four levels of mindfulness is mindfulness of one's mind, especially the unskillful qualities. Now, my mind had these basic unskillful categories (over-indulgence, a strong dislike for certain situations and people, and delusional thinking) that I somehow thought had been designed especially for me. These were just a few of the busload of unskillful qualities that I possessed. Samuel L. Jackson coined a popular phrase in one of his movies, "I can do that." Well, perhaps he could, but it's delusional when you don't have any insight into what you are doing. Insight comes from practice. Delusion occurs when you can't experience things as they are. There were times when I could bring my delusion into reality, but mostly it remained pie-in-the-sky. I had learned that the best medicine for delusion, or any unskillful state of mind, was to skillfully practice, practice, and practice. That was why I needed to practice mindfulness as my personal trainer, to help me accept that these qualities existed inside of me. Sometimes I thought it was one of the prerequisites for being human.

The fourth level of mindfulness is noticing the various mental qualities in your mind and the objects of the mind, including images. In this situation I needed to be mindful of several things. One was to ask myself, "Will I be creating more suffering or working toward healing it when this action is taken?" Through experience and consistency of working with these levels, one becomes mindful of Dharma, which is the traditional name of the fourth level.

Mahasi Sayadaw 1904 -1982 pp. 21, 99,111, photos

One of the most influential Vipassana/Insight meditation teachers in Myanmar and other countries in Asia, including the western world. He is the Elder at the Insight Meditation Society in Massachusetts, as *Ajahn* Chah is the Elder at Spirit Rock Meditation Center in California.

Meditation Applications p. 263

The preparation and intent can be the most significant part of the practice. There are basically two things going on. One is nature, which includes the body (elements), and the other is what quality of consciousness is happening (this has an influence on the body).

This can be difficult if anger or animosity is already on the surface of one's consciousness. However, if good intention is applied, the intensity of a mind poisoned by Mara is decreased. I can vouch for this.

Next comes the expression of our loving kindness—in words, songs, chanting, mantras, dancing, yoga, playing a musical instrument, listening to a wonderful talk, or eating healthy food. These experiences are our own creative expression verbally or non-verbally toward our inner world. The more sweet love we can generate inward, the greater will be our self-assurance for riding the tiger of meditation, and for simply living our lives.

After these preparations, we are ready to get inside what I call the space module where we practice concentration and insight. Concentration attends to all the various items or control buttons of the space module. As I said earlier, there are four basic postures—lying, standing, walking and sitting. A posture should be assumed that is not too comfortable or uncomfortable. If you are looking for a posture that's overly comfortable, the intent becomes comfort seeking, so that when discomfort arises we have to deal with mental constructs—like being pissed off and pushing away the discomfort to seek comfort. Some level of discomfort is going to arise, because it is natural, and we accept this. Seeking comfort is unintentionally setting oneself up for disappointment in any of the postures.

Now we bring our awareness to the sensation of the breath. This awareness should hold an investigative quality about what flavor of breath is happening. There are four basic ways our bodies constantly breathe: long in-breath and long out-breath, long in-breath and short out-breath, short out-breath and long in-breath, short in-breath and short out-breath. The ancient teachings speak of this. Within these four basic ways, there are at least one hundred different flavors; for example, coarse, heavy, slight, soft, misty, cool, warm, long, or short. There are also breaths for which your brain can't find words, and that's okay too. It is the knowing within the experience that's insightful.

Back in the space module, we have been through the safety checks—setting our intent for this meditation session, acknowledging our elders, sending good will to all people, sending loving kindness to those that are close, doing a few minutes of yoga, assuming an alert and comfortable posture, and being mindful of our surroundings. There is no specific order for the safety checks—and we may want to add or delete some checks—but eventually the controls of our space module are ready. As we notice the various qualities of the breath and making subtle inner physical adjustments, we are finally in the air, headed for inner space. We are finally ready to settle into the posture of choice and now being mindful of breath.

It is important to maintain a subtle level of concentration, for various unknown or surprising obstacles (physical or mental) can arise. I like to always keep the Four Noble Truths in the heart of my consciousness—that there is suffering, the cause of it, stopping it, and cultivating The Eightfold Path. This is like keeping your hands on the wheel or keeping God in your heart. If you are prepared for obstacles that may arise, the meditation can be simple. Learning to concentrate with mindfulness of body, feelings, mind, and objects of mind is an excellent way to begin.

Eventually your defilements arise in the form of mental and/or physical discomfort. The dark side of our sense of self, from the most subtle to the most disgusting, inevitably comes to the surface. These are the things that you do not like about yourself, things that you have been avoiding, suppressing, or covering up.

All this takes precision, heartfelt kindness to oneself, joy, and patience—especially if we have fallen into a place of self-hatred, because of doing something that is wrong! It is serious hard work; however, we can bring inner joy with just a slight smile for example. The result is a great treasure— generosity towards ourselves and towards our community.

Mingun Sayadaw 1911-1993 photos

Known for the embodiment of the Buddhist Canonical Text. At the sixth Buddhist Council in Myanmar, 1954-1956, a question was on the floor. He began responding, and according to my monastic elders, about seventy-four hours later Sayadaw had repeated word for word, page for page (16,000 pages), the Buddhist Canonical Text. Mingun's hometown is where I received the blessing from this one hundred years of age Venerable Shwe U'Min Taw Ya. In this town, now known as Mingun, each of these monks is referred to as the Great Sayadaw.

Seven Factors for Enlightenment or Awakening p. 225

The seven factors for enlightenment provide a brilliant process for training the mind. It is also a process within a process. The first factor, mindfulness, can be looked upon as one's personal trainer, meaning that it is a skill that applies to the entire practice. The other six are grouped in two pairs of three. The second to the fourth factors— persistence, investigation, and rapture—are wonderful skills to raise one's level of alertness and energy. The fifth to seventh factors—bliss, concentration, and equanimity—are skills to even out one's energy or to bring stabilization into the practice.

The first factor is cultivating a state of mindfulness. With regard to walking with my friend, I had been mindless in awareness of my breath, the movement of my feet and my body, my speech, my environment, and including my friend. After I decided to establish skillful mindfulness in my walking, this led me into the second factor.

The second factor includes an investigation of the qualities in one's body and mind. The pain in my feet and my complaining had only made things worse—because of the increase in muscular tension, thus inviting more of "my cousins" in, meaning *Mara* or the forces of unskillful thoughts and behaviors.

The third factor arises because of "wanting"—it is the persistence to see things through. Pain has a way of making one gather up right effort for this. As I began to investigate the various qualities of my mental state, the desire of persistence and accepting the need to become skillful in keeping my belly soft had become my reality. Slowly, the hardness of my body began to melt down and muscle tension decreased as the breath energy and sound of silence became dominant.

The fourth factor is rapture, which results from the breath energy. Rapture has an assortment of feelings and sensations. It is like going into an ice cream store and finding many different flavors or qualities. Those qualities include a feeling of warmth to tremendous heat all over your body, a feeling of being cool to very cold, a sensation of stepping through a spider web, a sensation of flying, a feeling that your body is spinning, a sensation of warm rain coming from all directions, and a feeling of being stabbed many times. With rapture, what feels good to one person may not feel good to another person. Also, what may feel wonderful in the beginning may change to unpleasant feelings, and the other way around.

The fifth factor has a few names—serenity, calmness, peacefulness, and bliss. I like to refer to it as getting a dose of moonshine, the kind of alcohol we made in the swamps that could start an automobile. It can be like sitting in a hot tub or a nice bath where mindfulness turns into mindlessness. One needs to be aware of this state of absorption. Having awareness of one's body and viewing it as a container helps because you need to know when your container is full. At that point mindfulness shifts to the sixth factor.

The sixth factor is the cultivation of concentration, which results in tranquility. The clarity or acuteness of the sense doors is unbelievable until you are used to it. Understanding concentration is a process.

Equanimity is the seventh and final factor, which I like to refer to as the essence of mindfulness. It comes with practice, because it has a multitask function. For example, it enhances an awareness of the quality of breath and inner speech, and awareness of the arising and passing away of body tension, thoughts, emotions and sensations, to name a few. Like a wheel with many spokes that's turning, it appears as if a lot is going on. However, if you are the center of the wheel, the spokes all come to oneness; the wheel turns without effort as we mindfully bring awareness to the rising and falling away of thoughts, emotions, and sensations in the great space of mind.

Sound Meditation p. 48

To explore sound meditation, you need to begin by finding a comfortable sitting, lying, or standing posture, as opposed to walking. When you feel comfortable, begin to feel and hear whatever sound the body is making, like the sound and/or sensation of the heart beating or the continuous hum; then extend to the sound outside of the body. If you are inside of a building, begin with the sound that feels closest to you. In the beginning, acknowledge with your inner voice the word "softly," or whatever kind of sound is registering for you. For example, "bubbles" is the sound that I am hearing coming from my fish tank.

What's the importance of the acknowledgement? Understanding that the mind has the ability to perceive itself, which is what we call "I, self, or me." I perceive it as a spoiled child that at times "can't get no satisfaction," as Mick Jagger of the Rolling Stones sings. Some people have referred to this "I" as "monkey mind," and pointed out that it is only satisfied from moment to moment. However, if you satisfy its curiosity, it will eventually leave you alone. That's why it is important to make the acknowledgement. You are letting the "I" know that you know what is happening.

The acknowledgement needs to happen only a few times and then you can go to another new sound, and then another. For some people, depending on their temperament, the acknowledgement may need to happen for several years. That is what happened to me. Because of various traumas during my life, the mental states were at times like a wolf pack to my perception. I had migraine headaches at least twice a month. I would get angry at anything, go to bed and wake up with anger. Those mental states would cloud my view of seeing things as they are. I would make a delusional comment without knowing that I was out of touch with reality. I believe that trauma of any magnitude is the biggest poison to one's body, speech, and mind, thus unintentionally fostering hatred, greed, and delusional thinking.

The sound of silence is a primary vehicle for healing. It is accessible when there is contact with nature, because you are not concerned about the sound of silence when there is contact with nature but the joy and quietude of being. After the Vietnam War many traumatized veterans lived as a group in the natural surroundings in Hawaii. Traumatized people seem to gravitate to nature. Nature produces a calming effect. After all, our physical body is from nature, and of course will eventually go back.

In tending your fire, you let your awareness expand to outside of the building, and so on. Continue to get in touch with hearing the sound and feeling the sensations of the sound. For example, feel the sensation of a vehicle moving through your awareness. You may come to the realization that the most predominant or constant sound is coming from within. The next level is to realize that there is no difference between the concept of inside and outside. Why? Because if you think about it, everything is registered within. That's why the duality between inside and outside can drop away, because it will become a hindrance at the point of practice. Eventually duality itself can be dropped.

The highest form of sound meditation comes from within our bodies; it is not created or uncreated. *Ajahn* Sumedho is the most senior Western Theravadin monk whose lineage stems from the Thai Forest tradition of *Ajahn* Chah. *Ajahn* Sumedho has described this practice in detail. *The Sound of Silence* is included in his discourses. (*The Sound of Silence*, *Ajahn* Sumedho, Publisher Wisdom, 2007).

In various cultures this application of meditation practice has different names. For example, in India, it is called Nada practice. A wonderful and simple way to get attuned to it is put a seashell to your ears, and then put it down and notice if you can still hear it. If you would like to become more exotic, then go and hang out with the whales, or take a trip up to the ice caps. Listen to the ringing of a bell, and notice if it ever stops ringing; listen to the sound of silence. There are an infinite number of ways to get attuned to this inner sound—just hanging out at the ocean, or at a waterfall, listening to a humming bird, or bees, or music. Once you are attuned to it, then that becomes your object of meditation for the day, week, or year—especially when you are in a noisy situation. After a while, when you are just hanging out in a peaceful setting or practicing, that sound will always be more dominant.

Sunlun Meditation p. 110

Sunlun Sayadaw 1878-1952, developed Sunlun Meditation; he was influenced by Ledi Sayadaw, the most influential teacher of the nineteenth century in Myanmar. One of Sunlun Sayadaw's students was U'Vinaya Sayadaw, 1914-2012; he was a healthy eighty-five years of age when I studied with him.

This breath lineage brings to the practice the cultivating of physical rapid breathing in order to quickly develop deep concentration by focusing one's attention at the nostril. After fifteen to forty-five minutes in sitting or standing posture, one should bring oneself to sitting posture and transition into Vipassana or insight practice, with the object of meditation being the breath and pleasant body sensations. As the nervous and muscular systems release tension, the pleasant body sensations will eventually override the unpleasant sensations. This system is known as "The Yoga and Vipassana" or Sunlun Meditation, resulting in a deepening of concentration, insight, and healing. The application is that simple.

Working with the breath is an ancient practice. This application is used in various meditation and yoga traditions, sound methods, chanting, or singing. The breath or oxygen has the highest nutritional value, with water second, and food third. Most cultures have a method and name for rapid breathing. It is an ancient practice. Learning to use it is like learning how to use butter in cooking.

These meditation breath methods cause a deepening of insight, compassion, tranquility, joy, psychic abilities, and wisdom, along with a purification of the body, mind, and chakra systems.

This is not an application with lots of written materials. To my knowledge, the only written material from Myanmar regarding the Sunlun method is on my website: www.lifetransition.com.

Thirty-Two Parts of the Body p. 234

Reading this list every day, once a week, monthly, a few times a year will help to put your life into perspective. This is what the body is made of:

hair of the head	liver	blood
hair of the body	membranes	sweat
nails	spleen	fat
teeth	lungs	tears
skin	bowels	grease
flesh	entrails	spittle
sinews	undigested food	mucus
bones	excrement	oil of the joints
bone marrow	bile	urine
kidneys	phlegm	brain
heart	pus	

The "Thirty Two Parts of the Body" meditation practice is to begin with the first five, which is head hair, body hair, nails, teeth, and skin. Mindfully note one, then move awareness to what was noted, then move to the next one. Find a rhythm with the mindful noting/moving awareness process. When self-assured (in the beginning this may take several practice periods), shift attention from noting to just moving awareness to the five body parts. After seven days, practice it in reverse for seven days. Then begin again by adding another group to this process.

This, then, is the body—from the soles of the feet up, and down from the crown of the head—a sealed bag of skin filled with unattractive things.

Walking Instruction p. 205

One of the first things to understand about walking is proper posture. As a child, I had trouble learning to walk. I remember people guiding me, and at times I was placed in some kind of walking contraption. As the body continues to grow, and if one doesn't enter any kind of military, police, or firefighter organization, and/or receive proper walking instructions, then poor walking posture often develops. Also, once a person becomes an adult, various therapies may be required, such as structural integration massage, chiropractic, osteopathic, Pilates, or physical therapy.

For walking meditation, I like to have the visualization that a silver thread is attached to the center top of my head, and the other end is attached to a star. I let that thread pull me up, which expands my spinal system. This inner movement decreases the stress from my lower back and stretches my torso upwards. Secondly, there is another silver thread attached to my sternum, which is the breastbone of the chest. The other end of that thread is attached to a star that is far in front of me, and I feel a pull upwards at an angle. This lifts my chest, sets my shoulders more on top, and lowers my shoulder blades toward the earth. With the help of these two silver threads, I sense my body being weightless, soft, and strong.

The next point is putting awareness on the feet, because they are the farthest body parts from the brain. One is either paying attention to the feet by tracking the touch of the heels or to something else like the rhythm of breathing. Another level of walking meditation is to move the body slowly and acknowledge the motion of the feet.

The walking area should be level and between fifteen to twenty-seven steps in length. If it's shorter, the mind engages toward the end; if it's longer, the mind thinks that it is going somewhere. Both too short and too long have the tendency to create mental activities about things other than walking. For the purpose of training the mind, this formal practice should be done in the same area each time if you can.

One's awareness is focused on the feet, tracking the foot that's in the rear to the front, and feeling the touch of the heel. The feet may be inside a pair of shoes, yet the sensation of touch is still there. You can feel the contact-point when the weight of the body is on that spot.

With every step, you make a mental note of what is happening. This "noting" is important for several reasons. One is that we are letting the mind know that we know what is happening. Another reason is so that we won't be distracted by other thoughts. By creating this "noting" thought, our awareness is given something to be interested in. You acknowledge each movement of the foot with a deep, soft in-breath, saying with your inner voice the word "intention," and feeling the sensations of the body changing for the event that is about to happen.

Saying "lifting," you feel the muscular system supporting that event of the foot and the sensation of the foot rising up.

Saying "moving," you feel a different group of muscles supporting that event and the sensation of the foot moving forward through the air.

Saying "dropping," you feel another set of muscles supporting that event and the sensation of the foot going down with gravity.

Saying "touching," you feel another set of different muscles engaging to support that event and the sensation of the touch of the heel, even if it is inside a shoe.

Saying "placing," you feel another set of muscular tensions and the sensation of the foot getting grounded with the earth, even if it is inside a shoe on a different surface.

Saying "aligning," without moving the feet, and you feel the sensation of the body as it aligns itself for an upright posture.

Then you shift awareness to the foot in the rear, and begin a new cycle of sequences, and you notice that each sequence and each cycle is indeed new or original.

As the mind becomes trained, the noting can shift to being a choice, and the full emphasis can return to the touch. But this takes time. It may take three months.

When you are comfortable with the basic sequence of any of the two mentioned levels, you can do variations, which include adding one of the sense doors to the end of the sequence. For example, for the sense of smell you would say to yourself at the end of the sequence of placing: "smelling" and you would take a long in-breath, smelling and feeling the sensation of that particular air quality. This helps you to see that all along your walking path there are different qualities of smell.

After working with the smelling qualities for at least one round of walking, you bring in "tasting" along with the noting cycle. With your mouth slightly open, you take in a breath to taste the Air Element and notice the different qualities of taste during your round. The same process applies to hearing, seeing, and touching. All of these qualities are wonderful to work with and deepen our mindfulness of the body. In some cultures, certain sense doors are more developed than others. The various cultures that live in the forest or jungle and depend on that environment for food usually have a strong sense of smell. One needs to be careful when using these sense doors. I recall walking through the airport corridor, taking in a deep breath for smelling, and almost passing out. I instantly became nauseated because of the various mixtures of smells coming from whatever fragrances people were wearing.

Glossary

Abhidhamma. The Abhidhamma is the last of the three *pitakas* (Pali for basket) in the Pali Canon, the scriptures of Theravada Buddhism. It is an intricate scholastic analysis of the impersonal phenomena happening form moment to moment, containing psychology and philosophy.

ajahn. A monk who has completed ten rains retreats; the title *Ajahn* means the monk has authority to give meditation instructions.

Anathapindika's Park. The park known as Anathapindika's Park is in Jeta Grove. Anthapindika was a wealthy financier, who became a leading devotee of the Buddha. He gave Jeta Grove to the Buddha, having purchased it from Prince Jeta.

baba. Name given to an elder on Pawleys Island that exemplifies a mature person. In India they would also be called *Babaji* or *Baba* referring to an enlightened person. The name comes from the community; it is not a name given to oneself.

breath energy. This has been referenced as the light body, energy body, causal body, juice, smitten, the kayas. In current academic language, it is referred to as the subtle body (in the book *Religion and the Subtle Body in Asia and the West: Between Mind and Body* by Geoffrey Samuel and Jay Johnston, 2013).

Buddha Rupa. The Sanskrit and Pali term used in Buddhism for statues or models of the Buddha.

chedi. One of the alternative terms mainly used in Thailand for a Buddhist shrine. Other names: stupa in India and *pogoda* in Myanmar.

devotee. One who is ardently devoted to something, in this case a student of a spiritual teacher.

dharma, dhamma. Dhamma or dharma, in the language of Pali and Sanskrit, can have the following meanings in Buddhism: the practice of Sila, (conduct) Samadhi (highest level of concentration), Panna, (wisdom, discernment, discrimination) and the Laws of Nature. The Laws of Nature are a motherly tending to nature from a micro and macro perspective; also, this refers to the teachings of the Buddha. Therapeutically, it is cultivating peace inside one's self, relationship, families, communities, country, and our planet.

diang. A monk's bed outside.

japa mala or mala. A garland or set of beads used by Hindus and Buddhists, usually made from 108 beads. There are numerous explanations why there are 108 beads, with the number 108 bearing special religious significance in a number of Hindu and Buddhist traditions. There are also 108 beads in a rosary.

In practice, *malas* are used for keeping count while reciting, chanting, or mentally repeating a mantra or the name or names of a deity. One repetition is usually said for each bead while turning the thumb clockwise around each bead, though some traditions or practices may call for counterclockwise motion or specific finger usage. When arriving at the head bead, one turns the mala around and then goes back in the opposite direction. If more than 108 repetitions are to be done, then sometimes in Tibetan traditions, grains of rice are counted out before the chanting begins, and one grain is placed in a bowl for each 108 repetitions. Each time a full *mala* of repetitions has been completed, one grain of rice is removed from the bowl. Often, practitioners add extra counters to their *malas*, usually in strings of ten. These may be positioned differently depending on the tradition. For example some traditions place these strings after every tenth bead. This is an alternative way to keep track of large numbers, sometimes going into the hundreds of thousands, and even millions. Therapeutically, this practice can enhance memory, focus, and peacefulness, just to name a few. Mantras are typically repeated hundreds or even thousands of times per day.

Kyaiktiyo (gye-te-o) Pagoda. The Kyaukthanban Pagoda or stupa (literal meaning: stone boat stupa) is located in the small town called Kyaikhto, in the Mon State, Burma. It is home to the famous Golden Rock. According to the legend associated with the *pagoda*, the Buddha, on one of his many visits to Earth, gave a strand of his hair to the hermit Taik Tha. The hermit, in turn, gave the strand to his adopted son, King Tissa, an eleventh century Burmese king, with the dying wish that the hair be enshrined in a boulder shaped like the hermit's head. Tissa, with the help of the Thagyamin, the king of the Nats, found the perfect place for the *pagoda* at Kyaiktiyo, a town at the base of the mountain with the same name; the strand was enshrined on top of a gigantic rock. It is this strand of hair that, according to the legend, prevents the rock from tumbling down the hill.

Luang Por. A title meaning "Venerable Father" used as a title for respected senior Buddhist monastics. *Luang* is a Thai word meaning "royal" or "venerable." It is used in both family context and to express respect for monastics. *Por* is the Thai word for "father." For instance, Luang Por *Ajahn* Chah was a well-known and widely respected monk. In his middle and older years as respect for him grew, people sometimes referred to him simply as "Luang Por." Today in Thailand, very few non-monastics know *Ajahn* Chah by that name; they know him as Luang Por Chah.

Mara. The demon who tempted Gautama Buddha by trying to seduce him with the vision of beautiful women, an army of warriors, and many other mental distractions. In Buddhist cosmology, *Mara* personifies unwholesome impulses, lack of skillfulness, and the "death" of the spiritual life. It is a tempter, distracting humans from practicing the spiritual life by making the mundane alluring or the negative seem positive. *Mara* is the embodiment of all unskillful emotions that can disrupt spiritual practice.

right. This word is associated with The Eightfold Path: Right View, Right Resolve, Right Speech, Right Action, Right Livelihood, Right Persistence, Right Mindfulness, and Right Concentration. The Pali word for right, *samma*, is used when there is understanding of the cause and effect in that "moment," because these factors give good results, whereas their opposite—wrong view, etc.—give bad results.

Rinzai Zen. One of two major Zen Buddhist sects in Japan, it stresses the abrupt awakening of transcendental wisdom, or enlightenment. Among the methods it practices are shouts (*katsu*) or blows delivered by the master on the disciple, question-and-answer sessions (*mondo*), and meditation on paradoxical statements (koan), all intended to accelerate a breakthrough of the normal boundaries of consciousness and to awaken insight that transcends logical distinctions.

Sangre de Cristo. Meaning the blood of Christ, this refers to the Sangre de Cristo Mountains near Santa Fe, New Mexico.

senior monk. An Arhat, enlightened, mature, or awakened person.

Shiva. This word means "the Auspicious One," also known as Parameshwara (the Supreme God), Mahadeva ("Great God"), or Bholenath ("Simple Lord"). Shiva is a popular Hindu deity and considered as the Supreme God within Shaivism, one of the three most influential denominations in Hinduism. Shiva is regarded as one of the primary forms of God; he is "the Destroyer" or "the Transformer" among the Hindu Trinity of the primary aspects of the divine. Shiva is also regarded as the patron god of yoga and arts.

Shiva of the highest level is limitless, transcendent, unchanging, and formless. In benevolent aspects, he is depicted as an omniscient yogi who lives an ascetic life on Mount Kailash, as well as a householder with wife Parvati and two sons, Ganesha and Kartikeya, or as the Cosmic Dancer. In fierce aspects, he is often depicted slaying demons. The most recognizable iconographical attributes of the god are: a third eye on his forehead, a snake around his neck, the crescent moon adorning and the river Ganges flowing from his matted hair, the *trishula* (the-three-pointed trident) as his weapon, and the damaru as his instrument.

Theravada, Theravadan, Theravadin. These words mean "The Way of the Elder" or "The Old Way." The first word is the noun and the second two words are adjectives. The publishing industry, over a period of time, went from spelling this foreign word from Theravadin to Theravadan, attempting to bring it into the English language. Please note the newly revised Theravada monastic code uses *Theravadin* as an adjective. Therefore, I have chosen to use Theravadin throughout this book in honor of its use in the countries where I did my monastic training.

Tibeten Bon Po. The indigenous religion of Tibet, pre-dating the introduction of Buddhism. It influenced Tibetan Buddhism and is still practiced as a minority religion. The earliest surviving documents come from the ninth and tenth centuries, well after Buddhists began the suppression of indigenous beliefs and practices. Bon-Po includes the best practices and ideas from other spiritual disciplines. Today it is a mixture of Buddhism, shamanism, and magic rituals. It is the old faith of Tibet.

torch. Flashlight.

Visuddhimagga. A large treatise explaining the major steps in the Buddhist path, arranged around seven purifications. Written by Buddhaghosa in Sir Lanka approximately in 430 CE, it contains very detailed instructions on concentration and insight practice.

Yahman. Everything is all right; it's all good. During my childhood years, the spoken language on Pawleys Island was Gullah. It is an English-based Creole language containing many African loan words and significant influences from African languages in grammar and sentence structure. Properly referred to as "Sea Island Creole," the Gullah language is related to Jamaican Patois, Barbadian Dialect, Bahamian Dialect, Belizean Creole, and the Krio language of Sierra Leone in West Africa.

Yeshe. A person who is endowed with wisdom and absorption. The Pali word for absorption is Jhana and in Sanskrit it is Jnana. This is a meditative state of profound stillness and concentration in which the mind is fully immersed and absorbed in the chosen object of attention.

yogi. A yogi is a practitioner of yoga. The term "yogi" is also used to refer specifically to siddhas, which are spiritual powers, and broadly refers to ascetic practitioners of meditation in a number of Indian religions, including Hinduism, Jainism, and Buddhism.

zen. The word *Zen* is derived from the Japanese pronunciation of the Middle Chinese word (pinyin: Chan), which in turn is derived from the Sanskrit word *dhyanan* (which can be approximately translated as "absorption" or "meditative" state). Also Zen is a school in Mahayana Buddhism that developed in China during the sixth century as Chan. From China, it spread south to Vietnam, northeast to Korea, east to Japan, and west to North America and Europe.

Acknowledgments

Editors:
When I embarked on this journey, I thought that I had set a great schedule for myself, one that would allow me to attend to my daily duties, leave time for the unpredictable, and write. I assumed it would take five years to complete the book. My first agent and publisher suggested that I use a ghost writer if I wanted to complete the task in fewer years. After six editors and eleven years I came to realize that the book would be completed when the time was right. All I needed to do was write and listen to my editors.

Dennis Jarrett, Ph.D., the recipient of several literary awards, was familiar with the Gullah language because of his work at Morehouse College as professor of literature. Having had the honor to observe his passion for writing was a gift that allowed me to embrace this magical craft. Neither one of us knew that I would be Dennis's last student. His priceless guidance will forever stay with me.

Joan Kaiser, M.A., LPCC, who guided me with kind and invaluable advice to perfect my craftsmanship. She never wavered in her encouragement and kept me going on the right path. I offer a deep bow of gratitude.

Caroline Wareham, M.Ed., LPCC, who supported my voice and humor and taught me how to write, nourishing me with her wisdom. We have enjoyed a great creative dance during our thirty-five years of friendship. I will forever credit her with inspiring me during our early collaboration on the hospice program. What a joy to have worked with a person who is so heartfelt and generous. Thank you, my friend.

Michael Schwab, Ph.D., who offered technical knowledge and radical insight and, at the same time, showed me that writing is an art. He opened a new window and assisted in sculpting my manuscript into a book. I will forever be grateful.

Thanissaro Bhikkhu, who validated the Buddhist Psychology and offered support to a finer style of writing and, most importantly, reinforced my intention to make sure that every line, paragraph, and chapter is about release from suffering. Thank you for taking the time from your busy schedule. *Anjali.*

Alexandra Kennedy, M.A., LMFT, who gave endless support and took me to an even more refined form of writing, giving me the diamond insight that each and every one of us has our own writing style and need not conform to anyone else's. Thanks for opening me up to the fact that every author adds to the standard of writing. Thanks for taking the time away from finishing your fifth book. You helped me see that writing is a dance with language, in bringing the right combination of notes or words to give juice to the story. You have demonstrated skillfully the art of compassion with a sword of sweetness. Our forty-plus years of continued friendship, practice, and shared spiritual quest have been a great gift. Thank you for teaching me how to put it into print.

Readers:
Jon Kennedy, Bruce Smith, Lori Paras, Sabine Schulze-Steele, Gail Sweeney, Amadea Morningstar: Enough can't be said for my readers who have so generously offered their time and feedback. I will always be grateful for your wisdom.

Inspiration:
I would like to thank Joel and Michelle Levey for their insight and contributions to the title of the book; Debra Chamberlin-Taylor for her wittiness and encouragement; Jack Kornfield for teaching me the academics of meditation, supporting me in my struggle with PTSD, being my senior advisor into the monastic life, and instructing me how to teach the Dharma. Jack, you have been an impeccable teacher to me.

To my life partner, Sabine, who put up with me and unconditionally loved me throughout this process. I offer infinite love and deep gratitude, as we continue to grow together and support each other's creativity. Sabine's heartfelt inspiration, wisdom, tender loving kindness, and criticism are just good medicine. Enough can't be said for her strength and for not letting cancer drown her personality. She is and has been a personal mentor for so many women, especially those who have also faced a life-threatening diagnosis. Sabine will always be my mentor.

I made the right decision to disrobe and choose a life with my wife and son. He has been released from prison after twenty years, and now wakes me up to the challenges of parenting in the later years of my life.

I would like to thank all those that endorsed this book. It is rare to find a true friend, a person that embraces you unconditionally. That is priceless.

I would also like to thank my parents and teachers, and their teacher's teachers for giving me authorization to strive for the best in this life.

Sacred Life Publishers:
I humbly thank Sharon Lund, Miko Radcliffe, Mary Myers, and the rest of her staff. Sharon went above and beyond what is customary in supporting this book through her diligent research and editing, which brought it to publication. She knows how to listen and give authoritative advice with great kindness; it's a writer's dream. I look forward to working with her again.

Photo credits:
David Hoptman, who combines great awareness and compassion with tremendous professionalism. This makes for an awesome work experience.

Sabine Schulze-Steele, who has taught me to document life in pictures. Sabine and I both owe our photographic ability to David: Thank you, sir.

I would like to humbly thank Venerable Pannavuddho Bhikkhu for coming to me in my sleep with regard to the cover photo a few days before the book went to print. For months I could not remember who took that photo. Now I know it was you. You will always be remembered. Blessings to your family.

Final Comments: After completing this book, I realized that I am giving a large part of my personal life to the public, the world. I also realized how delusional a world I was living in and that no one is all good or all bad, and it is a personal decision if one chooses to tend their fire.

I take full responsibility for all the words in this book, and if any harm has been caused, I humbly ask for your forgiveness. *Yahman.*

About the Author

Ralph Steele

Ralph Steele, M.A., has degrees in Religious Studies (with Board Honors) and Humanistic Psychology and is a Licensed Marriage and Family Therapist. He is the founder and director of Life Transition Therapy, Inc., which is a meditation-based, multi-disciplinary trauma healing center. Ralph is also the founder and guiding teacher of Life Transition Meditation Center based in Santa Fe, where he teaches Sunlun Meditation and other intensive meditation practices. He also works internationally as a consultant in stress management.

Ralph practiced as an ordained monk in the monasteries of Myanmar and Thailand. He has taught meditation retreats since 1987. Ralph founded the first Elisabeth Kubler-Ross Hospice Program (an Associate Degree) at Northern New Mexico College in El Rito, New Mexico, in 1986. He was instrumental in establishing People of Color Retreats at Spirit Rock Meditation Center in Woodacre, California, and the Insight Meditation Society in Barre, Massachusetts.

Ralph and his life partner, Sabine, have been together for over twenty-eight years. He proudly provides moral support to his forty-one-year-old son, Clarence, who was released from prison in the spring of 2014, after being convicted at a very young age.

Ralph is a Vietnam veteran.

For further information: www.lifetransition.com.